Going My Way

Bing Crosby in 1936 on NBC Radio. (Courtesy of Photofest. Used with permission.)

Going My Way

Bing Crosby and American Culture

Edited by
Ruth Prigozy and Walter Raubicheck

UNIVERSITY OF ROCHESTER PRESS

HOFSTRA
UNIVERSITY.

First published 2007

University of Rochester Press
668 Mt. Hope Avenue, Rochester, NY 14620, USA
www.urpress.com
and Boydell & Brewer Limited
PO Box 9, Woodbridge, Suffolk IP12 3DF, UK
www.boydellandbrewer.com

ISBN-13: 978–1–58046–261–7
ISBN-10: 1–58046–261–8

Library of Congress Cataloging-in-Publication Data

Going My Way : Bing Crosby and American culture / edited by Ruth Prigozy and Walter Raubicheck.
  p. cm.
 Papers originally presented at a conference at Hofstra University.
 Includes bibliographical references and index.
 ISBN-13: 978–1–58046–261–7 (hardcover : alk. paper)
 ISBN-10: 1–58046–261–8
 1. Bing Crosby, 1903–1977—Criticism and interpretation. I. Prigozy,
Ruth. II. Raubicheck, Walter, 1950–
  ML420.C93G65 2007
  782.42164092—dc22
                                        2007030561

A catalogue record for this title is available from the British Library.

This publication is printed on acid-free paper.

Printed in the United States of America.

To Kathryn T. Nicholson

Contents

List of Illustrations

Foreword

The statistics on Bing Crosby's career are dazzling and extremely revealing regarding his success and influence on the many millions whose lives he affected. He created a legacy that is unequalled in its scope and achievement, yet is obscure by today's standards. It is puzzling to think that his image has diminished in popular memory to that of being the singer of "White Christmas" and little else.

As an ardent fan of his recorded works, ranging from the earliest to the last, and as an admirer of his filmography and acting prowess, I never lose hope that he will be re-discovered by future generations. The gift of modern technology lies in our ability to reach many people who might not otherwise have access to a particular record or film performance, but might very well discover either one by surfing the Internet. What Bing Crosby achieved is so singular and unique that it simply has to live on. Like a multitude of other forgotten stars, Bing's time will again come. This belief is not proffered in a Pollyanna fashion but is borne out of the belief that what is good will survive and what is not, will not.

Some have surmised that Crosby's recordings are not as popular today as Sinatra's because of their technical limitations, having been recorded decades before modern sound engineering was perfected. If Crosby had been in his prime during the fifties, perhaps his recordings would be regarded in the same way that the fifties output of Sinatra is accepted: as the hallmark of his work and technically quite acceptable. As it stands, Crosby in the fifties was affected by changing times and an attempt to blandly compete with Sinatra, the result diminishing his reputation. He cared deeply about having hit records and the fifties were an increasingly tough time for him artistically, even though he succeeded in making some fine recordings in that decade.

As an artist who loves and reveres American Popular Song, I find Bing Crosby of supreme importance, and his influence is incalculable. Would that others were able to recognize his lasting gift!

Michael Feinstein

Preface

In the summer of 2002 the American media, predictably, gave extensive coverage to the twenty-fifth anniversary of Elvis Presley's death. Journalists and pundits analyzed the remarkable influence that Presley's music and image still wields over popular culture; concurrently, the "Elvis Number Ones" CD headed straight to the top of the Billboard chart. Yet little notice was taken in October of the same anniversary of the death of the most successful and influential American entertainer of the first half of the twentieth century—Bing Crosby. Though they both died in the same year, by 1977 Crosby's music had come to seem hopelessly anachronistic to the younger generations of record buyers, and to them his image had faded into that of a kindly old man who did occasional Christmas specials with other aging crooners of a bygone era. Elvis's early, sad self-destruction and death created for him an instantaneous, immortal place, alongside the other tragic American icons Marilyn Monroe and James Dean, while his music continued to be the archetypal basis of all rock 'n' roll, from rockabilly to punk. Elvis impersonators have become a staple of the American entertainment scene—who has heard lately of a Crosby impersonator?

Yet the truth is, all American popular singers, including Elvis, are Crosby impersonators of one kind or another. Bing emerged as a solo act in the very early 1930s just as the microphone became available to show business, and he quickly learned to use it as an instrument that allowed him to create a new, intimate kind of singing that was both masculine and sensitive to the emotions implicit in the melodies and lyrics. Instead of "belting" like Al Jolson or Eddie Cantor, Crosby—well—he "crooned" the song, of course. Meanwhile, his up-tempo records jumped and jived as much as the best jazz recordings of the time. There had been no one like him before and his achievement inspired countless young singers to follow his musical path—including his most famous "son," Frank Sinatra. And through Sinatra, Dean Martin, Nat King Cole, and many others, the Crosby style eventually became an ingredient in the musical mix that was rock 'n' roll.

In the fall of 2002 Hofstra University hosted a conference on "Crosby and American Culture." The anniversary of his death (which was also six months before the centennial of his birth) seemed to be an appropriate time to try to redress the appalling neglect of the Crosby legacy, and so several hundred people—academics, musicians who had worked with Crosby, and fans—gathered to celebrate Bing. This volume of essays represents the depth and range of the discussions heard on that remarkable weekend at Hofstra.

Although jazz has become a legitimate field of serious academic study during the last few decades, it is only recently that the same attention has begun to be paid to American popular song, particularly the "standards" of the period 1910–50, which are referred to in the popular press as the Great American Songbook. Though derived partially from European operetta and folk song, these songs always had a symbiotic relationship with various forms of jazz, such as ragtime, Dixieland, and swing. Therefore, it was inevitable that the study of Ellington and Armstrong would be succeeded by serious appraisal of the art of the Gershwins, Cole Porter, and Irving Berlin, who created the music that was as central to the culture of the twenties and thirties as Fitzgerald's novels, Millay's poems, and O'Neill's plays. And the singer who introduced many of these songs to the public was Crosby, either on radio, phonograph records, or in the movies. His interpretations of what are now "standards" contributed significantly to their timeless appeal.

In a sense, Bing Crosby was the first twentieth-century singer of popular song. His immediate predecessors, in particular Al Jolson, represented the culmination of nineteenth-century popular music traditions such as minstrelsy, parlor song, and musical theater. Jolson's unamplified belting, reaching the back seats of the Broadway or regional vaudeville theater, belongs to a pre-modern era, the era that antedated talking pictures (ironically, given his performance in *The Jazz Singer*), records, and radio. Crosby belonged to the world of the nightclub, the recording studio, and the soundstage. His message was that singing could be intimate and personal, appealing to each individual audience member listening to the radio, playing his records, or sitting in the dark watching his movies. And with his mellow baritone, Crosby demonstrated that male popular singing could be virile and seductive.

Rudy Vallee was the transitional performer between Jolson and Crosby but his megaphone-enhanced voice ultimately could not compete with Crosby's confident use of the microphone. Crosby's first hits as a solo performer in 1931, after he had left Paul Whiteman's Rhythm Boys, highlighted his personal approach to the music allowed by the microphone, his talent for making the lyric seem as if it were addressed to a particular "you," rather than a generalized theater audience. "Please," "Out of Nowhere," and "Just One More Chance" may not be great songs, but Crosby's delivery makes them into great records and gave birth to a new sound in

American music, one that captivated the public the way the early records of Elvis and the Beatles captivated audiences of the fifties and sixties because of the novelty and excitement of new ways to express emotion through song. As with these two later acts, Crosby synthesized his influences—in his case Armstrong, Jolson, and Dixieland—and then added something new to the music's presentation, the displacement of theatricality in favor of direct, conversational singing.

In particular, Crosby was intensely attuned to the latest developments in jazz, represented especially by Louis Armstrong and Bix Beiderbecke, the latter being another musician in Whiteman's orchestra. The rhythms of Crosby's up-tempo material swung rather than marched, and even his ballads barely contained their rhythmic impulses. The improvisations of his jazz heroes released his own intuitive creativity with beat and melody line, enabling him to vary his delivery of the choruses, to make his whistling into a jazz instrument, and to adapt Armstrong's scatting into his own nonsense syllables (the source of the constant parodies of the early Bing). And the blues, always an essential part of the jazz styles of the twenties and thirties, came as naturally to Crosby as the Dixieland he loved so much.

One often-overlooked aspect of Crosby's achievement was his impact on Hollywood movies in the thirties and forties. It can truly be said that Crosby helped sound pictures to mature. His first movies were comedy shorts directed by Mack Sennett, the silent legend, and immediately Crosby proved himself to be adept at slapstick and farce, as well as in his ability to laugh at his own matinee-idol image. (In the latter, he was followed thirty years later by the Beatles, who also impressed movie critics with their wit, comic timing, and self-parody in *A Hard Day's Night*.) He then established the pattern for the Hollywood musical of the thirties, playing a light comedy lead in relatively slight films that showcased a new batch of potential hit songs. In the forties his true acting talent began to emerge, first as a comedian opposite Bob Hope in the immensely successful "Road" pictures and then as the young, modern priest in the Father O'Malley films *Going My Way* and *The Bells of Saint Mary's*, dramatic films, which featured one or two Crosby vocal performances, rather than straight musicals. His success in these movies, notably his Academy Award for *Going My Way*, led to his being cast in the early fifties as the aging, alcoholic trooper in Clifford Odets's *The Country Girl,* the role that won him another Oscar nomination. After another hit film, *High Society* in 1956 (a musical version of *The Philadelphia Story*), Crosby made several films, ending his film career in a remake of *Stagecoach* (1966), where he played the role of Doc Boone, made famous in the 1939 original by Thomas Mitchell.

But Bing Crosby's work in television continued throughout the 1960s and indeed, until his death in 1977, his annual Christmas television special featuring his wife Kathryn and their three children drew wide audiences. What many today do not know is that since his death, Bing Crosby's voice has been heard in over fifty films and television programs including *The Talented Mr. Ripley* (1999) and in the pilot episode of the popular HBO series, *Six Feet Under* (2002). Bing Crosby's recording of "White Christmas" remains at the top of the list of best sellers of all time, and it is virtually impossible to miss hearing his voice intoning the classic Irving Berlin lyrics from early December through the holiday season. In the fol-

lowing pages, we hope to demonstrate the enduring legacy of Bing Crosby, a legacy that reflects American culture as it developed throughout the last century and
continues to inspire our admiration and contemplation today.

In this wide-ranging survey of Bing Crosby's life and career, our contributors
have approached the subject from many points of view so that, after the introduc-
tory remarks, we have divided the chapters according to their emphases: theoretical, cultural, and historical perspectives.

Michael Feinstein, the most important performer of the Great American Songbook today, reveres Bing Crosby, and expresses his disappointment that Crosby is
not better known to contemporary audiences. His remarks reflect the effort of this
volume to reintroduce and reassess the man who was the most important figure in
American popular culture for more than two decades of the twentieth century.

Gary Giddins, who provides the introduction to this volume, published the first
volume of his seminal biography in 2000: *Bing Crosby: A Pocketful of Dreams,
The Early Years, 1903–1940,* and began the contemporary reassessment of the entertainer that continues to this day. In this essay he offers the reader a look at the of-
ten-negative mythology that surrounded Crosby the man, in contrast with the
idealized figure of the 1940s, and explains how he attempted, in writing his biography, to find the truth behind both images. Crosby the man is "more layered than a
handful of stories," he concludes.

David E. White sees in the Father O'Malley films examples of "the analogies of
ignorance" that Bishop Butler, an eighteenth-century Anglican divine, expounded
in his apologetic works. Butler argued that the religious person trusts in God's
Providence so completely that he/she can accept cheerfully human ignorance
about its operations. Crosby's O'Malley is supremely confident in God's governance of the world and accepts that good will results from human behavior if one
permits God to operate, however inscrutably.

Eric Mazur takes a sociological view of Bing Crosby's portrayals of Roman
Catholic priests in three of his films, most notably, of course, *Going My Way.* In
his presentation of the priest as an American clearly in tune with the country's popular culture and its prevailing mores, Crosby's priest implicitly deflects anti-Catholic prejudices. The Catholic immigrant, as these films seem to say, is no danger to
the cultural identity of America and in fact enhances it.

Elaine Anderson Phillips examines the Crosby persona onscreen: his "coolness" that allowed male viewers to identify with him as well as a "desiring but
unaggressive male whom women viewers could desire without threat of male violence." Phillips explores the effect of Crosby's voice on his male and female audiences and how he symbolized *apatheia,* the control of passions. She studies
closely three Crosby films: *Going My Way, Holiday Inn,* and *High Society.*

Linda Robinson demonstrates how the effectiveness of Crosby's performance
in *The Country Girl* depends on "departure casting," the carefully constructed
variations from his typical screen persona. This extra-filmic element was essential
to both the publicity for the film and the reviewers' response to it. Robinson shows
how the persona of any screen actor is by definition multi-textual since it depends
on both physical appearance and screen image, the public knowledge of the actor's

life, and the combined effect of his/her previous screen performances. Crosby as a desperate alcoholic challenged the established persona in complex ways, to great acclaim.

John Dempsey demonstrates that Bing Crosby's music, while it was ostensibly left behind in popular taste by the advent of rock 'n' roll, actually had a lasting effect on many of rock's greatest performers, especially Elvis Presley, the Beatles, and Bob Dylan. In so doing, Crosby influenced several later generations of music lovers who may only be fully aware of him as the seasonal singer of "White Christmas." He concludes by analyzing the iconic duet Crosby performed on television with David Bowie in 1977.

Walter Raubicheck explores the inner dynamic of the Bing Crosby/Bob Hope comedy partnership in the "Road" pictures, identifying their "Americanness" as crucial to their appeal in the war and post–war years. Unlike Chaplin and the Marx Brothers with their obviously European comedic sources, Crosby and Hope developed a wisecracking brand of comedy that derives from the contrast between the exotic settings and cultures they encounter and their stubbornly working-class American attitudes.

Bernard F. Dick notes, "if Crosby had never spent a quarter of a century at Paramount, he would still have been the recording artist, but never the Oscar-winning movie star." He focuses on the role of Paramount studios in creating a new kind of movie "that was neither a musical nor a straight film, but one with musical numbers that were rarely integrated with the plot and were, for the most part, diversions. In other words, not musical comedies, but comedy musicals," that lasted well into the 1950s. Dick traces the way the studio marketed Crosby, and he provides a detailed history of his work for Paramount.

M. Thomas Inge analyzes Crosby's performance in the Walt Disney cartoon film adaptation of Washington Irving's 1820 story, "The Legend of Sleepy Hollow," where he is the vocal embodiment of Ichabod Crane. Inge's detailed discussion of the film illuminates how Crosby's appeal to the audience resulted in a shift in identification with the character who is not as attractive in the original story as in the Disney creation.

Jeanne Fuchs writes about the screen relationship of two of America's most beloved stars, Bing Crosby and Fred Astaire. In the two films they made together in the 1940s, both men used their particular talents, as singer and dancer respectively, to engage in rival courtships, even though each projected a potential "husband" image that made them much less threatening than their contemporaries, such as Gene Kelly and Frank Sinatra. Fuchs shows how Crosby and Astaire complemented each other effectively, especially in their duets, in these two films that she examines in detail.

Samuel L. Chell discusses the professional rivalry of Bing Crosby and Frank Sinatra on radio, in the movies, and on television. He shows how this rivalry was based on a traditionalist/modernist dichotomy, but also how, beneath these apparent dissimilarities, both singers agree on a tradition of American popular song that should be preserved, and together they are the tradition's greatest interpreters.

Steven Shafer looks at the cartoons over a thirty-year period—the ones coinciding with Bing Crosby's greatest popularity—that demonstrate how Crosby's public image changed dramatically. At first Crosby was portrayed in these short films as the archetypal "crooner," dangerous to young females and to the established order. During the war years and after, the sexual threat of the crooner was replaced by the safe, American respectability of the iconic Crosby.

In the final section of this volume, we focus on the importance of Bing Crosby in the context of American history as a key figure in the war effort, as a force behind the technical revolution, and as an entertainer whose achievements went far beyond the music, film, radio, and television work that made him famous. Deborah Dolan describes the Crosby Research Foundation, headed by Bing and his two brothers, where over fifteen thousand inventions to further the war effort, as well as for civilian use, were tested. She also describes the Del Mar Turf Club in San Diego, which became a major site for the government's use during the war.

Malcolm Macfarlane continues the discussion of Crosby's wartime activities, providing important information about his war-bond tours, his USO trips to entertain servicemen, and perhaps most notably, his importance to the troops overseas whose longing for home was expressed so acutely by Bing Crosby as he sang "White Christmas," a song that seemed to have been written and recorded just for them.

Martin McQuade and Pete Hammar describe Bing Crosby's instrumental role in the development of magnetic tape for use in radio. Frustrated by the time demands of live broadcasts, Crosby invested heavily in the new process of making effective tape recordings of live shows that could be broadcast at any time later. In so doing he proved his expertise as a businessman and transformed the entire entertainment industry.

F. W. Wiggins sums up the reputation and importance of Bing Crosby today, as he describes the history and current status of the Bing Crosby Fan Clubs, and reflected in the monthly publication that reports on virtually every event involving Crosby in our time. His remarks signify the ongoing importance of Bing Crosby to audiences around the globe.

Music critic Will Friedwald offers a summation of the views of anyone who has studied American popular music, indeed American culture of the modern era: Bing Crosby was the "architect" of twentieth-century style; as Friedwald states, "Crosby forever changed the way we hear the human voice, and he was the first great musician to develop a performance style largely in response to technology—specifically the advent of electrical recording in the twenties. It was the microphone that made the modern mass media possible—recordings, talking pictures and broadcasting—and Crosby was the first to fully fathom their implications." But it was not simply the technical innovations that made Crosby one of the major figures in American cultural history—as Friedwald says, "It was the heart behind the voice."

Finally, Kathryn Crosby, Bing's widow, his grandson Steven, and music producer and writer Ken Barnes provide personal accounts of Crosby from three very different perspectives. Kathryn Crosby offers a brief but poignant appraisal of her late husband; Steven Crosby looks back to his relationship with his grandfather with candor regarding his father's troubled interaction with Bing Crosby, and his own genuine appreciation and fondness for the cultural icon whose generosity to his grandson cannot be forgotten. Ken Barnes worked with Bing Crosby during the last three years of his life, and he offers a personal insight into the man whom so many regarded as an enigma throughout his life. Barnes's account of the last performances and recordings is particularly revealing of the professionalism that Crosby personified.

In the following pages, we hope to demonstrate how much we owe to Bing Crosby, and we trust that the readers will agree that he forever changed our world.

Ruth Prigozy
Walter Raubicheck

Acknowledgments

The editors wish to thank the Hofstra Cultural Center and Hofstra University, sponsors of the 2002 conference devoted to the life and career of Bing Crosby. In addition to Natalie Datlof, Athelene Collins, Marge Berko, Carol Dollisons, and Lai Ling Li, Alexei Ugrinsky has been most helpful, notably in matters related to publication. At the University of Rochester Press, editor Suzanne Guiod has overseen the details of manuscript preparation and has promptly answered our many questions. We also thank Terri Jennings of Jennings Publishing Services for her work on the design and layout of this book. The staff of Photofest is not only congenial, but also thoroughly knowledgeable and they have given us excellent advice in the selection of our illustrations. And our final thanks go to the many fans of Bing Crosby located both in the United States and abroad; they have been ardent supporters of our efforts, and they help to ensure that the man who is the subject of this book will be remembered as a legendary figure in music, film, and American life.

Bing Crosby and Barry Fitzgerald in *Going My Way*, Paramount, 1944. (Courtesy of Photofest. Used with permission.)

Bob Hope and Bing Crosby in *Road to Singapore,* Paramount, 1940. (Courtesy of Photofest. Used with permission.)

Marjorie Reynolds, Bing Crosby, and Fred Astaire in *Holiday Inn*, Paramount, 1942.
(Courtesy of Photofest. Used with permission.)

William Holden and Bing Crosby in *The Country Girl*, Paramount, 1954. (Courtesy of
Photofest. Used with permission.)

Bing Crosby and Grace Kelly in *High Society*, Metro-Goldwyn-Mayer, 1956. (Courtesy of Photofest. Used with permission.)

Introduction: Bring Crosby—Nothing Is What It Seems

Gary Giddins

No one in the mid-twentieth century was better known or more beloved than Bing Crosby, yet more than twenty-five years after his death he is often forgotten, or worse, misremembered. During the decade I spent researching his life I often thought of a theme that runs throughout the films of the great German filmmaker Fritz Lang: *Nothing is what it seems.* Of course, that's what Bing's detractors, including his eldest son and a biographer, told us when they revealed Crosby as a hard-drinking, child-beating, pinchpenny tyrant whose beloved persona was a carefully nourished fraud. When I wrote the initial proposal for my biography, I not only believed that he deserved to be knocked off the pedestal erected for him in the 1940s, but chose to develop the disconnect between public and private as a central theme. The idea of duality fascinated me. Here was a man perceived by the world as the soul of warmth but who in reality was cold, difficult, and remote. Among other things, that split would help define his achievement as the great actor he surely was.

Chiefly interested in Crosby as an artist, I wanted to defend the artistry against the irrational response that it, too, was somehow fraudulent. We live in an age of clay feet, and there are those who discount Frost and Hemingway because they were cruel and dishonest, or scorn the Roosevelts because Franklin and Eleanor were unfaithful. Entertainers are especially vulnerable to revisionist contempt; generations no longer vulnerable to their original charm may be indifferent to portrayals of Errol Flynn as a Nazi spy or Cary Grant as a self-hating closet-homosexual batterer. In time, of course, we learn to distinguish between art and artist, if the art continues to speak to us. Yet in the case of Crosby, the piling on had been relentless, perhaps because he had an especially long way to fall. No entertainer in our time has achieved quite the emotional hold Crosby had on his.

But nothing was what it seemed, and for awhile I was deeply troubled about the difficulty in nailing down the private horrors that I believed were more than counterbalanced by the public generosity and undeniable gifts that distinguished him as a defining figure of his time and one of the most influential musicians in the development of popular song. During my first research trip to Los Angeles, when I had been out there for several days and had done maybe fifteen or twenty interviews, I met a documentary filmmaker named Bryan Johnson who had been signed to make a film about Crosby—we shared some research. One night, after a particularly busy day of driving from one source to another—writing biography is very much like a Ross MacDonald novel, in which the detective interviews a series of interested parties, each one suggesting another person to visit—I phoned Bryan and asked, "Am I talking to all the wrong people?" I had heard nothing that day but testimony to Crosby as an admirable, loyal, brilliant, professional, unpretentious man. Bryan said, "I've been worrying about that myself."

So I began raking the muck, only to find much of it fall away. Crosby was hardly a saint, and the four boys of his first marriage did not have an easy time of it—Bing was often absent and strict when present, while his wife Dixie was alcoholic and reclusive. But he was a man of more parts than I anticipated, and a biographer is obliged to go with what he or she uncovers, because one soon learns that no one can be trusted and everything must be checked. You have to build the character of your subject from something very like a blank slate, accepting what you find even—or especially—when it contradicts what you believe. Let me give an example from the early period of my research. On the plane to Los Angeles, I read a biography of Grace Kelly by the reliable biographer, James Spada. Yet his book recounted an anecdote involving Bing, Grace Kelly, and Sue Carol (the wife of Alan Ladd and a close friend of Bing's first wife, Dixie Lee) that didn't ring true to me. Unlike most incidents in the book, this story was unsourced. I called Spada to ask him about it, and had hardly started when he said, "Don't tell me." He was way ahead of me. The story had been told to him by Robert Slatzer, a notorious source of Hollywood misinformation whose name appears in the indexes of several scurrilous books; his own books include one, turned into a miniseries, about his own secret marriage to Marilyn Monroe, who, according to her subsequent biographer, he most likely never met.

Spada said that Slatzer kept promising him a tape of his interview with Sue Carol but never produced it and as the book was going to press Spada decided to go with the story, to his regret. I pointed out to him that the year before his Kelly biography was published, Slatzer had co-authored *The Hollow Man*, a relentless Crosby hatchet job that did not include the anecdote in question. Spada was speechless. I pointed out also that when Slatzer's book came out, Sue Carol was still alive—she died while the Kelly book was in progress. Here's the punchline. Years later I made a routine visit to New York's gigantic used-books emporium, the Strand, to see if there were new relevant works on the film-related shelves. There were now four or five books on Kelly, and each one of them had the dubious story and each dutifully sourced it to Spada's book. Now if you were writing a bi- ography of Kelly or Crosby and found the same story in several books, wouldn't you assume its veracity? Yet there's not a word of truth to it—and this sort of thing happens frequently.

Another pitfall concerns tales related by word of mouth. People like to believe the worst of famous persons they dislike, and these tales take on the impenetrable certainty of urban myths. One person I spoke to, who did know Crosby, mentioned an incident he had heard about, in which Bing was given an untrained hunting dog. While out shooting birds with his son Gary, the dog failed to fetch a dead bird; Bing raised his rifle over his head and smashed the dog's skull. To anyone who knew Crosby, this story was laughably misguided and unspeakably vicious. Crosby was a devoted breeder of dogs, an animal lover, and, in any case, a man not given to flamboyant displays of temper. But in the aftermath of Gary Crosby's memoir and *The Hollow Man*, he was frequently depicted as a monster and this tale simply underscored the growing presumption. When I heard the hunting dog story a second time, I asked for the source and was given the name of a historian in Los Angeles. I then called the first person who had told it to me, and he too said he heard it from the historian, who was on my list of people to interview. The histo- rian told me he did not remember where he had learned the story, but knew it to be true. How? Because he once encountered Gary Crosby at a party and asked him; Gary didn't say anything, but he grimaced and nodded his head. "Great," I told him, "I'm having lunch with Gary tomorrow." Gary was incredulous. He told me to get the guy on the phone, daring him to say such a thing in his presence. I told him that wouldn't be necessary.

The illusory Crosby, however, is more layered than a handful of stories. Con- sider his famous self-effacement, especially his modesty about acting. According to Crosby, he wasn't really an actor at all—just a lucky crooner who played him- self. Crosby even said he won his Oscar because the good actors were off doing war work. In truth, few worked harder for the war effort than he did, and his rivals for the prize were Cary Grant, Charles Boyer, Barry Fitzgerald, and Alexander Knox. He would be nominated twice more, in competition with such actors as Ray Milland, Gregory Peck, Marlon Brando, Humphrey Bogart, and James Mason. He worked hard to become a film actor and to maintain his standing. One fascinating aspect of his career is his confidence that he might become a film star. True, sound was on the horizon when he first arrived in Hollywood and good voices were at a premium. But beyond vaudeville routines, Bing had enjoyed no success on stage.

Most performers of his generation who hoped to become film actors had either worked in the silent era or apprenticed in theater. Those who came from vaudeville expected to cash in on distinctive personalities they had developed on the road. Bing's one obvious talent was his voice; he had no professional personality be- yond that of a fresh-faced young man with a quick wit. Still, he wrote his mother of his determination to conquer the screen and talked himself into a series of audi- tions—we don't really know how many, three at least—in 1930, during the long layoff that preceded the filming of the Paul Whiteman revue, *The King of Jazz*. Be- fore joining with Whiteman, Bing had spent only a year in vaudeville, touring the

West Coast with Al Rinker. Before that, he had appeared in many school productions, where he was known for his excellent elocution and ability to get laughs. But there is no evidence that he developed a Bing Crosby persona, or that those closest to him thought he had potential as an actor. He was a singer of jazz and ballads, a man who liked to drink, carouse, and hang out with musicians. He was not known as a genuine comedian, and he lacked the looks that characterized matinee idols.

Yet he projected himself onto the screen; he believed—and this is an essential aspect of his genius—that he had something new to offer, something no one else could see. He was promptly rejected—not least by the very executive who signed Dixie Lee as a starlet and spent time and money developing her into a screen personality—because he had wingy ears, a receding hairline, and a round midsection. Fred Astaire was also rejected during this period because of his looks, but his talent was bracingly physical; no one had ever achieved enduring stardom on the screen by standing still and singing, and with the demise of musical revues, it seemed unlikely anyone would. Fortunately for Bing, however, having failed in Hollywood, he succeeded in initiating a rage for radio singers. In 1932, Paramount signed him on the assumption that radio fans might pay to see what the idols of the airwaves looked like.

Two years earlier, a run-in with the police over a drunk driving incident caused Crosby to lose a number in *The King of Jazz* to John Boles, who, with square jaw, dark good looks, and dapper mustache, was a walking cliché of a 1930s romantic hero. That look brought fame to Clark Gable, Ronald Colman, and Errol Flynn, but it did little for Boles, a dull performer, lacking in charm or emotional magnetism. In time, the cliché canceled itself out, and leading men found the better part of valor in shaving. Crosby's sparkling quality—funny and appealing and, for all his confidence, lacking in arrogance or self-importance—offered something new and clean-cut, and just when Hollywood was about to surrender its vitality to a censorship code. With his drollness and improvisational flair, Crosby soon mastered filmic space: He proved completely at home on a soundstage. Frank Capra once named him one of the ten greatest actors he ever worked with because of the kinds of business Crosby invented while singing. In long close-ups, he romanced the camera—the audience could not take its eyes off him.

In his first feature film, Paramount's pre-code *The Big Broadcast*, a splendid and long-unavailable film, Crosby played an irresponsible, alcoholic scamp. Yet he must have radiated a deeper truth, because neither audiences nor critics accepted the interpretation at face value. In the final reel, Bing (playing a character named Bing Crosby) abandons the "good girl" to hapless Stu Erwin and happily walks away with the sexy, scheming trollop. The public cheered. Directed by the now largely forgotten Frank Tuttle, an A-list Paramount director who helped create movie personae for Eddie Cantor, Alan Ladd, and Veronica Lake as well as Crosby, the film combined musical numbers with surreal visuals and black humor involving suicide, hallucination, mistaken sexual identity, and drunken reverie. Tuttle's style involved techniques introduced by the pioneer French filmmaker René Clair, but Crosby's presence guaranteed a uniquely American glow.

On the basis of *The Big Broadcast*, Paramount signed him to a three-picture deal; he was the only major radio star (until Bob Hope, seven years later) to enjoy a major success in the movies. The utter failure of Bing's CBS colleague, Kate Smith, and the relative failure of his NBC rival, Russ Columbo, was typical. Even radio comedians who enjoyed box-office success in 1930s films, including Jack Benny, Burns and Allen, and Joe Penner, demonstrated far less staying power than Crosby, who would go on to dominate the Quigley poll for the better part of two decades. He achieved his long run by inventing and refining a Bing Crosby persona, an overall personality that subsumed virtually all the characters he played.

Artie Shaw once remarked, "Bing Crosby was no more Bing Crosby than Humphrey Bogart was Humphrey Bogart." This may seem rather obvious today, when we are accustomed to movie gossip designed to humanize, at best, and belittle, at worse, celebrities we simultaneously mock and support. That was not the case in the 1930s, when fan magazines and newspapers reported on the stars as dictated by studio public relations departments. In that era, when studio chiefs nurtured stars by approving their films (sometimes detrimentally), performers often played versions of themselves; a Fredric March or Paul Muni might win plaudits for disappearing behind makeup and character, but most major stars were types, readily identifiable. Audiences wanted Gary Cooper to be Gary Cooper, whether he was wearing a cowboy hat or a baseball cap. If a movie tough guy made a guest appearance on radio, he'd be given lines that mined his tough-guy reputation. Jack Benny played a character named Jack Benny, a notoriously vain tightwad. A fan once asked the professionally crazy Gracie Allen, "Is Jack Benny cheap?" She said, "Am I stupid?" People enjoyed believing in personae they found attractive. This was especially true of Crosby.

His unparalleled achievement in this regard has been strangely forgotten. When the American Film Institute recently compiled a list of the hundred most important film stars, Crosby was conspicuously absent. Yet he ranked in the top-ten for the better part of two decades and scored as the nation's most popular film star five years running, something no one else in his generation, or those that followed—until the 1970s—accomplished. In short, he created the most successful of all prewar and wartime personae, as shown by the unbroken success of his pictures between 1932 and 1956. He outpolled Gable, Cooper, Spencer Tracy, James Cagney, Edward G. Robinson, John Wayne, and others who made better and more durable films. It was the Crosby persona that packed theaters, whether he played a rich heir, poor gadabout, minstrel, wag, or priest.

His persona was, needless to say, a contradiction, predicated on the idea fostered in the press, that Crosby was the laziest actor in Hollywood. In his interviews and publicity appearances—and he didn't do many—Bing presented himself as a guy who hated to work. Indolence was his skinflint routine, his craziness. He was extremely cool, relaxed at all times, so laid-back that the very tempo of his existence appeared to shape his singsong speech patterns, not to mention his highly personal patois, which combined fancy words with an inventive slang. He was constantly photographed at the track or in informal family settings. His clothing was aggressively casual: loud shirts with the tails hanging out, mismatched socks, a pipe, and always a hat, a constant prop designed to mask his unwillingness to paste on the "scalp doily," the "divot," the hated hairpiece required of every leading man who lacked real locks. Crosby's toupee-maker told me that his other clients, including Bogart and Wayne, would rather have been shot than appear without a piece. Bing didn't care. Too self-possessed to worry about that kind of vanity, he was a grown-up Tom Sawyer, lucky in all things, a singer whose unmannered style every amateur fancied he could do as well, an actor so secure in his own skin he made men and women alike feel secure in theirs. Surely, he didn't rehearse those wonderfully amiable radio shows or the lightly tossed off "Road" pictures. The public assumed he rolled out of bed and ad-libbed his career. In all American entertainment, there never was a cooler customer than Bing.

The reality was quite different. Crosby was one of the hardest-working men in show business. He made three movies a year. Most contract stars in Hollywood did that. But Bing also recorded on average forty records a year—no one else did that. He also did a live radio variety show every week. And he ruled in each medium. In addition to those tasks, he made numerous guest appearances on other radio shows and at charitable golf matches. During the war, he recorded more V-discs than any other performer and toured England and France in 1944, after participating in the Victory Caravan and other armed forces entertainments. On top of that, he played golf almost daily, often twice in a day, and found time to create the first Pro-Am golf tournament in show business history and launch the Del Mar racetrack. All without breaking a sweat, as far as the public—and for that matter, most of his intimates—could see.

The Bing Crosby whose early years are chronicled in *A Pocketful of Dreams*, as a hard-drinking carouser who stayed up all night listening to jazz, occasionally passing out in a speakeasy or nightclub, realized his maturity not in the standard 180-degree turn, but in a 360-degree turn back to the kind of boy he had been in Spokane. Even then, he was known to take it easy, to have a ready quip, to favor a good time; yet in those same years, he worked harder than anyone else in his family. At one point, he traveled several miles before sunup every morning to clean out a skid-row hostel, before delivering papers and singing Mass, all before his first class in school. After marrying Dixie Lee, who delivered an ultimatum about his drinking, he reverted to his old ways, when he had to work to pay for anything beyond bed and board. He became resolutely responsible. He went to sleep early—even when a party was in progress at his home—and woke with the rooster. Bob Hope marveled that Bing would spend an hour at the driving range before arriving on the film set. He was known for being the first in a recording studio or at a rehearsal, and the first to leave. He lived by the clock, refusing to be late for anything or anyone.

Bing's love of horse racing is an example of his commitment and another instance of fact countering a popular fiction. I interviewed two trainers from the early days at Del Mar and Santa Anita who remembered Bing padding around the stables first thing in the morning. Many stars invested in horses, attended races, and posed in the winning circle; but only Crosby came out in the small hours to be with the men who trained and cared for the horses. Crosby knew every aspect of the game. He understood horses, was himself an excellent rider, owned stables in Argentina, and raised several important horses, including Ligorati, whose match race with Seabiscuit was national news. The prevalent myth was quite different: Bing only owned nags. Bob Hope and others told hundreds of jokes about them—you could recognize Bing's horses because they were standing still. It was also assumed that Crosby was unassailably wealthy, when, in fact, he hemorrhaged so much money maintaining and betting on horses that his accountant had to rein him in.

The question I am most frequently asked (after, "How is the second volume coming?") concerns Crosby's precipitous decline in popularity in the 1960s. In the age of rock 'n' roll, Crosby gracefully absented himself in a semi-retirement, though it must be said that for Crosby semi-retirement meant a fairly constant regimen of work. He continued to make films until the mid-1960s, and never abandoned TV—there were, in addition to the annual Christmas specials, a mercifully short-lived situation comedy as well as gleaming variety hour specials, among them some thirty stints as host of *The Hollywood Palace*, and frequent guest shots. He never ceased recording. When the major American labels turned away from him, he financed a couple of albums on his own, and later turned to England, where he recorded prolifically until his last days. At the time of his death, he was on tour with his family show and preparing a new film with Hope.

Still, here was a man beloved the world over, the most successful recording star in history, with an unbeatable number of hits; a man who as late as 1954 starred in the highest grossing movie of the year (*White Christmas*) and enjoyed a greater triumph two years later in *High Society*, which gave him his last gold record ("True Love"). Yet quite suddenly he was left behind. Why? I think the answer lies in the ingenious persona that centered his long triumph. The qualities that endeared him to America and the world—the easeful optimism in the face of adversity, the willingness to embrace the public's appetite for a tuneful if occasionally sentimental view of life, the spiritual resilience that guided him but did not judge others, the likeably aloof warmth that was at once neighborly and reticent, never presuming more than was apt—made him the indispensable man of the 1930s and 1940s, an entertainer who represented stability in an age of turmoil.

The insouciant confidence never left him, but the world moved on, picking up speed. In the face of not war but of imminent annihilation, the tempo of life rocked into overdrive. Crosby, whose influence on technology had been so profound, from his fashioning a freestanding microphone into a musical instrument, to his contribution in the development of audiotape, now faced a technology that could vaporize entire cities with the push of a button. In the land of Sputnik, the bomb, TV, a stalemate cold war, desperate consumerism, prefabricated housing, liberated sexual mores, and the hammering beat of rock, Bing now seemed remote, grandfatherly, and irrelevant. The towering years of his career were not during the war (another widespread assumption), but in its aftermath, as thousands of servicemen acknowledged the balm he had provided by filling theaters that showed his movies and buying his records. "Kiss me once and kiss me twice and kiss me once again, it's been a long, long time." As late as 1949, he had no rivals.

A year later, silly novelties and jaunty rhythms took over the airwaves, and soon the entertainment world embraced youth above all else. Crosby was the last of the nineteenth-century men, an entertainer who conflated new and old and reached his contemporaries, their parents, and their children. By 1956, the entertainment world had split in two: Elvis for the young, Sinatra (whose career had been eclipsed in the postwar years) for their parents. Crosby often said that his favorite moment in any of his films was the *High Society* duet with Sinatra. He surely enjoyed the universal acclaim that judged him an old pro who could still wrap up a scene like no one else. Many reviews saw the scene as a competition and put Crosby on top. How did he do it? For the most part, by sitting still, while Sinatra nervously chewed the scenery. The days of Crosby's quiet command were numbered—but one has only to return to his records and films and broadcasts to realize that excellence never really disappears, however much fashions change. Crosby's art speaks to us still. It has only to be rediscovered or relearned. It's so old it's new. Nothing is what it seems.

Part 1

THEORETICAL PERSPECTIVES ON CROSBY

1

Analogies of Ignorance in
Going My Way

David E. White

Going My Way (1944) was one of the most successful promotions of Catholicism in American history; successful in part because of its suppression not only of the dark, judgmental aspects of religion, but also because there is almost no reference to the supernatural, the sacramental, or the theological. Rather than characterize Catholicism as superficial and sentimental, or impose some alien theory on a simple story, those looking for the basis of the religious appeal might better consider the numerous analogies of ignorance and its resolution in the film. The religious themes found in *Going My Way* continue, and in some ways are enhanced, in the sequel *The Bells of St. Mary's* (1945).

In theology, the analogical method seeks to remove objections to religion by showing that the opponent has already accepted the disputed point in a different context. Once the analogy is made explicit, the objection evaporates—nothing objectionable is left. *Going My Way* concentrates on one particular analogy of experience: the analogy of ignorance. Ignorance was also a favorite theme of Joseph Butler, author of the *Analogy of Religion* (1736). Although an Anglican, Butler was accused of Catholic sympathies and John Henry Newman explicitly credits Butler with his own conversion from the Church of England to Rome. The thesis of this paper is not that Butler's work influenced the making of the Father O'Malley films, but rather that Butler provides the clearest theological explanation of their appeal. In other words, there are certain themes the emphasis on which made Butler's works enormously popular, and those same themes are responsible for the popularity of the films.

The most general description of this quality is that the religion in Butler and in the films is naturalized. In Butler one is struck by the many appeals to nature. Even when he appeals to revelation, Butler is careful to stress the analogies between what we experience in the natural world and what we are taught by revelation. Rather than being at odds with what we experience in this world, religion is largely in accord with the course of nature and this is only what we should expect given that the author of divine revelation is also the author of nature. Thus, when Father O'Malley explains the meaning of *Going My Way,* he might as well have used Butler's phrase and said that he was acting naturally, acting in accord with the constitution and course of nature. As stated above, the connection between Butler and the films is not one of direct influence, at least I can find no evidence of such and any direct influence is antecedently unlikely.

Critics have generally assumed that the Father O'Malley character is so appealing primarily because Bing Crosby the actor is so appealing. My thesis is that Chuck O'Malley is appealing primarily because he represents a certain religious way of life that is appealing and that Crosby, somewhat incidentally, is the ideal actor to portray this way of life on the screen. At first viewing, Father O'Malley seems to be the embodiment of what William James called the religion of healthy-mindedness.[1] This attitude is characterized by high spirits, optimism, and a general denial or disregard for the tragic aspects of life. The contrasting type, which James calls the sick soul, often appears in a state of depression as a result of having faced up to the worst that life has to offer.[2] James's pragmatic solution, finding the religion that works best for whichever type one happens to be, is inappropriate in the context of Catholic theology, but the passages from Bishop Butler all belong to natural theology or that department of religious thought shared not only by Roman Catholic and Anglican, but by all people, Christian and non-Christian, who have thought clearly about the implications of belief in God (or so the proponents of this view will claim).

The way of life so well personified by, first and foremost, the Father O'Malley character and then secondarily, so well portrayed by Bing Crosby, may be called personal providentialism. To accept providence is to accept God's governance of the world. How one is personally related to this providence is a topic to be discussed with one's priest or spiritual advisor. In applying the concepts of providence to individual life situations, Father O'Malley brilliantly succeeds by both affirming the providential design while also acknowledging his personal ignorance of what that design is. What most viewers of *Going My Way* and *The Bells of St. Mary's* see as the happy-go-lucky and oh-so charming Bing Crosby, is actually a type of the Catholic saint or of the religious person generally, who has been brought to a state of (somewhat subdued) ecstasy by first totally surrendering the personal will to the divine will, and secondly by cultivating an extremely vivid and personal sense of the divine presence. Primarily we are shown that Father O'Malley is in this state, we are not told that he is in the state, and neither are we given much information on how he got there. From what is said, we can only surmise that he was brought to this ecstatic state through his Catholic upbringing, through attending Catholic schools, and through learning from Catholic priests, such as the priest he was to become. Certainly this is the way the films were taken by the many

Catholics (and non-Catholics) who found these films to be inspirational and such a great promotion of Catholicism.

The popularity of both *Going My Way* and *The Bells of Saint Mary's* was immediate. They were successful with audiences, with critics, and with the Academy of Motion Picture Arts and Sciences. The time of their influence on young people seems to have passed. It is as difficult to find a person under twenty-five who has heard of these films as it is to find one over thirty-five who has not. The same variations apply to Butler's reputation. Butler quickly became famous when his sermons were first published in 1726 and when his treatise the *Analogy of Religion* was published in 1736, he soon became a bishop. Butler died in 1752 and by the end of the eighteenth century, his *Analogy* was well on its way to becoming the best-known work of Anglican apologetics. It was highly praised by all parties in the Church of England, by the dissenting denominations, and by the Anglo-Catholics. Even though Bishop Butler supposedly clashed with John Wesley, the Methodist Book Concern was one of many publishers to reprint Butler's work throughout the nineteenth century. For our purposes the most important themes of the *Analogy* are the analogies of ignorance, especially as applied to the problem of evil[3] and Butler's famous maxim that, for us, unlike God, "probability is the very guide of life."[4]

In both Father O'Malley films I find four specific themes with which Butler is so closely associated. The first and primary theme is that of ignorance. We may be able to see providence in certain cases, but since we are in a general state of ignorance we should never be guided by our own sense of providence but ought rather to trust in God's providence. This is the mistake the nuns make in dealing with Mr. Bogardus. Father O'Malley does not make this mistake even though he obviously believes in providence as much as the nuns do. (See discussion below.) This ignorance is the only major theme to which Butler gives a chapter in both his *Sermons*[5] and his *Analogy*.[6] Secondary points that are closely related are the paradox of hedonism, the refutation of utilitarianism (in the "Dissertation on Virtue" appended to the Analogy), and the notorious "cool hour" passage.[7] Briefly, the paradox of hedonism states that directly seeking pleasure is not the best strategy for gaining pleasure.[8]

Butler's refutation of hedonism is based on the claim that we can never know enough to do the hedonic calculations very well, so we are much better off following a well-developed conscience, having discerned that virtue and happiness are nearly always coincident. Again and again in the O'Malley films, we see fine examples of Father Chuck following his conscientious instincts. According to the cool hour passage, conscience is not quite enough to motivate behavior in difficult situations. As one calmly deliberates about what to do, one will follow what is in one's interest. Of course, given a providential design to the world, there will be a perfect coincidence between duty and interest. Here again, Father Chuck is willing to take risks without any assurance of how things will play out and what viewers see is not a miraculous intervention or some externally connected reward for being in divine favor; rather, what we see is the inevitable working out of a natural process itself created and governed by divinity.

Going My Way includes many analogies of ignorance that may be classified as follows: (1) there is no need for us to know (e.g., Chuck is never able to answer the repeated question of why he became a priest); (2) ignorance can enhance our pleasure (e.g., Genevieve smiles when she finally discovers Chuck is a priest); (3) human ignorance can serve a useful purpose (e.g., the need to keep from Father Fitzgibbon the fact that Chuck is really in charge).

Bing Crosby's own charm, wit, and affability are apparent, his singing and his golf are manifest as sources of the appeal of *Going My Way,* but they all count for less than the ensemble's easy acceptance of ignorance and its analogies. "Going my way" obviously refers indirectly to divine providence or the acceptance of providence, but the film succeeds by concentrating entirely on the commonplace ignorance we accept, allowing the audience to discover the tacit analogy.

From the opening scenes in which Chuck does not know where St. Dominic's is, to the climactic scenes in which Father Fitzgibbon is surprised to be reunited with his mother and to learn Timmy will be his new curate, and with Chuck heading off to an uncertain future the audience is led to believe that at each stage we know all we need to know but nothing more. And along the way, just as Chuck is ignorant that Genevieve is Carmen and she, of course, ignorant that Chuck is a priest, so Ted Sr. discovers that he was ranting first in ignorance of his son's marriage and then in his ignorance that Ted Jr. had joined the army. Finally, of course, Chuck and Timmy are delighted to discover that, unbeknownst to them, Max and his associates had been listening when the choir sang "Swinging on a Star" and as a result a hit record is born. As Bishop Butler says, "There is no manner of absurdity in supposing a veil on purpose drawn over some scenes of infinite power, wisdom, and goodness, the sight of which might some way or other strike us too strongly; or that better ends are designed and served by their being concealed, than could be by their being exposed to our knowledge."[9]

The ignorance themes of *Going My Way* repeat, sometimes with even more emphasis, in *The Bells of St. Mary's.* As usual, the theatrical purpose of Crosby's ignorance seems to be primarily comedic. Early scenes in the film show him being told ominously about his predecessor being taken away with nervous exhaustion; accidentally ringing the school bell an hour early; declaring a holiday while unaware of the consequences; and finally, having his audience of nuns laughing at everything he says not because what he says is funny but because they are watching a cat carry on behind him. Such trials hardly amount to martyrdom and audiences may not be expected to get more than a laugh out of them; nevertheless, they reveal essential details of Chuck's acceptance of providence. In the first, he faces a potentially serious situation with concern but without undue anxiety, in the second and third he calmly accepts how his own well-intentioned but ignorant action may have caused trouble for others, and in the fourth he shows a remarkable ability to accept good-naturedly being the butt of a joke. Later, there are more serious analogies of ignorance to come. Near the end of the film he learns that he has been ignorant of much of what Sister Benedict has been doing and of why his efforts with Patsy had not been working. That his efforts are failing only serves to reinforce O'Malley's confidence in divine providence.

Interestingly, there are only two explicitly religious scenes in the films. The first one comes in *Going My Way* when Mr. Bogardus and Sister Benedict are in prayer. She prays not that things be otherwise or simply that God's Will be done. Rather she prays that she understand God's Will; she asks for some relief from the blind obedience she has shown so far. Her request is granted, through Chuck O'Malley, of course, but it is clear from an earlier scene that he is acting out of his own self-interest. The second one comes in *The Bells of St. Mary's*. The conflict between Sister Benedict and Father O'Malley, which had been a major running plot line, ends up getting resolved when it is revealed that both of them were acting in complete ignorance of why Patsy was acting the way she was.

While both films have been greatly appreciated by audiences and critics, some have felt that *Bells* suffers from its status as a sequel. In fact, however, there are some striking ways in which the sequel adds importantly to the theme developed here. In discussing ignorance of divine providence, one of the most difficult themes to make clear is why it is the wise who are more likely to understand their ignorance. The theme itself is as old as Socrates but in *Bells* it is brought out cleverly by giving viewers details of Father O'Malley's highly-trained mind, and at the same time showing his ignorance. Thus the tutoring session and the paper he helps Patsy write are presented in full, while O'Malley is clearly puzzled as to how the one led to the other.

Finally, the main storyline of *Bells* has often been misunderstood. It is often assumed that Father O'Malley charms the industrialist Mr. Bogardus into donating his property to the school. Some have found the story sentimental or have assumed that supernatural intervention was involved in Bogardus's transformation. In fact, the line is more complex and more Butlerian, right along the lines of the cool hour passage. The point of the cool hour passage is that even when one has good moral reasons for acting to benefit others, people generally will not act on such motives until they are seen to be in accord with self-interest or at least not contrary to it. Father O'Malley knows he must appeal to self-interest as well as morality. He gets Dr. McKay to agree that charity toward others is good for the heart. He then lets the doctor persuade Mr. Bogardus, or at least so it seems. Admittedly, this argumentation is presented in a popular and simplistic way. The point is, neither O'Malley's famous charm nor the nuns' prayers are involved in the outcome. All that is involved is a claim about self-interest presented by what the patient takes to be a competent medical authority. The ignorance involved here is, of course, that O'Malley makes no claim regarding why or how duty and obedience correspond, and he certainly makes no appeal to divine intervention in favor of those who do the right thing. His only appeal is to what he claims to be the ordinary working of our human nature.

Many scenes follow that are not relevant to this theme, but there are two mentions of self-interest in the story about Patricia. When Patricia's mother talks to Father O'Malley about having Patricia admitted to St. Mary's, the conversation ends with O'Malley saying, "I'll take care of your daughter if you'll take care of yourself." This follows Butler's injunction that the problem is not that people care too much for themselves and too little for others but rather that they do not even care enough about their own happiness. Later, when Father O'Malley is helping Patricia with her essay (an essay that is eventually read in full), he tells her that if we use common sense we will be happy by virtue of using our powers in accord with right reason. Here again is the entirely naturalistic line that Butler favored. This time the philosophy, however simplistic, is at least fully explicit.

Bishop Butler in the eighteenth century and Bing Crosby two hundred years later presented the world with a rendition of the religious life that appealed to a very large audience. Butler's works were used in the training of Anglican priests, and the Father O'Malley films inspired young men to become Catholic priests. I have argued that the sources of this appeal are the same in both cases. Religion is presented as a providential view of life that is natural and practical as well as sophisticated in its understanding of our ignorance, and optimistic in anticipating a complete coincidence of goodness and happiness.

Notes

1. William James, *The Varieties of Religious Experience* (London: Longmans, 1902).
2. James, chapter 5.
3. Joseph Butler, *Analogy of Religion* (London: Knapton, 1736), part I, chapter 7.
4. Butler, introduction.
5. Joseph Butler, *Fifteen Sermons* (London: Knapton, 1726), sermon 15.
6. Butler, *Analogy,* part I, chapter 7.
7. Butler (1726), *Sermon* 11.
8. Butler (1726), *Sermon* 11.
9. Butler (1736), part I, chapter 7.

2

Going My Way?: Crosby and Catholicism on the Road to America

Eric Michael Mazur

Introduction

In his history of Irving Berlin's song "White Christmas," Jody Rosen reflects on the ironic fact that one of the most popular Christmas songs of the twentieth century had been written by a Russian Jewish immigrant.

> The pop-song industry was dominated in both its creative and commercial spheres by Jews—many of them, like Berlin, recent immigrants—and the music it gave the world was the music of assimilation, a New World concoction: the result of a people's striving for social acceptance and a piece of the American pie.[1]

In his own analysis of the early motion picture industry, Neal Gabler comes to much the same conclusion.[2] As Rosen puts it, "much of twentieth-century pop culture is a kind of Yankee Doodle Yiddishkeit." Members of this religious community, which was increasingly dominated by impoverished immigrants who were confronting the conflict between the American dream of success and the American reality of marginalization, sought out venues available to them—such as the emerging fields of recorded music and motion pictures—to recast themselves into a form more familiar, and thus more acceptable, to the American dominant culture. In so doing, argue both Gabler and Rosen, they "remade American pop culture in their own image" and recreated what it meant to be an "American."[3]

The history of religion in twentieth-century America reveals other groups, besides the Jewish community, whose members struggled with the forces of marginalization in an attempt to enter the cultural mainstream only to profoundly affect that culture in the process. However, one group that receives significantly less attention in the literature is the American Catholic community, which in its own way struggled "for social acceptance and a piece of the American pie." In the twentieth century, American Catholics, like their Jewish neighbors, sought admission into the American way of life and many of them did it in exactly the same (or parallel) venues, whether they were Catholic singers, actors, or—in their own way—critics of both of those industries.[4] Just as Jewish songwriters and moviemakers recast the image of America while they worked their way into the mainstream, American Catholics involved in American public culture also reworked what it meant to be an American.

The following argument begins with an analysis of several films, starring Bing Crosby, that showcase the image of American Catholicism in the mid-twentieth century, a period when the Catholic community sought to find its place in American culture. The analysis examines Crosby as a valuable role model, the Catholic characters he presented, and the possible messages they conveyed to the viewing audience—both Catholic and non-Catholic—about what Catholicism in America could be, regardless of whether it actually was as it was portrayed or not.

And yet, the fact that Catholics, like Jews, underwent this process of "Americanization"—as did other religious communities—suggests that there were larger forces at play than those related to one particular religious community.[5] In the twentieth century, "Americanization" meant more than becoming Protestant-like, it meant negotiating not just between different religious traditions, but also between particularistic religious identity and a public presence that superceded tradition. By maintaining focus on Crosby, we can examine how a paragon of public Catholicism, seen and admired by millions, also reflected the larger processes of "Americanization" in American religion, processes similar to those experienced by American Jews. These forces were part of an ongoing process within and across American culture that involved not just Jews and not just Catholics but all of American religious culture. This period of radical transformation—or as sociologist Robert Wuthnow describes it, the "restructuring" of American religion that took place during the middle decades of the twentieth century—was not simply a coincidence of events introduced by a variety of separate religious communities, but was a reorganization of what it meant to be an American and particularly what it meant to identify with religion in America.[6] Not only did American Catholics work to become part of the American mainstream, but in so doing they also participated in the larger transformation of American religion.

The Context of American Catholicism

By the time Al Smith had been defeated by Herbert Hoover in the presidential campaign of 1928, Catholicism had been a part of North American culture for over four hundred years. However, there is little doubt that life in the United States had always been difficult for most Catholics. Political limitations and prohibitions on voting, office-holding in a variety of states—in some cases through the nineteenth century—the rise of the nativist movement in the first half of the nineteenth century, the burning of the Charlestown monastery in 1834, the publication of the virulently anti-Catholic "Maria Monk" forgery in 1836, and the culturally- and religiously-charged debates related to alcohol use and Prohibition in the early twentieth century left the American Catholic community understandably uncomfortable.[7] American historian Arthur Schlesinger, Jr., noted that the prejudice against Catholicism was "the deepest bias in the history of the American people."[8] In the eyes of many American Protestants, by the second decade of the twentieth century, "to be a Catholic was to be a soldier of a secret army, sworn at the Pope's command to 'burn the nation, slaughter the Protestant men, outrage the Protestant women, and flog the Protestant children into being obedient Catholics.' "[9] It is therefore understandable why historian of American religion Martin Marty noted, in his three-volume history of religion in twentieth-century America, that although Catholics had "been in the hemisphere since the fifteenth century, on the continent since the sixteenth, in the colonies since the seventeenth, in the nation since the eighteenth, [and] in place as the largest denomination since the nineteenth," they were "still on the defensive through the first half of the twentieth."[10]

By 1965, things were very different. America had elected a Catholic president—albeit not without controversy—and had made Bishop Fulton Sheen its "first religious television celebrity."[11] By the second half of the twentieth century, Catholicism had evolved from an immigrant church into what sociologist Will Herberg would call "one of the three great 'American religions.' "[12] The change in climate was so profound that by 1972, in *A Religious History of the American People*, Sydney Ahlstrom felt the need to identify the period after World War II as "Post-Puritan America."[13]

Much had changed for American Catholicism in forty years. Immigration increases accounted for a larger Catholic presence in American society that, in the words of Martin Marty, "had grown to threatening size";[14] between 1900 and 1950, Catholic population increased from 10.8 million to 28.6 million, or from fourteen to nineteen percent of the total American population. The economic advancement of its immigrant and now-resident communities enabled those Catholics to participate in a greater diversity of American cultural pursuits. "By the mid-1960s," write Bryan Froehle and Mary Gautier, "the legacy of earlier European immigrants began to smooth out, and Catholics came to rank above Protestants on most Gallup poll indices of socioeconomic status. Within a decade," they conclude, "the average annual family income of white Catholics matched or exceeded white Protestant groups."[15] In addition, the public role of Catholic figures like Cardinal Francis Spellman during World War II and the "complete identification between divine and American purposes" in fighting that war and the Cold War that followed, brought Catholics and Protestants together in patriotism, and the increasingly visible role of Catholic lay-figures, such as Bing Crosby, Spencer Tracy, and Pat O'Brien, made Catholicism more familiar to the American non-Catholic public and eased the shift of Catholicism into the mainstream in American culture.[16] Writes historian of American Catholicism John Tracy Ellis, "if the first generation of these ethnic groups clung to their respective ghettos, their children were much less content to do so, and their grandchildren broke entirely with the Old World framework and sought—with striking success—to enter the mainstream of American life."[17]

Ironically, these changes in American Catholic numbers and attitudes represented more than the emergence of another major religious tradition into American public culture. As Marty noted, American Catholics had been members of the largest single religious denomination in America since the mid-nineteenth century, and had been recognized by the Vatican as an established national church since 1908.[18] But, as various scholars have argued, the changes in any one American religious tradition had as much to do with overall changes in views of religion as they did with changes in the religious makeup of American society. Historian Robert Handy describes what he identifies as the loss of a Protestant monopoly on American public culture beginning at the end of the nineteenth century and increasingly obvious in the early decades of the twentieth.[19] Sociologists such as Robert Wuthnow, Wade Clark Roof, and Phillip Hammond have described the transformations in the organization, contours, and practice of American religion, each focusing on the middle decades of the twentieth century.[20] All have suggested that, over the course of the twentieth century, religion for all Americans, Catholic or otherwise, was transforming. In other words, while Catholics were emerging into American public culture—which had been from its start heavily Protestant—that culture was itself transforming away from those Protestant roots and into a form of religious identity that would transcend particularistic and tradition-based religious identity.

Crosby as Representative

To be sure, Bing Crosby did not personally cause this transformation of American Catholicism, nor was he singly responsible for the transformation of how Protestant America saw Catholicism. He is, however, representative of these changes in American religious culture—both of Catholicism and of the American religious culture generally—even while he (like a handful of other Catholic public figures) participated in changing how non-Catholics perceived their Catholic neighbors. It is therefore easy enough to justify focusing on Crosby as representative of the transformations that took place in the environment surrounding American Catholicism.

First, there is his own identification with Catholicism. Born Harry Lillis Crosby, Jr., in Tacoma, Washington in 1903, and raised in Spokane from the time he was two, Bing Crosby was well-versed in Catholicism, having spent eight years in Jesuit institutions (including Gonzaga High School and Gonzaga University)—he even considered joining the priesthood.[21] Crosby remained "a practicing Catholic his whole life long" and, despite having descended from Protestant as well as Catholic lineage, publicly embraced his Irish Catholic identity by the early 1940s. Jody Rosen describes Crosby's reluctance early in his career to record two religious songs ("Silent Night" and "Adeste Fideles") until the record company agreed to donate the profits "to an American Catholic mission in China."[22]

Second, there is the public's strong perception of Crosby as a Catholic. After playing Father O'Malley in *Going My Way*, Crosby seemed to embody Catholicism in American culture.[23] Labeling him "the best known fictional priest in America," Les and Barbara Keyser argue, "when anyone in America thinks of Catholics in film, Father O'Malley is invariably the first name to come to mind."[24] Recalling his participation in *Going My Way*, Crosby himself noted that, while he was familiar with the habit of fans mistaking the role for the actor, "this was the first time I'd gotten the full treatment myself." He remembered receiving fan mail from around the world addressed to "Father Crosby or the Reverend Crosby." He was admonished for eating meat-filled hors d'oeuvres at a reception held on a Friday, and his wife's aunt expressed dismay that he would play golf with Humphrey Bogart, noting that she was shocked at the "idea of a priest and a gangster getting together on a golf course!"[25]

And third, there is the place of Crosby in American public culture. He was an enormously popular public figure with nearly fifty million listeners tuning in to his *Kraft Music Hall* radio broadcasts in the 1940s.[26] Notes his biographer Gary Giddins, by the end of the 1940s, Crosby had been voted "the most admired man alive" (according to the *Philadelphia Courier*), beating such figures as baseball great Jackie Robinson, World War II heroes General Eisenhower and General MacArthur, President Harry Truman, friend Bob Hope, and even the Pope. He was the "number one box-office attraction" between 1944 and 1948, and in the twenty years between 1934 and 1954, was in the top-ten fifteen times. His recording of Irving Berlin's "White Christmas" was on the music charts in twenty of the twenty-one years from 1942 to 1962, and he was also the first white artist to chart on *Billboard*'s Harlem Hit Parade.[27] Two films in which he starred, *Going My Way* and *The Bells of St. Mary's*, were the highest-grossing films for Paramount Pictures and RKO Pictures, respectively, until 1947, and a third, *White Christmas*, was the biggest money-making film of 1954, earning more than any previous Irving Berlin film. Over the course of his singing career, he would see nearly four hundred of his recordings make the charts with nearly forty of them becoming number one hits. By the end of the twentieth century, his recordings had sold more than four hundred million copies worldwide.[28]

His popularity can be linked, in part, to his personality; he was often seen as a sympathetic figure, an "Everyman."[29] According to one reviewer, ushers reported that, in the various "Road" movies Crosby made with Bob Hope, "the spectators all laugh at Hope and identify themselves with Crosby."[30] Rosen notes that Crosby credited his own success to fans' belief that "they could sing like him in the shower."[31] Writes Terry Teachout, by World War II, Crosby was "more than a pop singer, more than a movie star." He was "a member of the family."[32]

But just as important as the role Crosby played for his audiences, there is the role Crosby played in the development of American popular culture. While Rosen suggests that Crosby's popularity was the result of his recordings coinciding with the very moment recorded music overtook live performances in radio broadcasting; he also identifies his voice as "modern," suggesting more than coincidence.[33] Biographer Giddins takes the argument further, noting that Crosby could be used "to trace the whole development of American popular culture": how his career coincided with the development of the recording, radio, and film industries; how "the conversion from acoustic to electric recordings" was particularly conducive to Crosby, a baritone; how Crosby's "fabled skill with the mike fostered a more intimate singing style"; and how the transition from silent to sound films propelled Crosby as "one of the first major stars of talking pictures." Notes Giddins, Crosby "was at the center of so many different aspects of the cultural life of that period."[34]

"Father Crosby" and "Crosby Catholicism"

Given the import role Crosby played in mid-century American culture, it is not surprising to suggest that one facet of his most public persona—that is, his film characters—might have an influence on the viewing audience, even in the area of religion. John Shelton Lawrence and Robert Jewett call this the "Werther Effect," a phenomenon—named for the fictional Goethe character, who was the subject of much fascination in the late eighteenth and early nineteenth century—by which fans identify with fictional characters.[35] Nor is it a surprise to suggest that the most obvious films to provide us with information about American Catholicism are those in which Crosby most clearly represented the tradition to viewers—those films in which he played a Catholic priest modeling "Crosby Catholicism" to the audience. The most representative—*Going My Way*—was an enormous financial and artistic success for Paramount Pictures; in just over ten weeks at the Paramount Theater in New York the film had been seen by over a million people, earned just under $850,000, and, according to Charles Reagan (Paramount's vice president in charge of distribution), was "piling up box office receipts in such a way that it is clearly apparent that it would be the biggest grosser ever released by Paramount."[36] In Crosby's own words, it also "won a flock of Academy Awards," including best supporting actor (for Barry Fitzgerald), best picture, best original song ("Swinging On a Star"), and best original story, as well as an Oscar for best actor for Crosby himself.[37] It was voted best picture of the year by the New York Film Critics, and Crosby's performance was voted the best of the year in a national poll of reviewers conducted by *Film Daily*.[38] One critic noted that "the film's hosannahs, sung generously by the critics, the lay public and by the company, seem more than amply justified," while another called it a "top-notch film . . ." and declared it "the best show of [Crosby's] career."[39] The second film in this category—*The Bells of St. Mary's*, which was a sequel to *Going My Way*—was designed to capitalize on the success of the earlier film. This film also enjoyed some artistic success and received Oscar nominations for best motion picture, best director (Leo McCarey), best actor, and best actress (Ingrid Bergman).[40] The third film—*Say One for Me*—was not as well received but in many ways centers more consciously around the paradigmatic Crosby-as-priest, "Father Crosby."[41]

The image of Catholicism portrayed in these three films is powerful and the message—that Catholics are not that different from Protestants, that they are good Americans, and that they can be "hip"—is directed not just at non-Catholics in the audience but at Catholic moviegoers as well. For the non-Catholics, these films present a Catholicism that is demystified and Americanized, and they respond to the history of anti-Catholicism that had not too long before reached its zenith in

America. For the Catholics, these films offered a formula by which they could negotiate between their often-conflicting desires to fit into American culture on the one hand and their own cultural exceptionalism on the other, and to instruct Catholics on how members of the "immigrant church" could be the paradigmatic American citizens.[42]

Suggesting why *Going My Way* may have been such a success, scholar of religion and film Margaret Miles argues, "films that succeed at the box office are those that identify currently pressing social anxieties and examine a possible resolution."[43] Crosby, as Father O'Malley, is assigned to replace Father Fitzgibbon (Barry Fitzgerald), who has led St. Dominic's parish since it was founded in 1897. As *New York Times* critic Bosley Crowther summarized it, the film portrays "a progressive young Catholic priest who matches his wits and his ideas with those of the elderly pastor of a poor parish" in a story of "new versus old customs" and of "traditional age versus youth."[44]

The sequel—*The Bells of St. Mary's*—continues in the pattern of showcasing Catholicism established by *Going My Way*. Father O'Malley is reassigned to take control of an aging Catholic school, and while there is the familiar dilemma over "bricks and mortar" concerns (this time the expansion of the school into a new building rather than face foreclosure of the church), the central engine for the plot is another personality conflict; not between a young Crosby and an old Fitzgerald, but between a very masculine Crosby and a very feminine Ingrid Bergman.

The third film in this category, *Say One for Me*, is the story of Father Conroy, a priest in Manhattan's theater district whose parish caters to the theater crowd (by holding Mass at 2:00 a.m., for example). He promises to look out for the daughter of a parishioner who has fallen ill, and when she takes a job at a nightclub, Father Conroy comes to her rescue. Fortunately, he also secures enough talent for his ecumenical fundraiser as well.

Catholicism—as a religious tradition distinct from Protestantism—is treated very gingerly in all three "Father Crosby" films. Part of the reason might have been because of the restrictions spelled out in the Motion Picture Production Code, which was quite clear about the depiction of religion and clergy.[45] However, regardless of the reasons, the depictions have the effect of minimizing whatever exoticism—or fear—might have been associated with Catholicism. It is noteworthy that of the three "Father Crosby" films, neither of the first two depicts Crosby doing anything specifically liturgical. In both *Going My Way* and *The Bells of St. Mary's*, there are no significant scenes that include a group of Catholic worshippers actually engaging in prayer—for example, there are no depictions of Mass—but only portrayals of individual Catholics praying. There are, of course, very clear clues relating to Catholicism: priests in collars, nuns in habits, and the occasional use of terminology specific to Catholicism. But for the most part, the priests and nuns seem only to oversee the material aspect of running the Church. This has been a historic critique of religious portrayal—an emphasis on "bricks and mortar" issues diminishing the religiosity of the Church in favor of materialism.[46] However, as historian Garry Wills has noted, this was "surprisingly true to Catholic life," noting that the film "celebrated all the church's faults as if they were virtues."[47] One reviewer at the time noted favorably that the presentation of the clergy "as simple, human folk" made them "thoroughly honest and real," and "concerned with such things as are Caesar's—such things as we all understand."[48] It isn't until *Say One for Me*, made near the end of the 1950s, that we actually get to see "Father Crosby" performing rites and rituals central to the Catholic tradition. But even there, the depictions minimize Catholic difference: the scenes taking place during Mass are focused primarily on the Protestant-like homily, and the one baptism scene in the film is truncated, its action implied rather than portrayed.

Given the climate of anti-Catholicism during the first half of the century, these depictions have the effect of softening the image of Catholicism for the audience. As Les and Barbara Keyser observe, "Crosby made O'Malley's Roman collar a powerful and positive icon, undermining anti-Catholicism at the very primitive level where prejudices are formed, the level of memory, association, and emotion." They conclude that those seeing Crosby in this role understood that "his version of Catholicism is quite a religion." The depictions also have the effect of making Catholicism seem a bit more like Protestantism. Its presentation was so attractive that, after the release of *Going My Way*, "some Protestants even went so far as to complain to the Production Code Office that Catholic clergy were being given preferential treatment in movies and that there should be Protestant equivalents."[49]

On the other side of the aisle, the message to American Catholics in the audience is one of empowerment for those seeking to become more mainstream Americans—that is, more like their Protestant neighbors. The Catholicism of Father Fitzgibbon (in *Going My Way*) is "authoritarian," "loveable but doddering," and "admirable but a trifle too inflexible," while that of his replacement, Father O'Malley, is "athletic, musical, and cheerful" as well as "practical, up-to-date, and infectious."[50] Noted one reviewer, "he's the sort of padre that any tough kid would follow and respect."[51] The Catholicism of Father Conroy in *Say One for Me* is similar, albeit a dozen years older; the Father's comfort in the theater district suggests that he regards his own job as—at least in part—dependent upon theatrics for success, and he is as comfortable discussing show business with dancers, comedians, and drunks as he is discussing the life of the Church with his fellow clergy. One reviewer noted that Crosby was "just about as usual, a little less lively, perhaps, a little older looking, but still casual and sincere. He'll never make Monsignor. He'll always be a parish priest, whenever he turns his collar backward, because you always sense a sport shirt underneath."[52]

But to be honest, very little recognizable Catholic doctrine is mentioned in the "Father Crosby" movies, and what there is seems banal. Father O'Malley explains his devotion to one couple in *Going My Way* by telling them that he is a priest because he enjoys helping people. "Religion doesn't have to be this [he plays somber music on the piano], taking all the fun out of everything; it can be bright, and bring you closer to happiness." And while "Father Crosby" spends a significant time in all three films saving souls and collecting wayward Catholic sheep, it is only his character in *Say One for Me*, Father Conroy, who agrees to baptize the child of an unmarried show girl; however, as mentioned above, this ritual is only implied.

The presentation of Catholic doctrine notwithstanding, the image of a priest presented on the screen served both as a powerful affirmation for American Catholics as well as a relief for non-Catholics in how they might see Catholic clergy. One reviewer observed positively that *Going My Way* presented Catholic clergy in "a human and unaffected light." He observed that "the people out there in Hollywood" had a habit of portraying clergy with "an air of highly self-conscious informality which is as mushy as a plate of oatmeal," and expressed relief that this film did not resort to the "particularly annoying" portrayal of "the 'Pat O'Brien type' of Catholic priest, which [had] become on the screen as stock a character as the big-hearted Irish cop." Instead, the characters in this film "insinuate themselves into your heart and give you a new, respectful feeling for clergymen—at least, with regard to the screen."[53]

Crosby himself took the power of the role very seriously. In his autobiography he recalled an episode in which studio executives encouraged him to appear in clerical garb as a gag cameo in one of Bob Hope's films. He refused. He also recounted some of the negative reactions to his manner, noting:

Not everyone approved of the fashion in which the young priest was humanized. I'd gone to a Jesuit school and I'd always found priests very human and not unlike the boys they taught, but in South American and Latin countries moviegoers objected to the priest I portrayed wearing a sweatshirt and playing baseball. I got a sizable amount of critical mail from those countries, reproving me for my "undignified" conception of the role of a priest.

However, His Holiness, Pope Pius XII, saw the picture several times and wrote a letter in which he described his enjoyment of the film, and said he thought it good to have the priesthood so humanized.[54]

It is worth noting that, at least as far as Crosby's memory of the event is concerned, the bulk of criticism came not from the United States, but from "South America and Latin countries," where the climate for Catholicism, and the Catholic–Protestant dynamic, was very different.

This Catholic–Protestant dynamic is often represented in the films as a friendly competition—but a competition with a definite edge—to see who is the "better" American, and expressions like patriotism, athletics, and general worldly engagement become the proxy arenas for what, in a pluralistic democracy, passes for religious confrontation. For example, in *Going My Way,* Father O'Malley marries a young couple so that the groom can go off to fight in World War II. In *The Bells of St. Mary's,* he oversees the students at the Catholic school as they recite the "Pledge of Allegiance" only to declare a "holiday" by dismissing them for the day. In all three "Father Crosby" films, sports is a consistent theme: Father O'Malley is presented as an athlete and fan of professional (and college) athletics, takes local children to baseball games, and seems to approve when two students get into a schoolyard fight, noting that the "outside" (read: non-Catholic?) world is difficult, and the kids need to know how to defend themselves. Later, Ingrid Bergman's character purchases *The Art of Boxing* by boxing champion Gene Tunney—a Catholic boxing celebrity well known to the general audience of the day—for one of the students. Father Conroy receives tickets to a basketball game from a nightclub owner (and wayward Catholic) and is clearly knowledgeable about officiating and gambling procedures. The implication is that Catholicism doesn't have to be meek, and can compete with Protestant culture on the gridiron ("Go Notre Dame!"), in the ring, and in society in ways that are definitively and undeniably American. It is unclear exactly for whom this message was most important: it seems to put the non-Catholic audience on notice, making them aware of an emerging, increasingly self-confident American Catholicism, while providing encouragement to the American Catholics in the crowd. Most telling might be the scene in *The Bells of St. Mary's,* when Ingrid Bergman's character calls on a student named Luther to recite material while Father O'Malley observes. "Luther? How'd he get in here?" asks O'Malley quietly to the teacher, jokingly connecting the student to the sixteenth-century protester of Catholic practices. Replies Bergman, with tongue in cheek, "We never knew."

The Catholic–Protestant dynamic provides another form of competition, not on the playing field, but in the mission field. This missionary competition, however, takes a form more acceptable for a community on the cultural margins—it is missionary work among the "unchurched." The threat to the St. Dominic's Church in *Going My Way* is not from Protestants, but from non-religion; the church is threatened with destruction and replacement not by another church, but by a parking lot. Father O'Malley berates a man whose window has just been destroyed by children playing stickball in the street. "I'm an atheist," notes the man, when O'Malley offers his rosary as payment for the broken window. When the man throws the damaging ball under a parked truck, O'Malley responds pejoratively, "You even throw like an atheist." In *The Bells of St. Mary's,* the future of the school rests on Father O'Malley's ability to "convert" the neighboring landowner to donate his new office complex. In these exchanges, Catholicism does not directly challenge Protestantism; however, each exchange expresses contempt for unbelief and shows Catholicism's ability to move men's souls, signaling its power to both Catholic and Protestant audience members.

In addition to the action and the dialogue, the song lyrics become locations of Catholic confrontation with Protestant America. For example, while the eponymous title song from *Going My Way* expresses optimism and longing for companionship, it is sung by a priest and therefore could be interpreted in light of the Catholic–Protestant dynamic as articulating a desire for peaceful coexistence with American non-Catholics. It applies vaguely Christian symbols as it concludes: "I hope you're going my way, too." In *The Bells of St. Mary's,* the lyrics are similarly suggestive, speaking of a "land of beginning again where skies are always blue," where "we've made mistakes," but where we should "forget the past and start life anew." Either these songs are minimizing a priest's vows of celibacy by projecting sexual longing, or they are larger statements about bigger issues. In either case, the result is a moderating of Catholic difference and particularism in Protestant American culture.

"I'm Dreaming of a White(ned) Christmas":
Crosby and Religion in America

Karen Brodkin, in her work on Jewish assimilation, describes the process by which American Jews negotiated their marginality over the course of the late nineteenth and early twentieth centuries, working to become—as she puts it—"white."[55] That is, they were working at blending in and becoming part of the American (and predominantly Protestant) mainstream. In his analysis of Irving Berlin's "White Christmas," Jody Rosen uses identical terminology.[56] While this is a familiar enough concept in the discussion of American Judaism, the same could be argued for any number of American immigrant communities, particularly those marginalized by their identification (self- or imposed) as outside the Protestant-dominated mainstream. What is often overlooked in such analyses, however, is the notion that such processes affect the mainstream itself. That is, American Protestantism has also been affected by the attempted—and often successful—efforts of others to join what is presumed to be the American mainstream. If what it means to be an "American" is altered by the changing makeup of America, then all are affected, the dominant as well as the minority culture. Evidence of this can be found in the reactions of many conservative Christians, who write nostalgically about an America of days past and explain the discomfort many of them have felt over the past few decades as they look out at the American landscape to see that they no longer control the production or maintenance of public symbols or meaning. The myth that all peoples will become Protestant-like as we all become "white," overlooks the movement away from a Protestant cultural monopoly in American public culture.

As was earlier suggested, "Father Crosby's" role in representing Catholicism of the middle decades as socially equal to its Protestant neighbors, was only a part of the transformation that was occurring in the American religious environment of the twentieth century. The other part, related to the leveling of the playing field for traditionally-marginalized religious communities, was the development of an emerging religious identity, which retained elements from, but still transcending, its historic connection to Protestant culture. Crosby, not only as a Catholic but as a significant public figure, also participated in the representation of this new picture of what public religious culture in America could be. He therefore provides an important bridge between the two related processes of transformation in American religious culture.

A second set of films starring Crosby provides evidence of this bridge. These films—*Holiday Inn* and *White Christmas*—are not explicitly religious; they are certainly not "Catholic" films like the three from the first set.[57] But as Margaret Miles has observed, just because a film is not "explicitly religious" does not mean that it doesn't "fall within the purview of religion and film."[58] These films are religious because of the way in which they present attitudes about the place and role of holidays—holy days—in mid-century American culture. And while both films are now associated with the Christmas season, this was not the original intention of *Holiday Inn*.[59] We might even argue that the latter's association with Christmas was inevitable only when the meaning of Christmas—and religious identity in general—changed in American public culture.

As noted above, the first of the two films, *Holiday Inn,* starring Bing Crosby, Fred Astaire, Virginia Dale, and Marjorie Reynolds, features Irving Berlin songs, such as "White Christmas" and "Easter Parade." Crosby's character tires of the entertainer's life and decides to establish an inn that will only be open on the holidays. While he suggests that this would mean the inn would be open about fifteen times a year, the film itself only identifies eight holidays. Rather than focusing on the identity of the holidays not included in the film, what is most interesting is the nature of those eight that make it into the film. Only two of the eight are traditionally Christian (Christmas and Easter Sunday), with another two being Christian in origin but widely celebrated throughout American society (New Year's Eve and St. Valentine's Day). One holiday is not specifically Christian but is religious in a specifically American context (Thanksgiving), and the last three are entirely patriotic (Lincoln's Birthday, Washington's Birthday, and Independence Day). The emphasis is on American cultural observances, giving credence to the theory that Irving Berlin was writing his way into the American mainstream; the most traditionally religious occasions—Christmas and Easter—have been entirely cleansed of their Christian-specific referents. As presented, all of the holidays are entirely accessible to all Americans—Catholic, Protestant, or Jew—and are not the "property" of any religious tradition. They are transformed into the warp and woof of the American culture.

The integration of these holidays into the meaning of what it is to be American is reinforced throughout the film. Mark Glancy argues that only two of the eight holidays represented are portrayed in a serious way—Independence Day and Christmas—suggesting a parallelism between the two.[60] Historian Jody Rosen notes that the song "White Christmas," which was seen as the centerpiece of this film by Berlin if not immediately by the American viewing public, is played three times, all in vaguely romantic settings, and once—when Crosby proposes marriage to Marjorie Reynolds—in blackface, suggesting a connection not only between this particular holiday and romance, but also to that most American of dilemmas, race.[61] And a shot of a newspaper column called "Where to Go" announces the opening of the inn (on New Year's Eve): "Holiday Inn: Opens tonight: don't ask why; just go and God Bless America!" Even the mystery of the unidentified seven holidays suggests an open-endedness, reminiscent of Gen. Eisenhower's oft misquoted line: "Our form of government has no sense unless it is founded in a deeply felt religious faith, and I don't care what it is."[62]

The second film in this set, *White Christmas,* starring Crosby, Danny Kaye, Vera-Ellen, and Rosemary Clooney, revolves around two entertainer war buddies who decide to assist their former commander who has retired from the military to run an inn. This film, created to exploit the formula developed in *Holiday Inn,* reinforces the American nature of these holidays, particularly Christmas. The central events occur at the patriotically-named Columbia Inn (the figure represented across American history), and both times the song "White Christmas" is sung, the audience is filled with American servicemen—the first time at a USO-type event for combat soldiers in Europe and the second time at a military reunion at the inn. In each of these scenes, there is a strong connection made among the Christmas holiday, this particularly non-theological song, and American patriotism. In the first, American servicemen become silent as they recall a home far away, while in the second, American servicemen celebrate the triumphant return to that home. One scholar has even suggested that it is the American servicemen, stationed around the world during World War II, who made this song such a hit, going so far as to identify it as "America's wartime anthem."[63]

The association of these two films with Christmas—a holiday that has become increasingly associated with American culture rather than with a specific religious tradition—is particularly interesting in comparison with the films in the first set. Neither *Going My Way* nor *The Bells of St. Mary's* shares such seasonal associations—with any holiday—although *The Bells of St. Mary's* is connected to Christmas indirectly: Henry Travers (who plays Clarence the angel in *It's a Wonderful Life*) has a significant supporting role in *The Bells of St. Mary's*.[64] The one film from the first set that contains any substantial Christmas content—*Say One for Me*—is also the one film in which "Father Crosby" is most explicitly Catholic. But it was also the least successful of all five films discussed. Could it be that by the time this film is released, a Christmas song sung by the clearly Catholic "Father Crosby" is no longer in tune with the times, even though that song is as theologically amorphous as "White Christmas" or any of the other Irving Berlin songs from *Holiday Inn* or *White Christmas*? Maybe it wasn't as fine a song. But as Jody Rosen writes, "The celebration of the American Christmas—that magically sanctified and ostentatiously irreligious holiday—became a kind of patriotic act." Patriotism, like many other public expressions articulated in the beginning of the 1950s, emphasized communal, ecumenical identity rather than difference. "Not coincidentally," continues Rosen, "it was during this same period that Chanukah, a relatively minor holiday on the Jewish calendar, gained the status of the 'Jewish Christmas,' an effort not just to preserve a distinctive Jewish identity but to hitch together the two festivals in display of the nation's cultural oneness." The public celebration of Christmas, and maybe the entirety of the public religious calendar, had by the 1950s become disconnected from its Christian roots such that (to some it seemed) even Jews—but certainly Catholics—could join in. The only song with any specific theological reference ("all God's people shall be free"), presented in *Holiday Inn* on Lincoln's Birthday, is more clearly a statement about American exceptionalism than it is about theological preferences. "Father Crosby" had given way to "Santa Cros," and while the American public might appreciate minimized differences between Catholics, Protestants, and Jews, it could certainly celebrate itself across religious traditions in ways that were becoming primarily, if not uniquely, American in character.[65]

Conclusions

"Most filmgoers," agues Margaret Miles, "consciously or unconsciously, will see and discuss the film they watch in relation to the common quandaries of the moment."[66] Over the course of the twentieth century, one of those quandaries has been: How does America's diversity relate to its growing sense of pluralism? The first part was a socio-historical fact: America's diversity was expanding as a greater variety of people came to the United States, whether they were Catholics, Jews, Muslims, Hindus, or Buddhists. The second part was never certain; how does a society confront diversity and how does it grapple with difference?

These two processes are clearly evident in the films discussed above. In the first set, an American Catholic community, present on the continent since the beginning of the European encounter, struggles to find its place in a public culture dominated by Protestants. The Catholicism represented by "Father Crosby" is a Catholicism of confidence and patriotism, difference but not deviance. In the second set, an American religious community, represented as much by a Catholic actor as by his Jewish songwriter, articulates what America can look like if it is to accept them both as equals. Catholics and Jews, and over the course of the twentieth century a host of other traditionally marginalized communities, would struggle between the desire to maintain their particularistic identity on the one hand and the desire to participate in the larger public culture on the other. Of the first, they would assert themselves into the consciousness of America, and of the second, they would reconfigure the rules and traditions to justify their participation. Together, they would transform both the content and nature of religion in America.

By the end of the twentieth century, amid calls from some Christians to "put the Christ back in Christmas," television viewers would hear Bart Simpson, animated child star of *The Simpsons,* proclaim in reaction to a Christmas special hosted by a Jewish comedian, "Christmas is the time when people of all religions come together to worship Jesus Christ."[67] At the same time, in *Lynch v. Donnelly* (1984), the United States Supreme Court would pronounce a nativity scene—the representation of one of the most significant events in Christianity—merely a cultural symbol whose public maintenance did not offend the separation of church and state. While it is tempting to read this as the re-conquest of Christianity over American society, it may actually be the logical conclusion of Americanization of religion. As Catholicism and Judaism joined the American religious mainstream once controlled by Protestantism, the nature of that mainstream would be forever changed. Biographer Gary Giddins was right, not only was Bing Crosby "at the center of so many different aspects of the cultural life of that period," but his roles as both "Father Crosby" and "Santa Cros" illustrate one of the most profound religious transformations of American history.

Notes

My thanks to Kate McCarthy for her assistance developing the initial idea for this paper, and the staff at the Bertrand Library for their assistance securing (wink wink!) some of the research material covered in this paper.

1. Jody Rosen, *White Christmas: The Story of an American Song* (New York: Scribner, 2002), 12.

2. Neal Gabler, *An Empire of Their Own: How the Jews Invented Hollywood* (New York: Doubleday, 1988).

3. Rosen, *White Christmas*, 12.

4. See Gregory D. Black, *Hollywood Censored: Morality Codes, Catholics, and the Movies* (New York: Cambridge University Press, 1994); Gregory D. Black, *The Catholic Crusade Against the Movies, 1940–1975* (New York: Cambridge University Press, 1997).

5. See R. Laurence Moore, *Religious Outsiders and the Making of Americans* (New York: Oxford University Press, 1986); and Eric Michael Mazur, *The Americanization of Religious Minorities: Confronting the Constitutional Order* (Baltimore: The Johns Hopkins University Press, 1999).

6. Robert Wuthnow, *The Restructuring of American Religion: Society and Faith Since World War II* (Princeton, NJ: Princeton University Press, 1988).

7. See John K. Wilson, "Religion Under the State Constitutions, 1776–1800," *Journal of Church and State* 32, no. 4 (Autumn 1990): 753–73; H. Frank. Way, "Death of the Christian Nation: The Judiciary and Church-State Relations," *Journal of Church and State* 29, no. 3 (Autumn 1987): 509–29; Catherine L. Albanese, *America: Religions and Religion*, 3rd ed. (Belmont, CA: Wadsworth Publishing Company, 1999), 505–10; Joseph R. Gusfield, "Moral Passage: The Symbolic Process in Public Designations of Deviance," *Social Problems* 15, no. 2 (Fall 1967): 175–88.

8. John Tracy Ellis, *American Catholicism*, 2nd ed., rev. (Chicago: The University of Chicago Press, 1969), 151.

9. Martin E. Marty, *Modern American Religion, v. ii: The Noise of Conflict, 1919–1941* (Chicago: The University of Chicago Press, 1991), 102.

10. Martin E. Marty, *Modern American Religion, v. iii: Under God, Indivisible, 1941–1960* (Chicago: The University of Chicago Press, 1996), 157.

11. Martin E. Marty, *A Short History of American Catholicism* (Allen, TX: Thomas More, 1995), 171.

12. Will Herberg, *Protestant—Catholic—Jew: An Essay in American Religious Sociology*, rev. ed. (Garden City, NY: Anchor Books, 1960), 136.

13. Sydney E. Ahlstrom, *A Religious History of the American People* (New Haven, CT: Yale University Press, 1972), 965.

14. Marty, *The Noise of Conflict, 1919–1941*, 148.

15. Bryan T. Froehle and Mary L. Gautier, *Catholicism 2000: A Portrait of the Catholic Church in the United States*. Maryknoll, NY: Orbis Books, 2000), 3, 16.

16. Marty, *A Short History of American Catholicism*, 166.

17. Ellis, *American Catholicism*, 167–68.

18. Marty, *A Short History of American Catholicism*, 142.

19. Robert T. Handy, *A Christian America: Protestant Hopes and Historical Realities*, 2nd ed. (New York: Oxford University Press, 1984); Robert T. Handy, *Undermined Establishment: Church-State Relations in America, 1880–1920* (Princeton, NJ: Princeton University Press, 1991).

20. See Robert Wuthnow, *After Heaven: Spirituality in American Since the 1950s* (Berkeley: University of California Press, 1998); Wade Clark Roof, *A Generation of Seekers: The Spiritual Journeys of the Baby Boom Generation* (San Francisco: Harper San Francisco, 1993); Phillip E. Hammond, *Religion and Personal Autonomy: The Third Disestablishment in America* (Columbia, SC: University of South Carolina Press, 1992).

21. Gary Giddins, *Bing Crosby: A Pocketful of Dreams, The Early Years, 1903–1940* (Boston: Little, Brown and Company, 2001), 53; Rosen, *White Christmas*, 99.

22. Terry Teachout, "Bing Crosby" (book review), *Commentary* 111, 4 (April 2000): 49; Giddins, *Bing Crosby*, 11; Rosen, *White Christmas*, 99.

23. *Going My Way*, directed by Leo McCarey (Paramount Pictures, 1944).

24. Les Keyser and Barbara Keyser, *Hollywood and the Catholic Church: The Image of Roman Catholicism in American Movies* (Chicago: Loyola University Press, 1984), 94–95.

25. Bing Crosby, *Call Me Lucky* (New York: Simon and Schuster; reprinted 1993, New York: Da Capo Press, 1953), 186–87.

26. Rosen, *White Christmas*, 98.

27. Giddins, *Bing Crosby*, 6–9; see also Rosen, *White Christmas*, 137.

28. *The Bells of St. Mary's*, directed by Leo McCarey (RKO Radio Pictures, Inc., 1945); *White Christmas*, directed by Michael Curtiz (Paramount Pictures, 1954); Giddins, *Bing Crosby*, 9; Rosen, *White Christmas*, 97, 172.

29. Rosen, *White Christmas*, 69.

30. Wes Gehring, "On the 'Road' with Hope and Crosby," *USA Today Magazine* (November 2000), 72, quoting a reviewer of *On the Road to Utopia*.

31. Rosen, *White Christmas*, 97.

32. Teachout, "Bing Crosby," 51 (quoting Giddins).

33. Rosen, *White Christmas*, 96, 140–41, 175–77.

34. Wendy Smith, "Gary Giddins: The True Life of a Crooner," *Publishers Weekly* (11 December 2000): 58.

35. John Shelton Lawrence and Robert Jewett, *The Myth of the American Superhero* (Grand Rapids, MI: William B. Eerdmans, 2002).

36. A. H. Weiler, "Happenings Hereabout: 'Going My Way' Set Record—Giant Mural for the Roxy," *New York Times* (16 July 1944): X3.

37. Crosby, *Call Me Lucky*, 38; "Crosby, Bergman Win Film Awards," *New York Times* (16 March 1945): 17.

38. " 'Going My Way' Gets Film Critics' Honor," *New York Times* (28 December 1944): 31; "Crosby 'Best of 1944' in Trade Paper Poll," *New York Times* (8 January 1945): 15.

39. Weiler, "Happenings Hereabout," X3; Bosley Crowther, " 'Going My Way,' Comedy-Drama With Bing Crosby and Barry Fitzgerald, at Paramount—New Film Palace," *New York Times* (3 May 1944): 25.

40. " 'St. Mary's' Lists 4 on 'Oscar' Ballots," *New York Times* (28 January 1946): 16.

41. *Say One for Me,* directed by Frank Tashlin (Twentieth-Century Fox, 1959).

42. See Jay Dolan, *The Immigrant Church: New York's Irish and German Catholics, 1815–1865* (Notre Dame, IN: University of Notre Dame Press, 1983).

43. Margaret R. Miles, *Seeing and Believing: Religion and Values in the Movies* (Boston: Beacon Press, 1996), 18.

44. Crowther, "Going My Way," 25.

45. Black, *Hollywood Censored*, 302–8.

46. See Roger Finke and Rodney Stark, *The Churching of America, 1776–1990: Winners and Losers in Our Religious Economy* (New Brunswick, NJ: Rutgers University Press, 1992).

47. Garry Wills, *Bare Ruined Choirs: Doubt, Prophecy, and Radical Religion* (Garden City, NY: Doubleday and Company, Inc, 1972), 23.

48. Bosley Crowther, "Clerical Callers: 'Going My Way' Gives a Human Picture of Men of God for a Change," *New York Times* (7 May 1944): X3.

49. Keyser and Keyser, *Hollywood and the Catholic Church*, 95, 102.

50. Keyser and Keyser, *Hollywood and the Catholic Church*, 98, 101.

51. Crowther, "Clerical Callers," X3.

52. Bosley Crowther, "Screen: 'Say One for Me,'" *New York Times* (20 January 1959): 11.

53. Crowther, "Clerical Callers," X3.

54. Crosby, *Call Me Lucky*, 187.

55. Karen Brodkin, *How Jews Became White Folks, and What that Says about Race in America* (New Brunswick, NJ: Rutgers University Press, 1999).

56. Rosen, *White Christmas,* 90.

57. *Holiday Inn*, directed by Mark Sandrich (Paramount Pictures, 1942).

58. Miles, *Seeing and Believing*, xii.

59. See Rosen, *White Christmas*; H. Mark Glancy, "Dreaming of Christmas: Hollywood and the Second World War," in *Christmas at the Movies: Images of Christmas in American, British and European Cinema*, ed. Mark Connelly, 59–76 (New York: I. B. Tauris, 2000), 68.

60. Glancy, "Dreaming of Christmas," 66.

61. Rosen, *White Christmas,* 117.

62. Patrick Henry, " 'And I Don't Care What It Is': The Tradition-History of a Civil Religion Proof-Text," *Journal of the American Academy of Religion* 49, no. 1 (March 1981): 41.

63. Rosen, *White Christmas,* 143.

64. *It's a Wonderful Life,* directed by Frank Capra (Republic Pictures, 1946).

65. Rosen, *White Christmas,* 98, 147.

66. Miles, *Seeing and Believing*, xiii.

67. The line is from *The Simpsons* episode "Marge Be Not Proud," which originally aired on 17 December 1995. My thanks to Kaoru Yamamoto for her assistance locating this quote.

3

Saint Bing: Apatheia, Masculine Desire, and the Films of Bing Crosby

Elaine Anderson Phillips

Bing Crosby was a pervasive presence in the lives of many Americans during the 1930s and 1940s. As his musical personality progressed from a "hot" scatting jazz singer to a smooth genre-spanning "American troubadour," he also became more than a singing voice to the American public through his film and live appearances. Crosby's laid back personal style, coupled with a growing mellowness in vocal technique and song selections, branded him as "cool" before the rise of bebop and "cool" jazz. Crosby's "coolness"—a self-control and personal authority, tempered by a casual use of that authority—became his signifying trait.

In his article, "Masculinity as Spectacle: Reflections on Men and Mainstream Cinema," Steve Neale writes: "Inasmuch as films do involve gender identification, and inasmuch as current ideologies of masculinity involve so centrally notions and attitudes to do with aggression, power, and control, it seems to me that narcissism and narcissistic identification may be especially significant."[1] Crosby's star image apparently lacks these qualities, until we realize that his persona emphasizes a self-control that governs the masculine aggressive streak and eventually leads to power. Thus, if "narcissism and narcissistic identification both involved phantasies [*sic*] of power, omnipotence, mastery and control"[2] for filmgoers watching stars, then Crosby triggered male fantasies of achieving power while not blatantly desiring it and using this power to persuade rather than force people into compliance.

Bing Crosby's on-screen image not only operates as a sign of identification for male viewers, but also as an unusual object of desire for female viewers. Crosby is a desiring but unaggressive male whom women viewers could desire without threat of male violence. Crosby lacks the aggressive sexuality of Clark Gable, the energetic ambition of James Cagney, and the physical grace of Fred Astaire. He does not win women through physical appeal or force. He relies on his voice, which his biographer Gary Giddins credits with eroticizing American song, and passive-aggressive manipulation.[3] Despite his assured heterosexuality, Bing Crosby does share some traits with his feminine viewers: he must use intelligence, indirection, and guile, if necessary, to get what he wants. Thus, the same women spectators who desired Crosby could unconsciously identify with his means of seduction. Unthreatening to both men and women alike, Crosby would (and still does) enjoy popularity among both sexes. As Crosby admitted in his autobiography, a great deal of his appeal to both sexes was that it did not seem elitist or belabored; he figured people liked him because he sounded the way the average man believed he sounded in the shower.[4] This "natural" phrasing was key to his cultural persona as an "authentic" common man made good. As Richard Dyer has observed, "Authenticity is both a quality necessary to the star phenomenon to make it work, and also the quality that guarantees the authenticity of the other particular values a star embodies. . . . It is this effect of authenticating authenticity that gives the star charisma."[5] The revelation of Crosby's "authentic" off-screen personality reinforced his screen persona through a multimedia publicity mechanism:

Stars appear before us in media texts—films, advertisements, gossip columns, television interviews and so on—but unlike other forms of representation stars do not only exist in media texts. To say that stars exist outside of the media texts in real life would be misleading, but stars are carried in the person of people who do go on living away from their appearances in the media, and the point is that we know this. . . . In the first place then the question of the star's authenticity can be referred back to her/his existence in the real world."[6]

Through recordings, radio, and film, as well as the constant references in each to the others, Bing Crosby's "star image" (a phrase coined by Dyer) became a consistent image of the same values: an easygoing, intelligent (even devious), unthreatening, unpretentious, and modest man of average tastes and exceptional luck. Crosby's personal modesty, in spite of his talent and wealth, struck many interviewers and co-workers strongly, which also helped to shape the meaning of "Bing Crosby" to the American public. While Crosby, as a successful performer and businessman, seems to have achieved a great deal of worldly success, both his public persona and the characters he played on screen do not place an obvious value on achievement. The Bing Crosby persona is a part of the world but not ruled by it. In the 1940s, this moved beyond a mien of admirable self-command and confident modesty to a more serious and devout connotation. For many Americans of the postwar years, Bing Crosby was no longer a devil-may-care singer/radio host/actor/sportsman, but a man of moral probity and sincerity, with a specifically Christian cast. "Bing Crosby" came to signify a masculine self-control combined with a moral gravitas based on the Christian virtue of detachment, also known as *apatheia.*

Apatheia is not the absence or repression of passions but the control of them; it is the state of being free from compulsion, obsession, and domination by the passions.[7] The classical pagan ideal of temperance is related to apatheia. In *Nicomachean Ethics,* Aristotle defined temperance as a deliberate subjection of bodily appetites to the mind: "Hence the appetitive element in a temperate man should harmonize with the rational principle; for the noble is the mark at which both aim, and the temperate man craves for the things he ought, as he ought, as when he ought; and when he ought; and this is what rational principle directs."[8] Temperance is also a form of indifference to the lack or withholding of physical satisfaction: "the self-indulgent man is so called because he is pained more than he ought at not getting pleasant things (even his pain being caused by pleasure), and the temperate man is so called because he is not pained at the absence of what is pleasant and at his abstinence from it.[9] What distinguishes apatheia from temperance, however, is the ultimate goal. Apatheia intends to free oneself from one's appetites in order to be free to love the highest good (or God). Aristotle's temperance is aimed toward creating a person who acts rationally and with larger goals than his own pleasure in mind. Thus temperance emphasizes the subordination of the passions to the mind, whereas apatheia requires freedom from mind itself in order to know God.

Apatheia became one of the central spiritual virtues developed by the early Desert Fathers. St. John Climacus, also known as John Scholasticus, John of the Ladder, and John of Sinai (ca. 579–649 CE) wrote *The Ladder of Divine Ascent,* one of the most influential books on Orthodox Christian spirituality. In it he states: "By dispassion I mean a heaven of the mind within the heart . . . Its effect is to sanctify the mind and to detach it from material things, and it does so in such a way that, after entering this heavenly harbor, a man, for most of his earthly life, is enraptured, like someone already in heaven, and he is lifted up to the contemplation of God."[10]

While the Greek word apatheia did not survive in the vocabulary of the Roman Catholic Church, the concept flourished as "dispassion," or "detachment." St. Catherine of Siena recorded God's rationale for the proper use of the material world: "I made these things to serve my rational creatures;[11] I did not intend my creatures to make themselves servants and slaves to the world's pleasures . . . They owe their first love to me. Everything else they should love and possess, as I told you, not as if they owned it but as something lent them." This seems more closely related to temperance's governing of desire but other Catholic writers would explore freedom from desire itself. Thomas à Kempis wrote: "Keep yourself as a pilgrim and a stranger here in this world, as one to whom the world's business counts by little. Keep your heart free, and always lift it up to God."[12]

St. John of the Cross also identifies desire, not possession, as a sin that separates humanity from God:

For we are not treating here of the lack of things, since this implies no detachment on the part of the soul if it has a desire for them; but we are treating of the detachment from them of the taste and desire, for it is this that leaves the soul free and void of them, although it may have them; for it is not the things of this world that either occupy the soul or cause it harm, since they enter it not, but rather the will and desire for them, for it is these that dwell within it.[13]

Detachment does not necessarily equal lack of possessions; it does mean mastery over or even indifference to what one has. Envy, gluttony, avarice, and lust are the sins that are antithetical to detachment because they stem directly from appetites that eventually rule the individual's decisions and behavior. Despite his wealth, business, and sporting interests, Bing Crosby has not been associated in the public's mind with the traits of avarice and greed. Part of this may be because he hired people like his brother Everett to do the hard bargaining for him[14] but this would also have originated from his Christian education at Gonzaga High and Gonzaga University. His high marks in Christian Doctrine indicate that he understood Roman Catholic theology.[15] Crosby may not have encountered the Greek term apatheia in his Jesuit education but he would have learned about the virtue of detachment and a stoic approach to the world's vagaries.[16] He attributed to the Jesuit priests a form of masculine piety that he took to heart: "while under such men I learned virility and devoutness, mixed with the habit of facing whatever fate set in my path, squarely, with a cold blue eye."[17] The last part of this quotation is telling because it emphasizes an appraisal of life uncluttered by emotions. In order to view life "squarely," one must do so without the fog of emotional needs or attachments shaping one's perceptions and dictating one's actions. Crosby embraced the classical ideal of temperance and the Christian refinement of dispassion or apatheia.

This paper focuses on three of Crosby's films from the 1940s and 1950s. I chose this time period because the Crosby persona, as both celebrity and star performer, had already been cemented into the American consciousness; furthermore, Crosby was a top box-office draw during the 1940s and early 1950s. To be fair, not all of Crosby's film roles during this time period consistently reflected a morally upright character; we have the "Road" series in which Crosby perpetually manipulates Bob Hope. Even later films, such as *Here Comes the Groom* (1951), portray Crosby as a likable schemer. But the dominant public image of Crosby as a calm, confident man and a decent moral figure evolved during this period. The key film in this evolution of the Crosby persona is *Going My Way* (1944). Despite Crosby's initial reluctance to play a priest, he performed the role so creditably that he not only won an Oscar, but also became conflated in fans' minds with the character he played.[18] *Going My Way* can be considered the film in which Crosby's secular "coolness" is converted to Christian detachment or apatheia, which allows him to act unselfishly towards the other characters. In order to understand the importance of this transformation, we also need to examine Crosby in similar roles before and after *Going My Way*. First, *Holiday Inn* (1942) reveals the conflict between the active- and passive-desiring male. Fred Astaire's aggressive pursuit of Marjorie Reynolds threatens Crosby's utopia, the inn built around pleasure and noncompetitiveness. *High Society* (1956) revisits the earlier situation of *Holiday Inn,* but here the apatheia introduced in *Going My Way* removes the prospect of humiliation for Bing Crosby's character. Crosby, the ex-husband who still loves the character played by Grace Kelly, contains his desire for her out of a mixture of apatheia and agape. *High Society* thus portrays the triumph of apatheia in secular and sexual matters.

In *Holiday Inn,* Bing Crosby's character, Jim Hardy, reinforces the public Crosby persona of an easygoing, noncompetitive fellow who chooses country life and a reduced work schedule over the hectic glamour of show business. *Holiday Inn* becomes a bucolic utopia based on pleasure and lack of competition; as Jim explains to Hollywood types who want to buy the film rights to the *Holiday Inn* story, it is "a simple little layout where we could do our best at the work we know how without having any illusions of glory."[19] This contrasts the material ambitions of his former fiancée, Lila Dixon, and the manic energy of the dancing part of his former act, Ted Hanover (Fred Astaire). Jim, however, reveals the negative side of his character when Linda Mason (Marjorie Reynolds) emerges as a love interest and as a new attraction for the inn. While Ted Hanover pursues Linda as a new dance partner and lover, Jim resorts to passive-aggressive behavior. Since Ted danced with Linda in a drunken fog on New Year's Eve, he doesn't remember her; when he asks Jim for a description of her, Jim generalizes and digresses. Jim stages a blackface number on Lincoln's Birthday to disguise Linda from Ted, and when Ted and his manager Danny try to follow her outside, Jim gives them wrong directions. Ted inevitably discovers Linda's identity when he comes upon Jim rehearsing a new song ("Be Careful, It's My Heart") and sweeps her into a romantic dance. Now Jim resorts to childish tricks, such as mixing up the tempo of the Washington's Birthday number, and, most unforgivably, sabotaging Linda's arrival for the Fourth of July production, since men from Hollywood are there to watch her and Ted. Linda's confrontation of him reveals her awareness of his manipulative and dishonest behavior:

Linda: Well, Jim, you deliberately kept me from working at the Inn tonight, didn't you?

Jim: Yeah.

Linda: You knew there would be men from Hollywood who might offer me a chance in pictures. You decided I shouldn't have that opportunity, not even the opportunity to refuse.

Jim: I was afraid the offer might be too important for you to turn down.

Linda: The point is you don't trust me to make my own decisions because they might interfere with your own selfish plans.

While Ted has not been honest with Jim or Linda, he has at least directly pursued her, swiftly deciding to dance with her during "Be Careful, It's My Heart," and declaring himself in love with her. When Linda demurs that he doesn't even know her, he tries to appeal to her ambition by telling her to pursue her Hollywood dreams instead of staying at the inn with Jim. Ted represents an excess of male energy and the male as aggressor: "If anything, Astaire's numbers reverse the usual psychoanalytical terms for describing gender identification symbolically, since in their orchestration of the male body as a site of joy they display plenitude and not lack, presence and not absence."[20] It is tempting to follow this line of reasoning and see Jim's singing as a Lacanian fall into language, an indication of "lack." Despite his easygoing demeanor, Jim lacks confidence and is unable to tell Linda directly that he loves her or to tell Ted to stay away. He is only able to act after his maid Mamie (Louise Beavers) refuses to believe his protest that he is okay after Linda leaves. She says, "Well, why you close the inn and sit around like a jellyfish with the misery? 'Cause a slicker stole your gal and you ain't got fight enough to get her back!" When Jim protests that he tried, Mamie tells him that his efforts were "Nothin' but tricks! If you went to Hollywood and told Miss Linda how much you loves her and misses her . . . I bet she'd be the quickest ex-movie star that ever exed!" Mamie, an African American, works as a sign of naturalness and authenticity; Jim finally sees that she is correct and that he needs to go to Hollywood to turn the tables on Ted and to woo Linda. As Mamie puts it, "You could melt her heart right down to butter if you turn on the heat." Jim does that by wooing Linda on the set of her movie and bringing her back to *Holiday Inn.*

Holiday Inn shows the risks of an overly-controlling superego to the male-desiring ego. Jim wants to be "nice"—noncompetitive, unaggressive, nonconfrontational. This lack of action almost loses him everything. It also shows that without a grounding in Christian theology, apatheia merely becomes apathy, as we see in Jim's sulkiness when Linda leaves for Hollywood.

In *Going My Way* (1944), Crosby's Father O'Malley is male apatheia incarnate. The character's first entrance in the film establishes a sense of his difference from others around him. O'Malley appears in clericals and a boater, asking directions to St. Dominic's. He covers a position for a little boy in a stickball game and promptly gets blamed for a broken window. When the angry apartment dweller confronts O'Malley about appropriate behavior for a priest, O'Malley accepts the blame (although he did not throw the ball) and offers his rosary beads as collateral until he can pay for the repairs. The angry man spurns the offer and insists he has no use for the beads because he is an atheist. When the man tosses the ball past O'Malley, the priest retorts, "You even throw like an atheist."[21] This short exchange reveals both O'Malley's humanity (he doesn't bless the man or offer to pray for him), but more importantly, it demonstrates appropriate Christian behavior without making it seem unrealistic or saccharine. O'Malley acknowledges he has done wrong, asks for forgiveness, and offers retribution; he models the Christian pattern of penance.

O'Malley's trappings of worldliness—the straw boater, the sweatsuit he wears when he meets Father Fitzgibbon (Barry Fitzgerald), the sporting equipment that arrives with his luggage—initially cause raised eyebrows. As Father Fitzgibbon asks fruitlessly several times, "What made you become a priest?" a timely interruption prevents O'Malley from replying. Yet as the film progresses, we realize that one possible answer to the question lies in O'Malley's detachment from worldly appetites. Sure, he led a dance band in his youth, dated an opera singer before seminary, and used to work out with the St. Louis Browns, but compared to the other characters, he is not governed by any passion. As he explains later to the young lovers, he chose a path that would fulfill his authentic inner self rather than the one of worldly success: "I had to decide whether to write the nation's songs or go my way." "My way" is to be in the world but not of it, to use its resources and amusements to lead people to a happiness based on unselfishness. Father O'Malley now chooses to use his musical talent to write music that shows "Religion can be bright . . . lead people closer to happiness." The song he uses to illustrate this, "Going My Way," is not only about delayed gratification, but also about an invitation to travel to the New Jerusalem, the redeemed world of a loving community where the road leads to "Rainbowville," a place where "the smiles you gather will look well on you / Oh I hope you are going my way too."[22]

Eventually, Father O'Malley will develop *koinonia*, a community of faith and un-selfish action at St. Dominic's, but for now, he operates in a world where people act on their own desires. Ted Haynes, Sr. is governed by greed; he wants the church to foreclose in order to build a profitable parking lot. Mrs. Quilp, the neighborhood gos-sip, is motivated by a lust to control others through gathering and spreading informa-tion. Carol James, the runaway, admits she couldn't stand her parents' rules; she wants her own way, while Ted Haynes, Jr. initially seems motivated by sexual lust for Carol. Even the apparently harmless Father Fitzgibbon is not immune; his appetite for good food blinds him to Tony Scapone's juvenile delinquency. He willingly ac-cepts the turkey Tony has stolen and tells O'Malley that Tony is a fine boy from an upstanding Catholic family. When O'Malley tells him that Officer McCarthy has told him that Tony has been in trouble with the law, Fitzgibbon's parochial prejudices color his reply: "Patrick McCarthy hasn't been to Mass in the past ten years!" It's only when Officer McCarthy brings Tony to the rectory and O'Malley talks to him that Fitzgibbon finally sees his error in judgment.

Initially, many of these characters read O'Malley's diffidence as a form of weakness. Father Fitzgibbon obviously sees him as a pastoral lightweight, and worldly characters see him as ineffectual. As Ted Haynes, Jr. explains to O'Mal-ley, "You haven't got anything and don't want anything. That's your business. And people respect you for it." But the implication is that any "real" man has to want something (money, power, women) and those who don't may get lip service but not real respect or power. Apatheia is misunderstood as a form of weakness, a lack of will to gain anything, either for God or oneself. The real strength of apatheia will eventually reveal itself through the film.

Father O'Malley handles his encounters with others tactfully, uncannily identi-fying what people unconsciously desire. He listens attentively, keeps his questions to a minimum, and plays along with people's pretensions. Unlike Father Fitz-gibbon, he is not duped by others' lies or threats; his essential detachment allows him to handle them with a light, ironic sense of humor. It is not coincidental that the majority of musical numbers in *Going My Way* are small in scale and orchestra-tion. Like Father O'Malley's conversations with other characters, they are inti-mate attempts at reaching the hearts and minds of individuals, without sermons or theatrical performances from a pulpit or stage. For example, when Father O'Mal-ley talks with Carol James about why she ran away, he listens to her story, banters with her, and they eventually bond over an impromptu singing lesson. O'Malley never discourages her from her dream of a musical career; conversely, Father Fitz-gibbon scolds her and tells her to return home and embrace marriage and mother-hood. Fitzgibbon's scolding repeats the parental instructions Carol had mimicked earlier. While O'Malley may hear her proclamations of maturity skeptically, he listens to her rather than dictate what she "should" do. O'Malley is not interested in controlling Carol's behavior; he is only concerned in her welfare as a pretty young girl alone in New York.

Father O'Malley's preferred line of attack is through charm and indirection rather than through preaching or enforced obedience based on his priestly status. He succeeds in reforming Tony Scapone because he wins the teen's trust through his kindness, lack of sermonizing, and willingness to play along with Tony's assertion of dominance. Tony eventually chooses to control his violent temper because Father O'Malley models leadership through quiet confidence while appealing to the boys' innate appreciation of beauty when he introduces them to chorale singing. As Scapone realizes that there are alternative forms of leadership that do not involve implied or actual violence, he wins O'Malley's confidence and becomes the choir's leader after O'Malley leaves.

Finally, O'Malley's ability to read and fulfill people's deepest longings for understanding works on Father Fitzgibbon. When Fitzgibbon learns that O'Malley is there to help him because the bishop is concerned about his age and difficulty in leading St. Dominic's, he tries to abdicate as the rector, even though O'Malley sincerely insists that he is only there to assist temporarily. Father Fitzgibbon runs away, a form of regression; when Officer McCarthy returns him to the rectory, he instructs him to tell O'Malley "you've been a bad boy to run away from home and now you're sorry." Fitzgibbon is placed back in the bedroom of honor, given dinner on a tray, and basically fussed over and forgiven by a set of substitute parents—Father O'Malley and Mrs. Carmody, the housekeeper. Although the two priests share a manly drink of whiskey, they end up talking about their mothers and O'Malley returns to the nurturing, parental role when he sings Fitzgibbon to sleep with "Too-Ra-Loo-Ra-Loo-Ral": the same tune from the music box Fitzgibbon's mother sent him. Fitzgibbon's deepest wish—to feel young and wanted, part of a loving circle—has been fulfilled by O'Malley. And this fulfillment, which on the surface can seem like a seduction to win Fitzgibbon over to O'Malley's side, can only work as agape (selfless love) if apatheia exists. Since it has been established earlier that O'Malley is not here to replace Fitzgibbon as the parish priest and O'Malley himself does not want the position, we can view his loving behavior without suspicion about his motives. Later in the film, when his song "Swinging on a Star" is bought by a music publisher, O'Malley insists that they present the check to St. Dominic's and stage it as a contribution in response to a sermon by Father Fitzgibbon.

Since O'Malley does not desire to control other people for selfish purposes, he is able to show unconditional, nurturing love (agape) to many of the characters in the film. When he announces that the bishop has reassigned him to another parish, Father Fitzgibbon delivers a farewell sermon that sounds like a eulogy; he praises O'Malley's unselfishness and concern for other people. This is cemented with the memorable ending shot of Fitzgibbon being surprised by the arrival of his elderly mother from Ireland, a final, unselfish and loving act on O'Malley's part. O'Malley's apatheia—his disinterest in using the power the bishop has given him for his own career advancement—has allowed him to transform St. Dominic's into a community based on selflessness. Various characters have given up their own selfish agendas in order to help St. Dominic's thrive as a neighborhood institution. More importantly, outsiders have been transformed by their contact with O'Malley and brought into the inner circle; Carol James has a new family and a loving husband, and Father Tim, O'Malley's best friend from high school, will now assist Father Fitzgibbon, as well as provide him with the friendship he clearly needs.

Although *High Society* (1956) has, superficially, little to do with *Going My Way,* Bing Crosby's character has a moral gravitas that can only stem from the American public's identification of Crosby with Father O'Malley's cool detachment from worldly snares. C. K. Dexter-Haven's "coolness" might have more to do with his assured wealth, social position, and love of jazz but he also reveals aspects of apatheia and agape in his behavior. We know that Dexter still loves his ex-wife, Tracy Samantha Lord (Grace Kelly), but he does not lose control of his actions because of that. While he sets up the Newport Jazz Festival to coincide with Tracy's marriage to George Kittredge, he does not reveal any clear plan for how to win her. If anything, he seems more focused on stopping the wedding to Kittredge out of a concern for Tracy's emotional development than out of a belief that he is the better choice for her.

Tracy's first screen entrance establishes her fixation on outward appearances. She bears boxes of wedding gifts into a room already filled with presents. When she hears Louis Armstrong and his band practicing next door, she runs over and scolds Dexter for trying to ruin her life. He admits he's still in love with her and that he doesn't want her to get married again "because I still think you can become a wonderful woman."[23] Another of Tracy's problems emerges during this conversation. She wanted Dexter to fulfill an ideal that didn't suit him; when she accuses him of ruining her life, he replies, "Sure you didn't try to spoil mine but you were calling all the shots, dictating the sort of fella you wanted me to be." Crosby delivers these lines with detached good humor, leaving him in control of the situation when Tracy/Kelly storms out.

The film connects Tracy's beauty with her money and social status, and these attributes depict their combined effect on the three main male characters. Dexter has money and position, as well as an intimate knowledge of Tracy, so he is not intimidated. George Kittredge, a self-made man, reveals his insecurity about his status through his denigration of Dexter's "easy" life and through his idealization of Tracy as a perfect, virginal goddess. Finally, Macaulay, "Mike" Connor, the journalist who will cover the wedding (Frank Sinatra), initially resists the allure of Tracy's beauty and wealth, but then succumbs when he thinks he has glimpsed her real vulnerability. Initially, Tracy is an unattractive character: acquisitive, controlling, unforgiving towards her father, and manipulative towards Mike in their first interview and in a private performance of bitterness at her uncle's house. Tracy would like to appear cool but she prefers feeling no emotion rather than feeling emotion without succumbing to it, which is the more accurate definition of apatheia. She is actually controlled by her fear of imperfection in herself and others. It is significant that the two scenes, which try to psychoanalyze Tracy's coldness—one with Dexter and one with her father (both men who disappointed her)—occur close to each other.

Dexter arrives to present Tracy with a model of their honeymoon yacht, the True Love. Significantly, Tracy is dressed in a pool cover-up that resembles a Greek statue's robes. Dexter tries to explain to Tracy why he believes she is so hard on men. He attributes it to her father's infidelity and when Tracy snorts at this, he elaborates:

Dexter: So you started demanding perfection. Nobody was going to hurt you. You felt I tricked you. Gee, I didn't know you wanted a husband who would be kind of a high priest to a virgin goddess—

Tracy: Stop using those foul words!

Dexter: It's a real pity too, Tracy, because you'd be a wonderful woman if you'd just let your tiara slip a little. You'll never be a wonderful woman or even a wonderful human being until you learn to have some regard for human frailty.

After leaving, Tracy recalls their honeymoon on the True Love, and we see a flashback of her—comfortable, playful, and vulnerable with Dexter. As they sing "True Love," the song reveals a relationship based upon reciprocation—"You give to me and I give to you"—as well as a sacramental approach to marriage (a guardian angel with nothing to do but participate in the mutual exchange of the two lovers).[24] Again, Crosby's delivery of Dexter's lines is essential to the effect. He is not angry or pleading but calm and rueful, and there is no plea that he can make her a wonderful woman. He seems to realize that marriage to Kittredge would keep her increasingly unhappy on the pedestal she believes will protect her from pain. Tracy's father makes the same observation as Dexter that Tracy's coldness and refusal to forgive is her most serious flaw; he implies that if she had been the right kind of daughter, one who admired her father "with a kind of foolish, unquestioning, uncritical affection," he might not have left the family. Unlike Dexter's explanation, this one is a self-absorbed attempt to manipulate Tracy into changing through guilt and a perceived past failure on her part.

While Mike Connor seems to be the most attractive and logical choice to win Tracy, he does not for several reasons. His two songs, "You're Sensational" and "Mind If I Make Love to You" are beautifully sung romantic numbers, but a relationship with him will not teach Tracy anything about herself. Mike, like George, is fascinated with her beauty and mien; unlike George, he offers erotic pleasure without the social respectability Tracy needs. Next, while their attraction is based on infatuation and the initial breaking down of emotional borders, there is no promise of "true love" that is heaven-blessed or enduring. Tracy's response to "You're Sensational," reveals an ambivalent fear and attraction towards letting go sexually. Compare this reaction to when she hears Dexter sing the song he initially composed for her, "I Love You, Samantha." Dexter is the only person who calls her by her middle name, which indicates an intimacy that no other character has with her. Furthermore, while "You're Sensational" and "Mind If I Make Love to You" are seduction songs that could be sung to any woman, "I Love You, Samantha" is tailored to her and it promises a fidelity ("I'm a one-gal guy") that exists whether she reciprocates or not.[25] When Tracy hears the song, she seems to melt into a private, erotic reverie that reveals an affection and need for Dexter that her earlier outbursts tried to disguise.

After a drunken "bachelor's party," in which the appearance of impropriety with Mike teaches Tracy a lesson about human vulnerability and forgiveness (as well as conveniently removing George from the upcoming wedding), Tracy chooses to remarry Dexter rather than marry Mike. The audience has been prepared to accept this ending through the plot structure and the songs. Dexter, unlike George or even Mike, has demonstrated the deepest knowledge of Tracy's character; he has accepted her fully and has behaved without any conscious attempts to manipulate her into his arms. Unlike Mike or Tracy, he did not lose control and behave inappropriately at any point. The love he offers Tracy is based on his knowledge of both her virtues and her flaws, and the remarriage is a chance to continue and deepen their intimacy, in contrast to the short-lived, romantic illusion that both George and Mike offer. Apatheia—the ability to feel emotions, such as love, disappointment, pain and forgiveness, without being controlled by them—is what makes Dexter the coolest cat in Newport, Rhode Island.

"Coolness"—self-command, self-containment, invulnerability—promises to contain the threat of male energy that can either erupt into violence towards an object or lead to loss of control over oneself. As a performance alone, it risks revealing gaps of need and vulnerability; we can see this with Frank Sinatra, for example. Repression of desire leads to its eruption in culturally unacceptable form—an emerging theme in postwar films dealing with male roles and relationships—while lack of desire indicates lack of masculinity. The post-*Going My Way* Bing Crosby signifies a masculinity based on something more than secular cultural values and thus creates a culturally resonant ideal of an admirable, if almost impossible, union of the superego (self-control) and the id (desire). Crosby's easy negotiation of this union stems from his early religious education and personal piety, as well as other factors. But it was the public's yoking of him with the priest he played onscreen that gave his public persona a moral heft and made his star image (until the posthumous character assassinations) into not only a likable, but a morally admirable, public figure.

Notes

1. Steve Neale, "Masculinity as Spectacle: Reflections on Men and Mainstream Cinema," in *Screening the Male: Exploring Masculinities in Hollywood Cinema,* Steve Cohan and Ina Rae Hark, eds. (London: Routledge, 1993), 9–20. Originally published in *Screen,* 24, 6 (1983).

2. Neale, 9.

3. Gary Giddins, *Bing Crosby: A Pocketful of Dreams, The Early Years, 1903–1940* (Boston: Little, Brown and Company, 2001).

4. Bing Crosby, *Call Me Lucky* (New York: Simon and Schuster, 1953), 146.

5. Richard Dyer, "A Star is Born and the Construction of Authenticity," in *Stardom: Industry of Desire,* Christine Gledhill, ed. (London: Routledge, 1990), 133.

6. Ibid., 135.

7. Kenneth Swanson, *Uncommon Prayer* (Columbus, MS: Genesis Press, 1987), 139.

8. Aristotle, *Nicomachean Ethics,* trans. W. D. Ross (Oxford, UK: Oxford University Press, 1984), 78.

9. Ibid., 75.

10. John Climacus, *The Ladder of Divine Ascent,* trans. Cohn Luibheid and Norman Russell (Mahwah, NJ: Paulist Press, 1982), 282.

11. Catherine of Siena, *Catherine of Siena: The Dialogue,* trans. Suzanne Noffke, O. P. (Mahwah, NJ: Paulist Press, 1980), 97.

12. Thomas à Kempis, *Imitation of Christ*, trans. Richard Whitford and Harold C. Gardiner (New York: Doubleday, 1955), 65.

13. John of the Cross, *Ascent of Mount* Carmel, trans. E. Allison Peers. *Christian Classics Ethereal* Library: http://www.ccel.org/ccel/johncross/ascent.iv.ivhtml (9 April 2007), book 1, chapter 3, paragraph 4.

14. Crosby, 108–9.

15. Malcolm Macfarlane, *Bing Crosby Day by Day* (Lanham, MD: Scarecrow Press, 2001), 13.

16. Giddins, 57.

17. Crosby, 72.

18. Crosby, 186–87.

19. Claude Binyon and Elmer Rice, screenwriters, *Holiday Inn* (Paramount Pictures, 1942). All quotations from *Holiday Inn* are from this screenplay.

20. Steve Cohan, "Feminizing the Song-and-Dance Man: Fred Astaire and the Spectacle of Masculinity in the Hollywood Musical," in *Screening the Male,* 55.

21. Frank Butler, Frank Cavett, and Leo McCarey, screenwriters, *Going My Way* (Paramount Pictures, 1944). All quotations from *Going My Way* are from this screenplay.

22. Johnny Burke and Jimmy Van Heusen, "Going My Way" (Copyright Bourne Music, New York, 1944, all rights reserved).

23. John Patrick, screenwriter, *High Society* (MGM, 1956). All quotations from *High Society* are from this screenplay.

24. Cole Porter, "True Love" (Copyright 1956 Cole Porter. Copyright renewed. Assigned to Robert H. Montgomery, Jr., Trustee of the Cole Porter Musical and Literary Property Trusts. Chappell and Co., owner of publication and allied rights throughout the world. All rights reserved. Warner Bros. Publication U.S. Inc., Miami, FL 33014.)

25. Cole Porter, "I Love You, Samantha" (Copyright 1956 Cole Porter. Copyright renewed, assigned to Robert H. Montgomery, Jr., Trustee of the Cole Porter Musical and Literary Property Trusts. Chappell and Co., owner of publication and allied rights throughout the world. All rights reserved. Warner Bros. Publication U.S. Inc., Miami, FL 33014.

4

Bing on a Binge: Casting-Against-Type in *The Country Girl*

Linda A. Robinson

Premiering on December 21, 1954, *The Country Girl* (1954) enjoyed immediate critical success. It starred Bing Crosby as Frank Elgin, a former musical comedy star crippled by alcoholism and self-doubt, Grace Kelly as Georgie, Elgin's drab and weary wife, and William Holden as the Broadway producer who champions Elgin in a comeback role. The film was nominated for seven Academy Awards, including nominations for best picture, best director, best art direction (black and white), and best cinematography. Grace Kelly won the Oscar for best actress, and the film's writer-director, George Seaton, won for best screenplay. Crosby was nominated for best actor, and although he lost to Marlon Brando in *On the Waterfront* (1954), he did win the *Look* magazine award for best film performance of 1954.[1] Indeed, Crosby's performance in *The Country Girl* was heralded as (and generally continues to be considered) one of the best of his career. In fact, the role of Frank Elgin was a quintessential example of casting-against-type, or "departure casting," in that Elgin is unlike nearly every other character Crosby had portrayed on screen to that point in time. This case study of *The Country Girl* examines two factors that led to the favorable reception of Crosby's atypical casting: the manner in which Paramount used Crosby's established star persona to prepare audiences for—and sell audiences on—this casting-against-type, and the way in which the persona itself, both despite and because of its differences from the character Elgin, substantively contributed to the perceived quality of Crosby's performance.

As has long been recognized, the Hollywood star system—whereby studios used stars to differentiate, stratify, and market films—depends on a necessary stability in star personae as a sort of product quality control to ensure the value and effectiveness of any given star's "brand." Thus, during the studio era, the system gave rise to the preference for what Barry King calls *personification* (the creation and dissemination of a recognizable persona, usually based on physical type) over *impersonation* (naturalistic, "believable" performances of a wide variety of roles).[2] In theory, given this foundational necessity for star persona consistency, it would seem that, almost by definition, casting-against-type should result in films that audiences will reject. Indeed, casting-against-type can result, and has resulted, in box office fiascoes, such as Clark Gable's casting in *Parnell* (1937), John Belushi in *Neighbors* (1981), Steve Martin in *Pennies from Heaven* (1981), Bill Murray in *The Razor's Edge* (1984), and Jim Carrey in *The Majestic* (2001).

Nonetheless, casting-against-type can also result in critical and box office success, and has revived failing or faltering careers, as in the case of Marlene Dietrich in *Destry Rides Again* (1939) and Greta Garbo in the comedy *Ninotchka* (1939), or it has launched new careers, as in the case of Frank Sinatra in *From Here to Eternity* (1953) and *Suddenly* (1954).[3] Indeed, it is the preference for consistency built into the star system that provides the basis for the successful casting-against-type. The audience's pleasure in such departure casting derives from the novelty it offers, much like a child's glimpse into a teacher's personal life in some unexpected setting, such as a restaurant or amusement park. This novelty is pleasurable, however, only so long as it is achieved skillfully in a manner that offers no distraction other than the novelty itself. In fact, because of the pleasure it engenders, that novelty is often a key element in the studios' promotion of these films, albeit usually interwoven with the ostensibly contradictory but necessary promise of the familiar.[4] Indeed, a constant tension in promoting an actor in a departure role is the promise of just enough—but not too much—difference from the actor's established star persona.

The star persona itself is a multitextual construct, consisting of the film actor as a biological entity, the actor's visual image on screen, an amalgam of the characters portrayed, and the personality manufactured by extrafilmic discourse about the actor (e.g., biographical information published in newspapers and fan magazines). In effect, the persona "is itself a character, but one that transcends placement or containment in a particular narrative . . . and exists in cinematic rather than filmic time and space."[5] Because studios cultivate such personae as marketing tools for films, film actors deliberately manufacture these personae to increase their marketability to studios. Indeed, Hollywood actors are driven by an oversupply of actors to stabilize the relationship between person and on-screen image so as to develop marketable personas: "Actors seeking stardom begin to conduct themselves in public as though there is an unmediated existential connection between their person and their [star] image."[6]

Perhaps more so than any other star of his time, Crosby typified the deliberately self-developed star persona. By 1954, the year in which *The Country Girl* was released, Crosby had long been positioned as one of America's most popular entertainers. In addition to his successful recording and radio career, he had also been performing in musical comedy films since appearing in *The Big Broadcast* in 1932; in 1940, he starred with Bob Hope in *Road to Singapore* (1940)—the first of seven popular "Road" pictures the pair would make together—and in 1944,

Crosby received and Oscar for best actor for his performance as Father O'Malley in *Going My Way* (1944). In all, Crosby was among *Motion Picture Herald*'s top ten box office draws in fifteen of the twenty years between 1934 and 1954; his screen popularity hit its apex in the latter half of the 1940s, during which he was named the number one box office attraction for five years straight, from 1944 to 1948. Even thereafter, as he neared fifty and the youth market for popular entertainment began to splinter off from the "mass" audience on which his popularity had been based throughout the 1940s, Crosby remained in the top ten box office draws for the next six years.

Significantly, most of Crosby's screen roles were all the same role: in the 1930s, he was the easy-going crooner, never taking life too seriously, and with *Going My Way*, this on-screen character was enriched with a warm tolerance that enhanced his insouciant attitude toward formalities and unflappable calm in the face of life's difficulties. Admittedly, the irresponsible and somewhat unscrupulous brother in *Sing You Sinners* (1938) is a less-than-admirable character, a role Gary Giddins describes as "a determined effort to move beyond the standard Crosby [film] persona . . . that had grown increasingly similar."[7] Even earlier, Crosby's character's drunken bender in *Going Hollywood* (1933) is a darker episode than is usually associated with Crosby's light-hearted screen characters. Moreover, Crosby's character in the "Road" pictures, while personable, is also manipulative and deceitful in his interactions with Bob Hope, this victimization of Hope being the basis for much of the "Road" pictures' humor. Further, Crosby's casting in *Going My Way* was not without controversy—certain Catholics reportedly objected to a seemingly irreverent "playboy" crooner being cast as a priest—and it is accurate to say that this role marked the first casting-against-type or departure role in Crosby's career, one that his popular biographers perceive as a distinct turning point in that, as has been noted, it introduced an element of warmth, decency, and commitment into a cumulative screen character who, until that role, had been attractive but more superficial.[8] Nonetheless, the only other of Crosby's earlier screen roles that truly approximates the character of Frank Elgin is the straight dramatic role of Bill Wainwright in *Little Boy Lost* (1953), released roughly a year and a half before *The Country Girl*, which, while a departure for Crosby, generated less attention than *The Country Girl*'s Elgin. Much more often than not, the character moviegoers saw in any given Crosby picture was the relaxed, good-humored, charmingly irreverent, and basically decent guy they had seen in every other Crosby picture.

Not only were Crosby's roles similar to each other, but perhaps more so than any other Hollywood star, Crosby was also perceived to *be* the character he played or, putting it the other way, his film characters were perceived to *be* "Bing Crosby," the individual. Indeed, few stars made as great an effort to collapse his film "image" into the public perception of the man himself. This merger was reinforced by the personality he projected each week on his radio show (via his direct address to the audience and dialogue with guests, both scripted) in the casual, slang-filled tone of 1953 autobiography, *Call Me Lucky* (which, in fact, is nearly impossible to read without mentally hearing Crosby's voice saying the words), and in press reports that repeatedly quoted him as saying that in most films, he had always played "Bing Crosby": "I suppose it's pretty apparent to anyone who goes to the movies much that through a career of sixty-odd pictures, I have played one character—Bing Crosby."[9]

In this respect, Crosby's persona harkens back to Richard DeCordova's concept of the "picture personality." In his analysis of the origin of the Hollywood star system during the first two decades of the twentieth century, de Cordova traces the development of the film actor from a nameless on-screen entity, to the "picture personality" (a phase in the commodification of the film actor that lasted from approximately 1910 to 1913), and finally to the "star." The distinction he perceives between the "picture personality" and the "star" is that, while both are constructed from multiple discourses—predominantly screen roles and print coverage, such as in film magazines—the star construction includes information about the film actor's personal life that establishes him or her as someone distinct from his or her screen roles. For the picture personality, however, "personality existed as an effect of . . . the representation of character across a number of films" because the written discourse on the picture personality simply reinforced the actor's cumulative screen character, creating a redundancy such that "everything written about the players' real personalities would support, amplify, and, in effect, advertise, the representations for sale in the movies themselves."[10] The nature of Crosby's star persona suggests that in some instances, the picture personality was not simply a phase in the historical development of Hollywood stardom but survived into the studio era as one particular type of star construction.

More significant, perhaps, than the identification between Crosby the biological being and Crosby the star persona, however, was the extreme *likeableness* of that persona: the affable, easygoing, unpretentious "good guy" who was everybody's friend. The result of this strategy in constructing Crosby's star persona is illustrated in a humorous newspaper column from late 1955, in which the columnist's joke is his willingness to take over Crosby's life should Crosby ever tire of it:

[Bing] is looked upon as sort of an ideal American. Quiet, gracious, a bit shy, fun-loving to just the right extent, friendly, easygoing, and—well, just a nice, solid citizen—whom no one could be jealous of if he made $1,000,000 an hour. We can all probably pay Bing the highest compliment possible if we will just stop and try to think of anything unkind we have ever heard said about him, either by those who know him personally or those who know him only as a celebrity.[11]

Thus, by the 1950s, a Crosby persona had been constructed so as to induce the public not only to like it but to believe that it was the "real" personality of the "real" person Bing Crosby and not the result of acting. That this Crosby persona was in fact a construction seems evident not just from theoretical work on the star system and hostile biographical accounts of Crosby that appeared in the 1980s (the reliability of which admittedly can be questioned), but also in reports by Crosby's professional colleagues.[12] Crosby's 1975 authorized biography, for instance, describes him as "probably the most-loved character in the world apart from the creations of Walt Disney . . ." but adds that "[a] surprising side to Bing Crosby arises from conversations with some of his show business contemporaries" who indicate that "there is always a moment with Bing when an 'ice curtain' seems to descend. . . ."[13] Thus, Nelson Riddle describes Crosby as "a bit stand-offish and a bit non-committal"[14] and Dorothy Lamour states that "there were times . . . when for short intervals I would feel very close to Bing. Then there were other times when I felt that he looked upon me as a complete stranger."[15] As Artie Shaw describes it, "[Crosby] developed a screen personality that worked because it was based on who he wanted to be—casual, relaxed. But it was a tense sort of relaxing because you knew he was working at it. Bing wasn't Bing any more than Bogart was Bogart."[16]

Once established, however, the Crosby persona had to remain consistent to retain its marketing effectiveness, leading Paramount in its publicity and creative decisions to grant his fans an ostensible proprietary interest in that persona to which the studio deferred or purported to defer. Thus, Paramount's publicity materials indicate that the studio viewed Crosby's departure in *The Country Girl* as both alluring and risky,[17] a selling point for the film, but one that could not be pressed too far out of fear of disappointing or shocking—and hence alienating—Crosby's fans. Consequently, although Crosby's casting as the weak, duplicitous Frank Elgin was a marked departure from the Crosby persona, the studio's first decision in writing the script was to ensure that it was not as great a departure as it could have been. The film was an adaptation of Clifford Odets's successful Broadway stage play, in which Elgin was a straight dramatic actor. After casting Crosby, Paramount's initial change to the stage play was to convert Elgin into a Broadway musical comedy star so Crosby would have the opportunity to sing.

With this conservative measure, this hedging of the bet, however, Paramount simultaneously capitalized on the casting-against-type by creating in its publicity for *The Country Girl* a "departure narrative" that had the effect of preparing the audience for Crosby's atypical role while using the casting as a novelty to spark interest in and curiosity about the film. This departure narrative uses Crosby's star persona to differentiate not only the substance but also the nature of his performance in *The Country Girl* from that in his earlier films; that is, not only is Elgin a dramatic role as opposed to Crosby's usual comedic ones, but Crosby in the role is *actor* rather than *personality*. Moreover, this departure narrative follows for the most part the dramatic arc of a typical Hollywood script: Crosby takes on this risky new challenge (i.e., attempting to become a "real" actor), overcoming opposition and self-doubt to do so, and emerges (or promises to emerge) triumphant in the end. Implicit in this narrative is the expectation that if Crosby's work in *The Country Girl* is well-received, he will have achieved not only acclaim for execution of a task he had never undertaken before but a new career for himself—or at least added a new facet to his identity. Furthermore, the narrative does more than engender curiosity about his performance in *The Country Girl:* positioning the well-loved Crosby as the protagonist in this narrative seems calculated to align the audience *with* Crosby's effort in the film, to cause the audience to root for his success in this new role and thus be predisposed to like his performance long before actually seeing it.

And, indeed, Paramount launched this departure narrative approximately a year and a half before the film's release, in press releases issued for *Little Boy Lost,* a "dry run" for the departure that *The Country Girl* would prove to be. *Little Boy Lost,* the story of an American widower seeking his lost son in post-World War II Paris, is shot in a black-and-white, pseudo-documentary style, and Crosby is the only American in the cast. Although he sings two songs out of deference to audience expectations, the film is a straight drama and the role of the grieving and emotionally stunted widower is nothing like Crosby's roles in any of his previous films.

Both *Little Boy Lost* and *The Country Girl* were the products of the producer/writer-director team of William Perlberg and George Seaton. Seaton, who began his Hollywood career writing for the Marx Brothers, had been writing and directing movies in partnership with producer Perlberg since 1939. The pair worked together first at Columbia, then at Twentieth-Century Fox, and finally moved as a team to Paramount, where they had their own production company that produced two films a year.[18] According to contemporary press accounts, the partners' customary practice was to first finalize the screenplay and then to cast it: "We produce each script on paper as we believe it should be done and then go out to find the players. We'll pay the money to get the parts played right and we won't start a picture until we feel we have the right people."[19] In early March 1951, the *Hollywood Reporter* reported that Paramount had acquired the screen rights to Clifford Odets's stage play *The Country Girl*[20] and Paramount's publicity states that Seaton began work on a preliminary script for *The Country Girl* in December of 1952 during filming of *Little Boy Lost.*[21] By late June 1953, with shooting of *The Country Girl* scheduled to begin in December, Crosby had been cast as Frank Elgin.[22] Seaton has indicated that the decision to cast Crosby in *The Country Girl* resulted directly from his performance in *Little Boy Lost*:

I always felt that Bing Crosby was more than just a crooner. I think that he did a very creditable job in *Little Boy Lost*, but during that film, I could see that this man had a depth to him that he didn't want to admit. Having that experience with Bing in *Little Boy Lost,* I felt that he was just right for *Country Girl.*[23]

In turn, Crosby's willingness to take on the roles in *Little Boy Lost* and *The Country Girl* may be attributed to the state of his career in the early 1950s. As he approached fifty, there is some indication in contemporaneous press accounts that his singing career was starting to flag.[24] It was thus logical that, just as rival crooner Sinatra had recently achieved critical acclaim by turning to dramatic roles, Crosby should consider doing the same. In fact, some of *The Country Girl* publicity was to make this explicit comparison:

Last year when Frank Sinatra announced that he was going to play dramatic roles and followed that with "From Here to Eternity" and "Suddenly," Bing Crosby promptly accepted the implied challenge. "If Frankie boy can do it," said the *ex-crooner* . . . and radio and TV song-and-dance man, "so can I"—and proceeded to make good his threat.[25]

In any event, when Crosby was cast as the lead in *Little Boy Lost*, Paramount began to issue press releases intended to pave the way for a nonsinging, serious actor Crosby. One such press release, apparently issued in 1953 before *Little Boy Lost*'s July release, alerts moviegoers to Crosby's "first straight dramatic opus" and calls attention to the unexpected casting by allowing Seaton to respond to "repeated inquiries" as to why he chose Crosby for the role. Seaton purportedly states that he cast Crosby *not for his voice* (his usual appeal) but for his eyes: "Bing's eyes show what he thinks and how he feels and in close up . . . they tell the story."[26]

A second undated Paramount press release ("okayed" by Crosby in August 1953, shortly after *Little Boy Lost* premiered) offers a fuller introduction to the departure narrative, defining the challenge Crosby is taking on, establishing its necessity, and the admirable, intangible reward it offers, and—walking the departure-role tightrope—simultaneously promising not to eliminate the "old" Crosby altogether. First, Crosby recognizes that, given "the virtues of a change of pace—contrast, variety, etc., . . . I'm now convinced a performer must . . . alter his delivery once in a while to survive."[27] After reassuring the reader that he intends to continue singing in movies and on records, radio, and TV, Crosby describes both his return to musicals after winning the 1944 best actor Oscar for *Going My Way,* and then his decision several years later "to change pace at work."[28] Thus, he states that he was open to the role in *Little Boy Lost,* even though "it wasn't going to be easy, this *being a real actor* for a change."[29] Crosby then notes several ways in which, apart from calling for "real" acting, his role in *Little Boy Lost* was a departure from his usual material, such as the film's three songs in contrast to the seventeen planned for *White Christmas* (1954).[30] Ultimately, the role offered him "more satisfaction . . . than . . . playing Bing Crosby. But it's the satisfaction born of *tackling something completely different* in the way of work and seeing it come out all right."[31]

Even so, although the trade press spoke favorably of *Little Boy Lost,* with the *Hollywood Reporter,* for instance, calling Crosby's work "unquestionably the outstanding performance of his career, one that stamps him as an important dramatic actor,"[32] the film's impact on Crosby's career was minimal. *The Country Girl,* however, would prove to be a stronger vehicle than *Little Boy Lost* for the Crosby departure narrative. The source material, Odets's acclaimed Broadway play, was more prominent than Marghanita Laski's short story. Further, *The Country Girl* had not one but three major roles, allowing for the casting of three stars or potential stars. Thus, the casting of William Holden, who had won an Oscar for his performance in *Stalag 17* (1953), and Grace Kelly, who was attracting attention because of pre-release interest in *Rear Window* (1954)[33] (and whose portrayal of the drab, beaten-down Georgie also had casting-against-type promotional value), helped flag the film as a "major" production of the type to draw attention to Crosby's "new" role.

In fact, however, early in 1954, the film drew attention that, at least initially, was unwelcome. The decision to film *The Country Girl* was criticized because of Odets's apparent Communist affiliation, and Catholics protested the casting of Crosby, a Catholic, as an alcoholic. Specifically, in February 1954, *The Tidings* called upon its readers to express their objections:

Paramount . . . [has cast] Bing Crosby as the lush in "The Country Girl," a morally objectionable Broadway show by Clifford Odets whose Communist Party involvements never did come clean in the Congressional wash. Bing's folks tell him he shouldn't do it. If you agree write now to Mr. [Frank] Freeman at Paramount studios, Marathon Street, Hollywood.[34]

In April 1954, *Variety* reported that the studio had been "almost inundated" by letters from Catholics protesting Crosby's role as a drunk; Adolph Zukor, however, defended the film, offering to screen it for complainants upon its completion to establish its inoffensive nature.[35]

Even before the *Variety* article, it was reported that Seaton and Perlberg viewed the dual criticisms of *The Country Girl* as sufficiently serious to merit a public response. Thus, Perlberg explained:

When we purchased [the play], Odets had been mentioned as a Commie by witnesses in Washington. We agreed with Y. Frank Freeman, in charge of production here, president of the Producers' Association and certainly a bulwark against Communism, not to proceed with the film until—and unless—Odets cleared himself. Odets testified subsequently that he had quit the party after nine months in 1935, but continued to lend his name to left-wing causes. He stated he would be more careful about his endorsements and sponsorships in the future. We received a clean bill of health from the investigating committee and from the American Legion. . . .

"As for Crosby playing a lush,"—Seaton takes it up—"We see Bing take a drink in only one scene; anyhow, the drinking is a minor part of his neurosis, his 'escape' from it. As Bing himself said, 'If we do it honestly, there's a point to be made in this picture. It offers hope.' "[36]

Press reports published both before and after the *Variety* item—even as the film's general coverage increasingly focused on the novelty of Crosby's role—continued to reflect a contradictory need to reassure readers that it was not *too* seedy, at least with respect to alcohol. An example is the March 1954 report in the *Citizen News* that although "there have been reports of protests of the casting of Crosby as a drunk . . . 'there's just one scene in which I'm supposed to get a little tipsy,' [Crosby] assured. 'The rest of the time it is merely inferred.' "[37]

At the same time, groundwork began to be laid in the press for full development of the departure narrative. Repeating the suggestion from the *Little Boy Lost* press releases of a year earlier, a number of articles were published in early and mid-1954, upon Crosby's fiftieth birthday, positing the possibility of his retirement or predicting a shift in his career to serious, dramatic roles. For instance, the *Los Angeles Times* predicted that Crosby's fiftieth might "go down in show business history as the birth of a new Crosby—a serious, nonsinging actor." The article suggested that such a move might be necessary because of a drop in his popularity as a singer, evidenced by a dip in his record sales. Nonetheless, he was portrayed as eager to take on dramatic roles, even though the studio, purportedly acting in the audience's interest, had so far prevented him from doing so: "[Bing] was all for leaving songs out of 'Little Boy Lost,' but the Paramount front office said the public was not ready for a tuneless Crosby."[38]

That this departure narrative is apparent in contemporary press coverage and studio press releases is not to say that it was in every instance internally consistent or coherent. Certainly at times Paramount's strategy for publicizing the film takes on an elastic if not experimental quality. In the spring of 1954, for instance, the narrative took a curious detour as Crosby is repeatedly quoted as saying that dramatic roles were easier than his work in musicals. Thus, for example, he claims that the role of Frank Elgin is " 'the easiest kind of thing to play. It's much easier to portray other people than to play yourself,' [Bing] said. 'Maybe I'm getting tired of playing "Crosby," like I do in the "Road" pictures.' "[39]

These claims, while perhaps creating the impression that Crosby was capable of serious dramatic roles, work against the departure narrative, a key element of which is not only the unexpectedness of the star's "new" role but the accomplishment it represents. As every scenarist knows, at the heart of every drama is conflict, and a more dramatically satisfying and hence effective accomplishment occurs not when a performer effortlessly moves into a new role but when he or she has to face a challenge and overcome obstacles to do so. Moreover, suggesting that deliberate, conscious effort stood between the audience and the Crosby persona (something Crosby now implied was manufactured), his claim that it was difficult to "play himself" in musicals undercut the perception that Crosby's films gave audiences direct access to Crosby the man; further, the faint note of arrogance undermines his easygoing "everyman" persona. Whether or not Paramount was troubled by the implications of these interviews, or perceived a need to heighten the "drama" of Crosby's departure narrative, in fact the film's publicity later in the year, particularly in the weeks leading up to *The Country Girl*'s December 1954 release, abandoned for the most part his claim that serious acting was "easy" in favor of a narrative that emphasized the challenge the role had posed for him. Thus, a *New York Times* article attributed to Crosby himself says:

I must say that I had some serious qualms about my ability to accurately limn [Elgin]. . . . In fact, I told George Seaton two or three times that I didn't think I could cut it. . . . But George was firm. *I think really he just wanted to see if I had guts enough to try.* He told me if I carried it off I'd have done something of which I could really be proud. . . . And so, though I demurred a little and dug my toe in the carpet and simpered some, I finally saw the obvious merits of the proposal and took up the challenge.[40]

In addition, to further the departure narrative, Paramount was not above rewriting history or contradicting its own prior version of events. For instance, in Crosby's bylined press release on *Little Boy Lost* issued in August 1953, Crosby states that "it wasn't going to be easy, this being a real actor for a change. I knew that, remembering the toil on 'Going My Way.' "[41] Later in *The Country Girl* departure narrative, however, albeit as part of the lobbying effort to win the best actor Oscar, Crosby began to characterize his performance in *Going My Way* as nonacting: "I just walked through 'Going My Way.' "[42]

In another such instance, barefaced in its discrepancy from the actual development of Crosby's career, a press release, apparently issued during the shooting of *The Country Girl*, valorizes Crosby's boldness in taking the Elgin role by suggesting that such boldness underlies his long-standing popularity. This press release is also designed, however, to legitimize the practice of casting-against-type and to condition audiences to perceive Crosby's uncharacteristic role in a favorable light. Thus, despite the consistency in Crosby's roles during the 1940s and early 1950s (emphasized in other publicity for *The Country Girl)*, the press release hypothesizes one reason for Crosby's consistent placement among *Motion Picture Herald*'s top ten moneymakers for the past fifteen years:

Crosby dares to play such an off-beat character as Frank Elgin in Perlberg and Seaton's "The Country Girl." . . . The word "dares" is used advisedly. Crosby, who doesn't have to take orders from anyone, was certainly under no compulsion to leave his comfortable and well-loved singing and dancing roles to take on the stern job of straight, unrelenting drama in "The Country Girl," a job, incidentally, which may ultimately net him an Oscar. But being a smart showman, he thought the risk of completely changing his screen personality was a justified one.[43]

The press release then describes Seaton as surveying exhibitors to learn moviegoers' most common complaint, which the exhibitors identify as "the sameness" of motion pictures and "seeing the same actor 'in the same kind of picture." Seaton continues,

Too many good actors in Hollywood today are gradually losing their popularity because they don't dare, as Crosby did in "The Country Girl," to change the type of characterizations that brought them first fame. Actors must learn what studios like Paramount learned a long time ago—that "playing it safe" can too often mean playing with red ink.[44]

At the same time, promotion of *The Country Girl* began to use the film's pre-production controversy, which once caused sufficient concern to require a public denial, to raise the stakes in the Crosby departure narrative and thus heighten interest in the film. In publicity the film received in the weeks leading up to its release and immediately thereafter, the initial criticism of the film—and hence its ostensible potential to jeopardize Crosby's image and career—became part of the challenge Crosby had to face in deciding to take on the role. For instance, *Look* magazine reported that "Crosby was advised not to do *The Country Girl* at all because it might offend his fans,"[45] and the *Beverly Hills Newslife* reported that "the crooner, regarded as the most famous popular singer in the world, risked his fabulous career when he agreed to portray a preserved-in-alcohol singer in 'The Country Girl.' "[46]

In like manner, Elgin's alcoholism—which earlier in the year had engendered letters of protest and responsive disclaimers by Crosby and Seaton/Perlberg to downplay the character's drinking problem and to minimize its representation in the film—now became a key element in Crosby's accomplishment as a dramatic actor and, in turn, in the film's promotion. Several articles appeared alongside photographs of Crosby as Elgin, often looking unshaven and defeated, and described the role in terms of drinking or alcoholism. For example, in mid-November 1954, the *New York Times Magazine* published an article on *The Country Girl* accompanied with photographs of Crosby's "new look" in his role as "a drunken, washed-up stage actor struggling to regain his self-respect."[47] In other articles,

Elgin is a "lush . . . a weak, lying, excessive drinker";[48] "a spineless, cheating drunk";[49] and a "craven, drunken, deceitful husband."[50]

Upon the film's release in late December 1954 (and in pre-release reviews published in mid-December 1954), critics uniformly heralded Crosby's performance as his most impressive to date. For example, one reviewer declared that "Crosby is absolutely terrific as the drunkard whose mental cowardice impels him to use the death of his child as an excuse for failure";[51] another opined that "this is far and away the most difficult part Crosby has ever tackled and he gives it a performance that is deeper, more moving, and more authoritative than anything he has ever done."[52] Indeed, the reviews themselves took up the departure narrative by describing Crosby as having "become an actor." "Instead of his portrayal of a crooner, Crosby emerges as a dramatic actor. . . ."[53] "In [*The Country Girl*] the erstwhile crooner becomes a dramatic actor with a vengeance. . . ."[54] The headline for the *New York Times* review was simply, "Crosby Acts in *Country Girl*."[55]

Two of the most interesting reviews describe Crosby's work in terms of his *maturation* as a performer. Thus, the *Los Angeles Times* opines:

If there is a surprise in this film, it is doubtless the maturing of this bland little man, this Groaner, into an actor. It has been coming, this adulthood, a long time now—Seaton permitted him some less-than-upright straying glances in "Little Boy Lost," you remember—and the shock of discovering that he is capable of such moral weakness is more than counterbalanced by the inner strength with which he finally rises above it to "stand on his own two feet."[56]

Similarly, the *Los Angeles Examiner* describes *The Country Girl* as "a completely adult picture" and Crosby's performance as reflecting a corresponding maturity:

I guess it's the true artist in a man which makes him want to go against everything he's stood for previously in his work—as Crosby does in this particular characterization. The beguiling Bing, the clowning Bing, the charming Bing are all absent here. This man, a very unpleasant man, if you will, *but an adult,* tough in his drunken individuality, cruel in his crafty deceitfulness, finally bringing your tears of compassion as he comes to terms with himself and life.[57]

Presumably, and indeed as these reviews indicate, contemporary critics were not immune to the effect of Paramount's departure narrative on their perception of the film, although the degree to which they were influenced by it is impossible to determine. Even so, few would argue today that those reviewers were wrong in their assessment of Crosby's performance. At the same time, however, to the extent that critics fell into step with the departure narrative, they largely failed to recognize how Crosby's persona—from which his performance was such a departure—contributed to the perception of the quality of that performance. It was not simply a matter that the *role* of Frank Elgin was such a contrast to Crosby's prior *role* of "Bing Crosby." Rather, the favorable reception of Crosby's performance was the result not only of Paramount's departure narrative having predisposed viewers to want to see it as a good one or of Crosby's ability (as a film actor) to produce a good performance, but of Crosby's persona itself, which helped to *create* viewers' perception of his performance in at least two other ways, largely unacknowledged (and perhaps unrecognized) at the time.

First, because his star persona was "Bing Crosby," the public's perception of Crosby's "standard" film performances was that they were not performances—i.e., the result of acting—at all. Thus, *any* performance Crosby produced for *The Country Girl* that seemed different from the "Bing Crosby" persona would necessarily be perceived as acting; if that performance were "naturalistically" convincing, it would be perceived as excellent acting, as indeed it was.

Second, and more significantly, Crosby's persona and, in particular, the *likeableness* of that persona and the resulting decades of good will he had established with the audience—the "colossal, enveloping warmth of affection" that his authorized biographer describes as having "come his way through the years"[58]—are necessarily part of Crosby's performance in *The Country Girl*. As noted previously, one component of a star's persona is his or her cumulative on-screen character, and this aspect of the star persona is designed to foster regular moviegoing by encouraging audiences to construct this cumulative character film by film from the totality of the star's on-screen roles;[59] for the construction to take place, however, the audience must necessarily bring into each film the star's pre-existing character construction, which then blends into or incorporates the new character presented in the new film. Given that Crosby's previous on-screen characters were so consistent, it is impossible to watch Crosby as Frank Elgin and not see within the character of Elgin the decency and good nature that had been repeatedly imprinted onto the Crosby screen image during the previous twenty years.

Moreover, while such imprinting would have affected any dramatic role Crosby undertook, it was particularly effective in *The Country Girl* because Elgin was simultaneously both a departure from and a parallel to Crosby's star persona. Elgin is a former musical comedy star and recording artist who at one time enjoyed success comparable to Crosby's. Elgin is, in effect, an *ex-Crosby,* an identity effectively conveyed to the audience by a flashback showing the successful Elgin before his son's death. Thus, because Crosby's persona doesn't simply contrast with but parallels or underlies Elgin—because Crosby is playing a man who was once Crosby, exhibiting Crosby's breezy good humor and eliciting the same affectionate regard Crosby elicits himself—the Crosby persona is necessarily imprinted onto the character Elgin independently of any effort (indeed, without any effort whatsoever) on the part of Crosby the actor.

Thus, the Crosby persona imparts a sense of worth to the Crosby screen image, an underlying level of identity, that in the case of Elgin gives the character a subliminal diegetic past as a man with internal qualities that belie—and equip him to overcome—his current degradation. In short, the nature of Crosby's persona, the sense of comradeship it had long cultivated with the screen audience, automatically allies that audience *with* Elgin, despite his obvious weakness and duplicity, so that the audience is resistant to "believing" the worst of him (even as that worst is exhibited on screen) or, at the least, unconsciously predisposed to identify with him or to excuse his faults. Crosby's performance as Elgin is, indeed, sympathetic, but that sympathetic quality is due as much to the pre-existing "relationship" between the audience and the Crosby persona as it is to Crosby's impersonation skills. In sum, Frank Elgin is a role that is different from Crosby's star persona and yet one in which that persona has a place. Moreover, Crosby's persona was such that its place or fit within the role necessarily complemented the role, adding dimension to it, rather than clashing with it or undermining it.

Indeed, in a further study and cataloging of factors likely to result in audience acceptance (and even embrace) of departure casting, it may prove that one such factor is the trajectory from a pre-existing sympathetic persona to an unsympathetic departure role. Similar instances of successful "nice guy" moves into darker roles are James Stewart's alienated, psychologically complex, and morally ambivalent roles of the 1950s and, more recently, Tom Hanks's performance as a hit man in *Road to Perdition* (2002). (In the latter case, of course, the character's mission through much of the film—protecting his son from a rival hit man—also serves to generate sympathy for him despite his profession and its attendant quality of cold calculation.) In contrast, when the trajectory is reversed, as from a relatively unsympathetic or unattractive (albeit possibly humorous) persona, such as Bill Murray's, to an ostensibly sympathetic or admirable role such as Larry Darrell in *The Razor's Edge* (1984), the imprinted, underlying persona can be inconsistent with the role in a way that hollows out the performance instead of reinforcing it with an implied but consistent underlying dimension.

Certainly, Seaton recognized the potency of Crosby's persona, which he states underlaid his decision to cast Crosby in the dramatic lead first in *Little Boy Lost* and then in *The Country Girl*:

> The character Crosby plays [in *Little Boy Lost*] is essentially a man against himself . . . both protagonist and antagonist in one body, an immature, indecisive man. . . . Our problem was to show the man for what he was—and yet not to make him appear too weak. . . . We felt this character must be played by an actor *who possessed a personal basic worthwhileness*. . . . This sort of *fundamental dignity and appeal* is not something which can be applied like a band-aid to just any performer. . . . We felt [Crosby] was *the only actor in Hollywood who could endow our script with this quality.*[60]

Similarly, with respect to the Elgin role, "Bing was right because he has a quality that wins the sympathy of an audience—no matter how low he sinks, or how much he lies and cheats. They hope that somehow he'll work it all out and be happy."[61]

Even when describing Elgin in unflattering terms, reviewers often reassured readers that Crosby's performance was nonetheless sympathetic, an achievement they attributed to his acting as Elgin rather than to the twenty years of acting he had put into the Crosby persona. This was so even for a critic who perceived a conscious, effective use of Crosby's persona in the Elgin role:

> [Frank Elgin] is a despicable character and it is a remarkable tribute to Crosby's genius that he never loses audience sympathy while playing it. George Seaton's script performs the writing miracle of capitalizing on all of Bing's personality assets by throwing them in reverse. Crosby's nonchalance is made to seem a mask for lack of guts. His charm is turned into shallowness. He performs a real tour de force of acting when in an audition scene, he

sings a perky number in a way that delights the audience, while letting you know at the same time that the singer is wracked with self-doubt.[62]

In this audition scene, in fact, an extraordinary layering of identities and performances occurs, similar to what DeCordova describes in Mary Pickford's dual roles in *Stella Marris* (1915). In a scene where Pickford as a homely orphan compares her mirrored image to that of Pickford's other role, a beautiful rich girl, one layer of identity is the contrast between the homely girl's character and Pickford's personal traits known to movie audiences of the time.[63] A similar contrast of identities occurs in the audition scene in *The Country Girl,* where the audience sees the familiar and self-confident Crosby playing a weak and uncertain performer resurrecting a Crosby-quality musical performance from a time earlier in his career when he was, in fact, a Crosby-equivalent. Further, just as audiences' "knowledge" of the real Pickford reinforced her portrayal of the beautiful girl, Crosby's performance of Elgin, the ex-musical comedy star, is given credence by Crosby's twenty-year career as a song-and-dance man. Indeed, by revising the Elgin character to parallel Crosby and in casting Crosby in the part, Seaton assured the audience's belief in Elgin's credentials as a genuine Broadway star (and hence an understanding of the extent to which he had "fallen" after his son's death). As Seaton has stated:

[In the stage play], it's an actor that is an alcoholic, but the thing that never stood up in my mind nor in the critics [*sic*] minds nor the audiences [*sic*] minds when they saw the play was the fact that you could believe that Paul Kelly, who played it in New York, was one of the great actors of all times—and I just couldn't believe this. So that's why we changed it from the play within the play to a straight dramatic play—a musical. Crosby came across like gangbusters in it.[64]

More intriguing, however, is to contemplate the (at least) four layers of identity—or perhaps, more accurately, of performance—that co-exist in Crosby's screen image during this audition scene. The base identity or performance is Crosby, the biological entity. The second layer of performance is, as in the case of all of Crosby's film roles, the Crosby star persona. The third layer of performance is the character of Elgin who, ten years earlier in the film's diegesis, *was* the Crosby persona. Elgin is, in effect, a degraded and defeated version of the Crosby persona, the Crosby persona robbed of its resilience, confidence, and good humor. The fourth layer of performance is the auditioning Elgin; that is, the degraded Crosby persona creating the illusion of the intact, functioning Crosby persona. In short, in this scene we see Crosby the man performing the Crosby persona performing the degraded Crosby persona performing the Crosby persona. The talent and professionalism Elgin exhibits in the audition number, despite the character's self-doubt evident just seconds prior, contains within it not just the diegetic moment but decades of similar Crosby numbers—numbers which, by their apparent ease of execution, offer a solid and comforting reassurance in the Hollywood myth of happily-ever-after. Thus, interestingly, although the audition convinces the audience that Elgin is, in fact, capable of the role for which he was auditioning (because, when pressed, he can be as good a song-and-dance man as Crosby), it could have had the effect of highlighting the (possible) artificiality and precariousness of that reassuringly confident, easygoing Crosby persona.

Similarly, watching scenes in which Elgin switches instantaneously from desperate, fearful, bullying complaints when alone with his wife to self-assured joking with the director or to generous reassurances to fellow cast members, today's audience perceives an eerie echo of what might have actually occurred on the film set: the distinct disconnect between the man and his public persona. Indeed, viewed today, these rather unsettling levels of identity give rise to the possible belief that, as Crosby implied in some of his press interviews at the time, the Elgin role called for less "acting" than that of "Bing Crosby," albeit for different reasons from those Crosby articulated. In late 1954, however, it was the departure narrative—emphasizing the distinction between Crosby's previous roles and the role of Elgin—that shaped perception of his performance, and therefore this unsettling layering was not generally discerned, at least as is reflected in reviews and Crosby's press coverage at the time, both of which celebrated the narrative's triumphant conclusion.

Indeed, the Crosby departure narrative concludes, after the release of *The Country Girl,* with Crosby's having found, in meeting the challenge of the role, a "new sense of ambition"; as an actor for whom Hollywood now "rates . . . at least an even chance with Brando" for the best actor Oscar, it is reported that he got "a lot more satisfaction out of playing a serious role in 'The Country Girl' than lighting his way through the song-dance-gag roles of most of his films."[65] Crosby's press coverage during the first months of 1955 is obviously part of Paramount's lobbying for the best actor Oscar; at the same time, however, it brings full-circle the departure narrative that was begun in mid-1953: Crosby, hitting fifty, was contemplating a major career change—retirement or a switch to straight, dramatic roles—and had taken risks, overcome obstacles, struggled with self-doubt, but boldly forged ahead and ultimately triumphed after opting for the latter.

In fact, however, *The Country Girl* did not launch Crosby into a new career as a serious actor, even though his departure narrative was designed to promote and legitimize such a possibility. In truth, in the years from 1954 to his death in 1977, Crosby did relatively little film work (and that work included a number of cameo appearances or appearances as himself).[66] Nonetheless, during those years, he played his long-standing "Bing Crosby" persona more often than serious, dramatic roles. While he sang and danced as usual in *High Society* (1956), *Anything Goes* (1956), *The Heart of Show Business* (1957), *Say One for Me* (1959), *High Time* (1960), *The Road to Hong Kong* (1962), and *Robin and the Seven Hoods* (1964), he attempted only three serious dramatic roles: *Man on Fire* (1957) (the first film in which he did not sing at all), *Stagecoach* (1966), and the made-for-television movie *Dr. Cook's Garden* (1971) (in which, in Crosby's only appearance as a villain, he portrays a small-town doctor who "weeds" the town's population by killing those he deems unworthy to live).

In terms of the film itself, however, Crosby's casting-against-type in *The Country Girl* was an unqualified success with audiences and critics at the time of its release, even as it represented a departure—albeit, as has been seen, not a complete departure—from the hugely popular star persona he had cultivated during the previous twenty years. King has noted that star personas are so durable that, once accepted and embraced by the public, they "will tend to survive discrepant casting and performances."[67] That survival is due, at least in part, to the fact that, even in a departure role, the star persona is not dormant but continues to operate through or within the performance. As Paramount recognized here, the persona's distinct existence also makes it available for use in positioning the departure role favorably in the public's mind. Thus, in the case of *The Country Girl,* Crosby's star persona—both in the way that Paramount capitalized on it in creating a departure narrative with which to engage the public's interest and sympathy and in the way the persona itself infused his performance with a dimension it would not otherwise have had—was a significant contributing factor to the favorable reception of Bing on a binge.

Notes

1. "Bing Crosby, Judy Garland Win Awards," *Los Angeles Times,* 2 March 1955.

2. Barry King, "Articulating Stardom," in *Star Texts: Image and Performance,* Jeremy G. Butler, ed. (Detroit: Wayne State University Press, 1991), 147.

3. Departure roles can also enhance a film actor's reputation by offering proof of his or her acting skill and versatility, and can in fact provide the basis for a particular type of star persona, as was the case with Bette Davis. Paul McDonald, *The Star System: Hollywood's Production of Popular Identities* (London: Wallflower, 2000), 55. Not addressed here is the artistic or occupational appeal of departure roles for the film actor, who in media interviews will often speak of the welcome change from type-casting and the satisfaction inherent in meeting challenges that his or her "regular" roles do not offer.

4. King, "Articulating Stardom," 147.

5. Ibid.

6. Ibid.

7. Gary Giddins, *Bing Crosby: A Pocketful of Dreams, The Early Years, 1903–1940* (Boston: Little, Brown and Company, 2001), 471.

8. See, for example, Barbara Bauer, *Bing Crosby: A Pyramid Illustrated History of the Movies* (New York: Pyramid Press, 1981), 120–21.

9. Bing Crosby, "Bing Scans His 'Elgin,' " *Los Angeles Times,* 12 December 1954.

10. Richard de Cordova, *Picture Personalities: The Emergence of the Star System in America* (Urbana: University of Illinois Press, 1990), 88–89.

11. Henry M. Lemore, "The Lighter Side," *Los Angeles Times,* 10 Nov. 1955 (emphasis added).

12. See Gary Crosby and Ross Firestone, *Going My Own Way* (Garden City, NJ: Doubleday, 1983); Donald Shepherd and Robert F. Slatzer, *Bing Crosby: The Hollow Man* (New York: St. Martin's Press, 1981).

13. Charles Thompson, *Bing: The Authorized Biography* (London: Allen, 1975), 235, 236.

14. Ibid., 243.

15. Ibid., 239.

16. Giddins, *Bing Crosby,* 264.

17. The publicity for *The Country Girl* described herein includes both published articles and Paramount press releases, usually undated, whose content indicates the approximate time of their issuance. As I did not always find evidence that these press releases had been

incorporated into published press accounts, they do not necessarily reflect information that was actually provided to the public. They do, however, reflect Paramount's strategy in publicizing the film. As Paul McDonald reports, studio publicity was not an "afterthought" in the production process but an integral component of a film's production from acquisition of the property through the film's release. McDonald, *The Star System*, 52.

18. Philip K. Scheur, "Producer-Director Stick But Not Stuck," *Los Angeles Times*, 4 April 1954.

29. Thomas M. Pryor, "Hollywood Scene: Perlberg-Seaton Portrait," *New York Times*, 19 August 1956.

20. "Paramount Buys Odets B'way Play," *Hollywood Reporter*, 2 March 1951.

21. *Little Boy Lost* undated press release, Paramount Studio, *Little Boy Lost* file, Margaret Herrick Library at the Center for Motion Picture Study ("MPA *Little Boy Lost* file").

22. "Bing's Country," *New York Times*, 21 June 1953.

23. J. D. Marshall, *Blueprint on Babylon* (Phoenix: Phoenix House 1978), 48.

24. James Bacon, "Bing May Sing Good-by to Song and Start as an Actor at Age 50," *Los Angeles Times*, 2 May 1954.

25. "Bing Goes Dramatic," *Cue*, 27 November 1954 (emphasis added).

26. *Little Boy Lost* undated press release.

27. *Little Boy Lost* press release, "okayed" August 1953, Paramount Studio, MPA *Little Boy Lost* file.

28. Ibid.

29. Ibid. (emphasis added).

30. *Little Boy Lost* press release.

31. Ibid. (emphasis added).

32. "Little Boy Lost," *Hollywood Reporter*, 8 July 1953.

33. James Spada, *Grace: The Secret Life of a Princess* (Garden City, NJ: Doubleday, 1987), 87.

34. William H. Mooring, "Hollywood in Focus: What Happened to the Anti-Red Pledge?" *The Tidings*, 5 February 1954.

35. "Squelching Campaign Against 'Country Girl,' " *Variety (D)*, 13 April 1954. See also "Strange Sensitivity About Crosby—Although Unreleased and Unseen, Paramount Gets Protests on Bing's Drunk Role," *Variety (W)*, 14 April 1954.

36. Philip K. Scheur, "Bing Crosby's Acting Comes of Age With Alcoholic Role in 'The Country Girl,' " *Los Angeles Times*, 12 December 1954.

37. Bob Thomas, "Bing Crosby, Nearing 50, Considers Retirement," *Citizen News*, 8 March 1954. See also Aline Mosby, "Alcoholic Role Had 'Groaner' Worried," *Beverly Hills Newslife*, 13 December 1954; "Bing Crosby and Grace Kelly Try for Academy Awards," *Look*, 14 December 1954.

38. James Bacon, "Bing May Sing Good-by." See also Bob Thomas, "Bing Crosby, Nearing 50" and "Bing Crosby Seen Exiting Radio, Too," *Variety*, 3 March 1954.

39. Hedda Hopper, "What Is Today's Bing Like?" *Los Angeles Times*, 13 June 1954; Hedda Hopper, "Bing's First Half Century," *Chicago Tribune*, 13 June 1954.

40. Bing Crosby, "Bing Scans His 'Elgin,' " *Los Angeles Times*, 12 December 1954 (emphasis added). See also Aline Mosby, "Alcoholic Role Had 'Groaner' Worried" and "Bing Goes Dramatic," *Cue*, 27 November 1954.

41. *Little Boy Lost*, undated press release.

42. Rochlen Kendis, "Candid Kendis: Bing Eyes Work With Combo," *Los Angeles Mirror-News*, 21 February 1955.

43. *The Country Girl* undated press release, Paramount Studio, *The Country Girl* file, Margaret Herrick Library at the Center for Motion Picture Study ("MPA *Country Girl* file").

44. Ibid.

45. "Bing Crosby and Grace Kelly Try for Academy Awards."

46. Aline Mosby, "Alcoholic Role Had 'Groaner' Worried." See also "Movie: Crosby Plays a Drunk," *Pix,* 15 January 1955; Philip K. Scheur, "Bing Crosby's Acting Comes of Age."

47. "The Country Girl," *New York Times Magazine,* 14 November 1954.

48. "The Country Girl," *Variety,* 29 November 1954.

49. "Bing Crosby and Grace Kelly Try for Academy Awards."

50. *New Yorker,* 25 December 1954. See also Margaret Harford, " 'The Country Girl' Wins Praise," *Hollywood Citizen News,* 22 December 1954; "Bing on Binge," *Life,* 6 December 1954; *Saturday Review,* 18 December 1954.

51. " 'Country Girl' is Powerful Drama with Superb Acting," *Hollywood Reporter,* 29 November 1954.

52. "The Country Girl," *Newsweek,* 6 December 1954. See also Margaret Harford, " 'The Country Girl' Wins Praise," *Hollywood Citizen News,* 22 December 1954; Jerry Pam, "'Country Girl' Hit—Crosby Excellent," *Newslife,* 23 December 1954; "Crosby Turns Actor," *Fortnight,* 19 January 1955; *New Yorker,* 25 December 1954; *Saturday Review,* 18 December 1954.

53. Jerry Pam, " 'Country Girl' Hit—Crosby Excellent."

54. "Crosby Turns Actor."

55. Bosley Crowther, "Crosby Acts in *Country Girl,*" *New York Times,* 16 December 1954.

56. Philip K. Scheur, "Bing Crosby's Acting Comes of Age."

57. Ruth Westbury, " 'Country Girl' Adult Picture," *Los Angeles Examiner,* 12 December 1954 (emphasis added).

58. Thompson, *Bing,* 235.

59. De Cordova, *Picture Personalities*, p. 112.

60. *Little Boy Lost* undated press release (emphasis added).

61. "Bing Crosby and Grace Kelly Try for Academy Awards."

62. " 'Country Girl' is Powerful Drama with Superb Acting."

63. De Cordova, *Picture Personalities,* 111.

64. Marshall, *Blueprint on Babylon,* 48.

65. Dick O'Connor, "Bing Crosby Views 30 Years of Success," *Herald Express,* 21 February 1955.

66. Crosby made cameo appearances in *Showdown at Ulcer Gulch* (1956) (Influential Man), *Alias Jesse James* (1959), *Let's Make Love* (1960), and *Pepe* (1960), and he appeared as himself in a number of films and television programs: *Hollywood Mothers and Fathers* (1955), *Bing Presents Oreste* (1956), *The Bing Crosby Show* (1961) (TV), *The Hollywood Palace* (1964) (host; TV series), *Bing Crosby in Dublin* (1965) (TV), *Cancel My Reservation* (1972), *The World of Sport Fishing* (1972), *Just One More Time* (1974), *That's Entertainment* (1974) (host/narrator), and *Bing Crosby and Fred Astaire: A Couple of Song and Dance Men* (1975) (TV). He also narrated the films and television programs *The Legend of Sleepy Hollow* (1958), *Cinerama's Russian Adventure* (1966), and *Bing Crosby's Washington State* (1968).

67. King, "Articulating Stardom," 147.

Part 2

CULTURAL PERSPECTIVES
ON CROSBY

5

Bing Crosby:
Rock 'n' Roll Godfather

John Mark Dempsey

The author of a recent exhaustive biography of Bing Crosby, Gary Giddins, laments that Crosby's imprint has badly faded in recent years. As one participant in a 2002 Crosby conference at Hofstra University in Hempstead, New York, commented: "The image of Frank Sinatra is that of a stylish man standing in the spotlight, in front of a microphone, but the image of Bing Crosby is a grandfatherly man wearing a floppy hat with a golf club on his shoulder." With the observation that, among other astonishing achievements, Crosby recorded more than four hundred hit songs over a period of thirty years, Giddins asks: "Could a man who spoke so deeply to so many for so long have nothing to say to us now?"[1] Crosby's true standing as an innovative artist, "the epitome of cool," has been diminished, in Giddins' view:

If children of the sixties knew his work at all, it was from his perennial hit record of "White Christmas," TV reruns of his "Road" pictures with Bob Hope, and his duet with David Bowie on "Little Drummer Boy." Bing's numbers—and the aesthetic they represented—were shaded by those of rock. His art was now as remote from demotic tastes as classical music or jazz.[2]

But while Giddins is right that Crosby's star has unquestionably dimmed, the preceding comment also points to the seeds of influence that Der Bingle indeed planted with baby-boomers. Crosby's influence on his grandchildren's generation—the rock 'n' roll generation—can be seen in a 1993 documentary hosted by comedian Dennis Miller, "Bing! His Legendary Years, 1931–1957," in which Miller, the "ranting" star of "Saturday Night Live," HBO specials, and "Monday Night Football," proclaims his admiration for Crosby. "Nowadays, people may not use the words 'Bing Crosby' and 'hip' in the same sentence, but the fact is, I think he embodied the word," Miller said. Miller described his mother dragging him out of a movie theater after watching one of the Bing Crosby-Bob Hope "Road" movies over and over.[3] As the one hundredth anniversary of Crosby's birth was observed in 2003, it would be foolish to assert that Crosby had as profound an influence on the development of rock as black bluesmen, such as Muddy Waters, or country music performers, such as Hank Williams. But even if the post–World War II generation had a very limited appreciation of Crosby's career, it seems Crosby still made his mark on their collective psyche through his influence on some of that generation's brightest lights. Meaningful connections to Bing Crosby and some of the most important rock performers of the 1950s and 1960s are not difficult to find. Crosby had a more noteworthy effect on the early wave of rock stars—who laid the foundation for much of today's popular culture scene—than one might have thought.

Through his recordings, radio programs, and movies, Bing Crosby's influence on American popular culture in the 1930s, 1940s, and 1950s is unquestioned. But in reality, Crosby's cultural influence has actually reached much farther, inspiring major rock musicians and other figures of popular culture up to the present day.

From the beginning, rock 'n' roll has had its "soft" and "hard" and "romantic" and "tough" qualities. The melodic ballad—seemingly incongruent with loud, rhythmic music—has always been accepted as an important aspect of rock 'n' roll. As "black" gives meaning to "white," rock's softer side helps to define its hard-edged quality. Crosby's music, by providing a grounding experience in traditional pop music, especially to Elvis Presley, the Beatles, and Bob Dylan, helped to create a kind of duality that provides texture and meaning to rock music.

Crosby is by no means the only pre-rock performer to have influenced rock 'n' roll. "Pop is a cornucopia and a continuum. . . . None of it excludes any of the rest," noted venerable rock critic Robert Christgau, who has written for the *Village Voice,* the *New Yorker,* and the *New York Times,* and authored numerous books on rock music. Frank Sinatra's singing style helped to pave the way for rock's informal style. Christgau points out: "Frank Sinatra and rock and roll aren't mutually exclusive. . . . His singing is every bit as colloquial as Bob Dylan's, Carole King's, or [hip-hop performer] Rakim's."[4] Christgau also credited Louis Armstrong with profoundly influencing rock: "His gravelly, sardonic vocal excursions cut singing loose from cornball beauty. . . . Rock would be unimaginable without solos or gravel or high-handed popwise fun."[5] But Christgau ("Consumer Guide") also recognized Bing Crosby's contributions to rock 'n' roll's characteristically defiant attitude: "He was hip to the jive at a time when declaring yourself a Rhythm Boy [Crosby's pre-fame vocal group] was rebellion aplenty."[6] A scene from one of Crosby's early movies refers to this by showing the outrage of two matronly women who see and hear a young Crosby performing what they derisively term "darkie" music.[7] Christgau asserted: "Rock and roll . . . couldn't have happened without him."[8]

Crosby's Connections to Rock

The outcry over the supposed moral degeneracy of rock 'n' roll that began with Elvis Presley in the 1950s (and has continued to this day) was nothing new. It had been preceded by similar outrage over other new forms of popular music, including the style that Bing Crosby helped to popularize in the 1930s. In this way, Crosby blazed a cultural trail for the daring popular singers and musicians who would follow decades later.

The phenomenon of the national pop star had its beginnings on network radio. On October 29, 1929, only two days after the Wall Street crash known as "Black Tuesday," Rudy Vallee sang "My Time is Your Time" for the first time as the host of "The Fleischmann Hour" on NBC. Vallee's greeting, "Heigh-ho, everybody," had already become familiar to New York listeners on WABC and WOR. Soon the fan mail was pouring in to NBC, so much so that the network bought the rights to "The Maine Stein Song" (which would become associated with Vallee) and gave it to him to record. The song became a huge hit, and earned a lot of money for NBC.[9] Christgau refers to Vallee as "the first pop heartthrob."[10] Vallee was the first well-known exponent of the singing style known as "crooning," which employed a soft, sensual style, in contrast to the booming, straightforward manner of singing that had existed before amplification.[11]

Although he is also one of the most influential jazz singers, crooning found its ultimate expression in the singing of Bing Crosby. Crosby had already found some measure of success as a vocalist with the Paul Whiteman orchestra, singing in a group called the Rhythm Boys. As part of Whiteman's band, they had sung on a CBS program; but Crosby came to the attention of CBS's young president, William Paley, who, while on board a cruise ship, repeatedly heard a recording of Crosby and the Rhythm Boys singing "I Surrender, Dear." He personally signed Crosby to a CBS contract and gave him a nightly program in the fall of 1931 and it quickly became a remarkable success. Soon, Crosby had a massive hit, "Just One More Chance," that established him as a phenomenon, just as "Heartbreak Hotel" did for Elvis Presley in 1956 and "I Want to Hold Your Hand" did for the Beatles in 1964. Crosby dominated the hit music charts for twenty years, placing twenty-seven songs on the charts in 1939 alone, an accomplishment excelled only by the Beatles with thirty hits in 1964.[12]

In the modern era, we have become accustomed to fervent attacks on rock music broadcast on radio and television. But crooning elicited similar reactions from traditionalists. Cardinal O'Connell of the Boston Archdiocese strongly denounced crooning in the January 1932 edition of *Literary Digest*:

Immoral and imbecile slush. A degenerate, low-down sort of interpretation of love. A love song is a beautiful thing in itself. . . . But listen again with this new idea in your head and see if you do not get a sensation of revolting disgust at a man whining a degenerate song, which is unworthy of any American man. . . . It is a sensuous, effeminate luxurious sort of paganism. . . . Think of the boys and girls who are brought up with that idea of music.[13]

It would be another twenty-five years before Elvis Presley would similarly shake the foundations of traditional culture with his sensual hip-shaking style. Significantly, while growing up in Memphis, one of Presley's favorite performers was Bing Crosby. Although known as "the king of rock 'n' roll," a major part of Presley's appeal was his ability to croon melodic ballads such as "Love Me Tender," "Lovin' You," and "Are You Lonesome Tonight?" Even though young Presley's favorite singer was Dean Martin, this aspect of Presley's style was certainly influenced by Crosby. (Of course, Martin himself owed much to Crosby's style.) In a National Public Radio interview, Gary Giddins put it succinctly: "No Bing, no Elvis."[14]

Sitting on the steps of the apartment house where he and his parents lived, young Presley would strum his guitar and sing songs such as "Moonlight Bay," a song Crosby recorded with his son Gary in 1951. At parties, Presley would ask that all of the lights be turned out while he sat in a corner, played his guitar, and sang. Among the performers whose songs he sang was Bing Crosby. When Elvis showed up to audition at the Sun recording studio on July 5, 1954, the first song he recorded was the Crosby hit, "Harbor Lights."[15] Presley sang the song in a crooning style similar to Crosby's, a style that Presley employed on many other recordings in his career. Giddins noted that in many of his ballads Presley imitated Crosby's "pianissimo head tones," or ethereal, high-pitched vocalizations.[16]

When Presley and Crosby died within weeks of each other in 1977, journalist Russell Baker commented on their similarities:

> Both came from obscurity to national recognition while quite young and became very rich. Both lacked formal musical education and went on to movie careers despite a lack of acting skills. Both developed distinctive musical styles that were originally scorned by critics and subsequently studied as pioneer developments in the art of popular song.[17]

When the "Million Dollar Quartet" of Elvis Presley, Johnny Cash, Jerry Lee Lewis, and Carl Perkins recorded together at Sun Studios in December 1956, one of the songs they recorded was "You Belong to My Heart," a Crosby hit from the 1945 Disney animated film, *The Three Caballeros.*[18] Presley later recorded "Blue Hawaii," more than two decades after Crosby recorded the number in 1937, and also covered the 1950 Crosby song "Beyond the Reef."[19]

Even more than Presley, the Everly Brothers brought a style to rock 'n' roll that emphasized melody and harmony. Like Presley, the Everly Brothers strongly influenced the Beatles and Simon and Garfunkel.[20] The Everly Brothers were clearly familiar with Bing Crosby's catalog. They scored a number-one British hit in 1961 with an up-tempo version of the Crosby hit "Temptation," from the 1933 movie *Going Hollywood.*[21] The brothers felt so strongly about "Temptation" that they split with their original manager, Wesley Rose, over releasing the song.[22] Around the same time, the Everly Brothers recorded two of Crosby's other hits, "True Love" and "Now Is the Hour."[23]

Bing Crosby's presence on the popular music scene had been so pervasive in the years leading up to the early rock 'n' roll era that it is not surprising that rock artists commonly recorded Crosby standards. "I came from a family where my people didn't like rhythm and blues. Bing Crosby—'Pennies from Heaven'—Ella Fitzgerald, was all I heard," said Little Richard, whose style seems to owe very little to Crosby.[24] Among the first songs Roy Orbison learned growing up in West Texas were Crosby's "You Are My Sunshine" and "San Antonio Rose," although surely Orbison was also familiar with country-style versions of the songs.[25]

Growing up in Great Britain, the Beatles, too, absorbed much of Crosby's music. Even after Elvis Presley's explosion on the scene in 1956, radio in England, dominated by the BBC, featured relatively little rock 'n' roll,[26] and so much of the music heard by the incipient Beatles was traditional pop. Ironically, Crosby seems to have had the greatest influence on John Lennon, the Beatle most associated with uncompromising rock 'n' roll.

Lennon said he was inspired to write the Beatles' first number-one British hit "Please Please Me"—the record that lit the fuse of Beatlemania—by Crosby's 1932 song "Please." Lennon explained: "I was always intrigued by the words to a Bing Crosby song that went, 'Please lend a little ear to my pleas.' The double use of the word 'please.'"[27] One account says that Lennon's mother Julia, though absent for most of his childhood, often sang the song to him when he was a small boy.[28] Also, Lennon—who had a keen ear for satire—may have heard the song in a late-1950s Crosby TV special, in which Crosby's sons parody the song and try to teach their dad how to sing it in rock 'n' roll style.[29]

Lennon's admiration for Crosby extended beyond this one particular song. After he moved to New York City, Lennon stocked the Wurlitzer jukebox in his Dakota apartment with "as many Bing Crosby records as he could get."[30] Lennon's songwriting partner, Paul McCartney, noted that while Lennon exhibited an exterior that was "tough, tough, tough," one of Lennon's favorite songs was Crosby's romantic ballad "Girl of My Dreams," and McCartney observed that it was this side of Lennon that produced such melodic Beatles ballads as the lush "Good Night."[31]

McCartney, more than Lennon, is associated with Crosby's style of traditional popular music. McCartney's father Jim had been a semi-professional musician in his youth and greatly admired Bing Crosby, among others. Jim McCartney often played the favorite songs of his youth on the piano and passed on his love of pop music to his son. This influence is apparent in McCartney's Beatles songs "When I'm Sixty-Four," "Your Mother Should Know," and "Honey Pie," which parody the 1930s style of pop music dominated by Crosby, if not Crosby's music itself. Beatles songs such as "Good Night" and "When I'm Sixty-Four," like Presley's "Love Me Tender" and "Lovin' You," provided the soft, romantic counterpoint to rock's hard and tough side.

George Harrison also professed an appreciation for Crosby's music. "We'd listen to anything that was played on the radio," Harrison said. "Irish tenors like Josef Locke, dance-band music, Bing Crosby, people like that."[32] From the beginning, a major aspect of the Beatles' appeal was the eclectic nature of their music, ranging from "tough" cover versions of Chuck Berry ("Rock and Roll Music," "Roll Over Beethoven") to "romantic" show tunes ("Til There Was You," "A Taste of Honey"). The pre-fame Beatles performed an energetic version of a 1935 number-one Crosby hit "Red Sails in the Sunset" in their stage act[33] —although they might also have been familiar with Nat King Cole's 1951 version of the song or the Platters' 1960 recording.[34]

Harrison rejected the narrow view that only rock music was worthwhile: "I don't understand people who say, 'I only like rock and roll,' or 'I only like the blues,' or whatever."[35] Among the first tunes that the young Harrison learned to play on guitar was Bing Crosby's 1932 hit, "Dinah."[36] As a solo performer in 1976, Harrison recorded "True Love," the Cole Porter song that was a major hit for Crosby (with Grace Kelly) in the 1950s.[37]

Like Harrison, another 1960s-era British rock superstar, Pete Townshend of The Who, has been known for the spiritual content of his work, especially in The Who's quintessential album, *Tommy*. In the late 1960s, Townsend became a follower of the Indian mystic Meher Baba. It would be foolish to suggest that Townsend's mystical tendency was strongly influenced by Bing Crosby, yet Townsend clearly was familiar with Crosby's music and drew some inspiration from it. In an interview at that time, Townsend said he found spirituality in Crosby's most famous song "White Christmas" and in doing so expressed his admiration for Crosby's performance: "It is, in effect, a spiritual song. It's effective on every spiritual level, and it's a complete, wonderful musical effort. It's got to be accepted for what it is. It's a piece of pure, wonderful existence."[38]

Another rock icon with the reputation for profoundly philosophical, if not mystical, lyrical themes, Bob Dylan, has drawn inspiration in recent years from Bing Crosby. But in Dylan's case, it was Crosby's vocal style that most impressed him. Interviewed in the mid-1980s, Dylan commented: "I tell you who I've really been listening to a lot lately—in fact, I'm thinking of recording one of his earlier songs—is Bing Crosby. I don't think you can find better phrasing anywhere."[39]

Dylan, to date, has not recorded a song closely associated with Bing Crosby. But rock journalist Paul Williams commented on the Crosby influence in Dylan's song "Emotionally Yours":

Dylan is sincere in his 1985 profession of admiration for Bing Crosby. . . . A song and performance like this is an expression of Dylan's search for a way to incorporate into his own work what he has learned from Crosby and others as a singer and as an interpreter of songs. . . . It is the work of a singer and songwriter who has been genuinely inspired to explore new ground, in his phrasing, his notions of what a song is, and particularly in his relationship (as a singer) with melody.[40]

Veteran rock writer Robert Hilburn has also likened Dylan's singing to Crosby. Hilburn commented on "the relaxed Bing Crosby-like croon of 'Moonlight,'" a song on Dylan's acclaimed album *Love and Theft*.[41]

Dylan biographer Tim Riley found a relationship between Crosby's relatively unsexual persona and Dylan's popularity. Like Crosby, Dylan "transcended the sexual mystique. . . . Bing Crosby . . . escaped the sexual trap with a golfer's smugness," Riley observed.[42] In the 1930s, Crosby was indeed the object of many a young woman's desires but tended to make fun of his image as "the great lover."[43]

Besides the influence of his music, Crosby's path to superstardom in the 1930s set a pattern that Elvis Presley and the Beatles were later to follow. Crosby parlayed early success in recordings and radio broadcasting into a very successful movie career. Likewise, Presley quickly moved from hit records into radio's off-spring, television, and then movies.[44] Presley's manager, "Colonel" Tom Parker, set out to follow the pattern established by Crosby, and later Frank Sinatra, of becoming a "family entertainer, at home on stage and screen."[45] Like Crosby, the Beatles received some early exposure on radio (they had a regular BBC show) before achieving their great recording success, then they set television-ratings records in Great Britain and the United States before making several successful movies. Even Dylan has tried his hand at movie acting, with less notable results.

Technical Influence

Besides the musical influence he provided, Crosby played a major role in the technology revolution that aided the development of rock music. After World War II, Crosby started Bing Crosby Enterprises to develop new products. An engineer for the new company, John Mullin, had been fascinated by the excellent fidelity of German radio programs during the war. The Germans had developed a method of recording on magnetic tape. Mullin brought home two German tape recorders, made refinements to them, and Bing Crosby Enterprises joined with the Ampex Company to begin marketing the devices.[46]

Crosby himself saw the immense potential for audiotape. He was dissatisfied with the way his weekly network radio show was produced. Robert Christgau noted:

Frustrated by the sound quality of his half-improvised radio shows, which had to be patched together from 78-rpm master discs so they could be scheduled through four time zones, he became the first entertainer—unless Adolf Hitler counts—to exploit the fidelity and editability of [magnetic tape] . . . . Musical "authenticity" would never be the same.[47]

On October 1, 1947 Crosby's ABC radio program became the first network program to be broadcast on tape. Soon, virtually all prime-time network programs were being recorded and broadcast on audiotape.[48] The improvement in technology made recording music easier and less expensive, promoting the emergence of rock 'n' roll and rhythm-and-blues music in the 1950s.[49]

Along with Crosby's contribution to the use of magnetic tape, Christgau noted Crosby's role in popularizing the long-playing (LP) record format,[50] which, of course, became a major outlet for the creativity of rock's greatest artists. Further, Crosby is credited with developing the use of the microphone as a tool in the singer's arsenal, bringing a "quiet intimacy" to singing, as author Robert Ray noted in an essay on technical advances that aided rock music.[51] As author Thomas A. DeLong explained, crooning was a natural consequence of technology: "In essence, it was an adaptation to the techniques of radio broadcasting. The highly sensitive mike demanded a different mode of vocal production. Singing into the delicate carbon microphones compelled artists to use soft, almost caressing tones lest a loud or high note shatter a transmitter tube."[52]

Columnist and cultural commentator Russell Baker noted that "Both Crosby and Presley were creations of the microphone. It made it possible for people with frail voices not only to be heard beyond the third row, but also to caress millions."[53] Christgau observed that Crosby brought a new "democratic" ethic to singing that contributed to the emergence of rock:

It was Crosby who mastered vocal amplification by developing a style appropriate to the microphones that defined radio and recording studios. . . . Soon the floodgates were opened to a host of singers who hadn't gone through the painful rituals whereby a few lucky, hard-working individuals train their freakishly exceptional "beautiful" voices to carry in a concert hall.[54]

Strange Duo

Of course, Crosby earned a unique place in modern rock history when he recorded a duet with David Bowie for Crosby's last major project, his 1977 Christmas television special. The song, a medley of "Little Drummer Boy" and a Bowie original "Peace on Earth," has become a modern-day Christmas classic.

In September 1977, only weeks before he died, Crosby prepared to record his twenty-first Christmas program in London and wanted a young guest star. He had not heard of Bowie, but his children were fans of the British "glam" rocker. Crosby invited Bowie to appear on the program and Bowie, "harboring a sneaking admiration for the 'old groaner,'" readily accepted. Bowie felt "Little Drummer Boy," as sung by Crosby, was out of his vocal range,[55] and wrote "Peace on Earth" on the spot as a countermelody.[56]

Bowie and Crosby engaged in some light banter before singing together. Their repartee seemed to acknowledge the odd nature of the pairing. Crosby asked Bowie what kind of songs he sang:

Bowie: Mostly the contemporary stuff. Do you, eh . . . like modern music?

Crosby: Oh, I think it's marvelous. Some of it's really fine. But tell me, have you ever listened to any of the older fellows?

Bowie: Oh yeah, sure. I like, ah . . . John Lennon and the other one with . . . eh, Harry Nilsson.

Crosby: Mmm . . . you go back that far, huh?

Bowie: Yeah, I'm not as young as I look.[57]

Crosby and Bowie completed the number in only three takes. Released as a single at Christmas 1982 in Great Britain, the song became a posthumous hit for Crosby, reaching number three on the charts.[58] Bowie presented a surprisingly conservative appearance for the performance, and Crosby, obviously unaware of Bowie's gender-bending persona up to that time, called him a "clean-cut kid." Crosby went on to praise Bowie's singing and astutely observed: "He could be a good actor if he wanted."[59]

Bowie's decision to perform on the Crosby Christmas program was a significant step in his career. Bowie's manager Ken Pitt (with some resistance from Bowie up to that point) had been trying to move Bowie in the direction of becoming a broad-based, popular entertainer. After the appearance on Crosby's television show, Bowie continued his move toward the mainstream, narrating Prokofiev's *Peter and the Wolf* for an RCA recording, guesting on Johnny Carson's Tonight Show, and appearing on the cover of *Time* in 1983. The *Time* article noted that Bowie had found a new role, "the teen-age rebel who makes good."[60]

The Crosby-Bowie duet has taken on legendary status. Dennis Miller observed that Bowie's appearance with Crosby represented an acknowledgment of respect from the rock generation: "Bowie knew something the rest of us didn't. By the end of the sixties, a lot of the younger generation was rejecting the family values Bing came to represent. This image overshadowed the way he had revolutionized pop culture."[61] One writer noted that the meeting of Bowie and Crosby "marked the point at which pop began to resolve the generational conflicts of the Sixties and Seventies."[62] Another writer observed of the duet between Crosby and Bowie that "It was hard to tell their voices apart: Suddenly, unaccountably, Bowie had become mainstream."[63]

Conclusion

If, as Middleton and Brackett suggest, popular music is a range of interrelated forms, it is possible to see how the music and career of Bing Crosby, while not as directly influential as blues and country music, still played a significant role in the development of rock music. Biographer Gary Giddins may be correct that modern audiences have lost sight of Crosby's rightful status as the "epitome of cool,"[64] but many rock performers have found inspiration, in one form or another, in Bing Crosby. Perhaps a new generation will come to see Crosby as Miller sees him: One of the "coolest performers of the century" and the "Mick Jagger of his day,"[65] ironically, a "godfather" of rock 'n' roll.

Notes

1. Gary Giddins, *Bing Crosby: A Pocketful of Dreams, The Early Years, 1903–1940* (Boston: Little, Brown and Company, 2001), 1.

2. Ibid., 14–15.

3. "Bing! His Legendary Years, 1931–1957," produced and directed by Bryan Johnson, 75 minutes, MCA Records, 1993, videocassette.

4. Robert Christgau, 1992, "B.E.: A Dozen Moments in the Prehistory of Rock and Roll" (http://www.robertchristgau.com/xg/music/ten-det.php, accessed 6 January 2006).

5. Christgau, "Either And" (http://www.robertchristgov.com/xg/music/sinatra_srphgp).

6. Robert Christgau, 1999, "Bing Crosby," *Consumer Guide Reviews* (http://www.robertchristgau.com/get_artist.php?id=146&name=Bing+Crosby, accessed 6 January 2006).

7. "Bing! His Legendary Years."

8. Christgau, "B.E.: A Dozen Moments."

9. Philip K. Eberly, *Music in the Air: America's Changing Tastes in Popular Music 1920–1980* (New York: Hastings House Publishers, 1982).

10. Christgau, "B.E.: A Dozen Moments."

11. Thomas A. DeLong, *The Mighty Music Box* (Los Angeles: Amber Crest Books, Inc., 1980).

12. Giddins, *Bing Crosby.*

13. Eberly, 103.

14. Harriet Baskas (interview), 14 October 2002, "Bing Crosby remembered a quarter century after his death," National Public Radio (http://www.npr.org/templates/story/story.php?storyId=1151660, accessed 3 January 2006).

15. Peter Guralnick, *Last Train to Memphis* (Boston: Little, Brown and Company, 1994).

16. Giddins, 417.

17. Russell Baker, *There's a Country in My Cellar* (New York: Morrow, 1990), 98.

18. Guralnick, 365–66.

19. Gene Santoro, "Lilt: Seductive Hawaiian musical forms have regularly swept the mainland and changed its music," *Atlantic Monthly* (November 1994), 128–32.

20. *The Beatles Anthology* (San Francisco: Chronicle Books, 2000); David Fricke, liner notes, Simon and Garfunkel, *Old Friends,* CD, Columbia Records, 1997.

21. *The Everly Brothers* (http://www.bellenet.com/everly.html, accessed 26 July 2002).

22. Consuelo Dodge, *The Everly Brothers: Ladies Love Outlaws* (Starke, FL: CIN-DAV, Inc., 1991).

23. Phyllis Karpp, *Ike's Boys: The Story of the Everly Brothers* (Ann Arbor, MI: Popular Culture, 1988).

24. Alec Wilder, *American Popular Song: The Great Innovators 1900–1950* (New York: Oxford University Press, 1972), quoted in Middleton, 110.

25. Ellis Amburn, *Dark Star: The Roy Orbison Story* (New York: Carol Publishing Group, 1990).

26. *The Beatles Anthology.*

27. *The Beatles Anthology,* 90.

28. Walter Everett, *The Beatles as Musicians: Revolver through Anthology* (New York: Oxford University Press, 1999).

29. Giddins, *Bing Crosby.*

30. Ray Coleman, *Lennon* (New York: McGraw-Hill Company, 1984), 478.

31. Ray Coleman, *McCartney: Yesterday . . . and Today* (Los Angeles: Dove Books, 1997).

32. *The Beatles Anthology,* 26.

33. *The Beatles First Live Recordings, Hamburg, Germany, 1962,* LP, Pickwick Records, 1979.

34. Giddins; "Nat King Cole Lyrics: 'Red Sails in the Sunset,' " *Lyrics Café* (http://www.lyricsafe.com, accessed 25 July 2002).

35. *The Beatles Anthology,* 26–27.

36. Everett, *The Beatles as Musicians.*

37. *George Harrison,* 33 1/3, LP, Dark Horse Records, 1976.

38. Jann Wenner, ed., *Twenty Years of Rolling Stone: What a Long, Strange Trip It's Been* (New York: Friendly Press, Inc., 1987), 46.

39. Mikal Gilmore, "Dylan at a Crossroads Once Again," in *The Bob Dylan Companion: Four Decades of Commentary,* ed. Carl Benson. (New York: Schirmer Books, 1998), 180.

40. Paul Williams, *Bob Dylan: Performing Artist, The Middle Years, 1974–1986* (Novato, CA: Underwood-Miller, 1992), 265.

41. Robert Hilburn, "Record Rack: This Year's Dylan is a Sonic Dynamo," *Los Angeles Times* (Calendar), 9 September 2001, 88.

42. Tim Riley, *Hard Rain: A Dylan Commentary* (New York: DaCapo Press, 1999), 7.

43. "Bing! His Legendary Years."

44. Giddins, *Bing Crosby.*
45. James Miller, *Flowers in the Dustbin: The Rise of Rock and Roll, 1947–1977* (New York: Simon and Schuster, 1999), 134.
46. Bob Thomas, *The One and Only Bing* (New York: Grosset and Dunlap, 1977).
47. Christgau, "B.E.: A Dozen Moments."
48. Sydney W. Head and Christopher H. Sterling, *Broadcasting in America* (Boston: Houghton Mifflin Co., 1991).
49. Paul Théberge, "'Plugged in': Technology and Popular Music," in *The Cambridge Companion to Pop and Rock,* eds. Simon Frith, Will Straw, and John Street (Cambridge, UK: Cambridge University Press, 3–25, 2001).
50. Christgau, "B.E.: A Dozen Moments."
51. Robert B. Ray, "Tracking," in *Present Tense: Rock and Roll and Culture,* ed. Anthony DeCurtis (Durham, NC: Duke University Press, 1992).
52. Thomas A. DeLong, *The Mighty Music Box,* 70.
53. Baker, 98.
54. Christgau, "B.E.: A Dozen Moments."
55. Robert Webb, "Pop: It's In the Mix: The Independent's Guide to Pop's Unlikeliest Collaborators," *The Independent* (London), 22 September 2000, 14; Steven Lewis, "Bing Crosby Meets David Bowie," Bing Crosby: Steven Lewis' Internet Museum (http://www.kcmetro.cc.mo.us/~crosby/bingbowie.htm, accessed 5 January 2006).
56. Kevin Chambers, *Peace on Earth* (http://www.chapel42.com/peace_on_earth/index.htm, accessed 16 October 2001).
57. "Peace on Earth/Little Drummer Boy," *Twin Music Lyrics* (http://www.twin-music.com/lyrics_file/bowie/extra/peace.html, accessed 5 January 2006).
58. Jim Davies, "Let's Duet Together," 19 August 1994, *The Guardian,* Section 2, 14–15.
59. Webb, 14.
60. Peter and Leni Gillman, *Alias David Bowie: A Biography* (New York: Henry Holt and Company, 1986), 466–67.
61. "Bing! His Legendary Years."
62. Webb, 14.
63. Peter R. Koenig, *The Laughing Gnostic: David Bowie and the Occult* (http://www.cyberlink.ch/~koenig/bowie.htm, accessed 5 January 2006).
64. Giddins, *Bing Crosby,* 14.
65. "Bing! His Legendary Years."

6

American Archetypes:
How Crosby and Hope Became
Hollywood's Greatest Comedy Team

Walter Raubicheck

In many ways Bob Hope and Bing Crosby are the most underrated comedy team in Hollywood history, probably because both performers achieved such tremendous success independently of their collaboration. But in terms of box-office success, cultural impact, and genuine innovation in screen comedy, Hope and Crosby rival, if not surpass, the great teams that come just before them and immediately follow them: the Marx Brothers in the thirties and Martin and Lewis in the fifties. The latter also achieved great success independently, but only after the team had irreparably split. Certainly it is time for a major "Road" picture revival, the kind the Marx Brothers enjoyed in the sixties. The recent DVD releases will help renew public interest, but my main point is that much of the success of the team stems from the fact that unlike Chaplin, the Marx Brothers, Laurel and Hardy, and others who maintained roots in European comic traditions and personae, Hope and Crosby created characters whose roots were distinctively American. In fact, much of the humor of the series stems from the clash between the boys' unshakeable Americanness and the traditions of the exotic cultures they encountered. Of course, by contemporary standards some of these conflicts can occasionally seem tasteless in their cartoonish stereotyping of other peoples. And their Americanness is certainly rooted primarily in the experience of nineteenth and early twentieth century white males. But the fact remains that the more genuinely American the boys' tastes and habits are, the funnier their reactions are to their surroundings.

Hope and Crosby made seven "Road" pictures between 1940 and 1962: *Singapore, Zanzibar, Morocco, Utopia, Rio, Bali, and Hong Kong.* An eighth film, *Road to the Fountain of Youth*, was being planned when Crosby died suddenly in 1977. Of course, they also performed numerous times together during those years on radio and television, embellishing the characters they had created on the screen. To the delight of the audience, Crosby often did cameo roles in other Hope films of the forties and fifties, always appearing in a way that emphasized their "rivalry." Though each actor made his greatest non-"Road" films during this twenty-year period, as far as comedies are concerned, they both reached their peak in the series.

On the silent screen Buster Keaton and Harold Lloyd created definite American personae, but Chaplin and Laurel and Hardy never completely abandoned the British Music Hall tradition that had nurtured them. That the Marx Brothers never strayed too far from their European influences is particularly evident in Harpo's mime and in Chico's clownish Italian impersonation. Only Groucho—though he rarely dressed like an American—presented a recognizably American character: the fast-talking, wise guy sharpie. But Hope and Crosby are almost aggressively American male personalities: down-and-out and desperate for money, totally vulnerable to classic sex appeal, ready to betray each other because of this primary need for a gorgeous female love object, but ultimately fair and even generous when not battling for a woman or for money. When the films begin, their characters are either carnies, vaudevillians, or sometimes both: performers in classic and distinctively American entertainments. But they are also carnies or vaudevillians with an outlaw angle—ready to dupe their audiences to make extra money or stay one step ahead of the cops—another tradition in American popular culture. Ultimately they portray talented con men who can only be conned each by the other (specifically Hope by Crosby) or a beautiful woman (usually Dorothy Lamour). The roots of these characters—whether or not Hope or Crosby or the screenwriters were aware of it—lie in nineteenth century cultural archetypes found in texts like Melville's *The Confidence Man* and Twain's *Huckleberry Finn*.

The comparison with the Marx Brothers is instructive. Implicitly the brothers were European immigrants who still reflect much of the behavior of the "old culture." Harpo and Chico were conspicuously alien to the American settings of their films, which provided much of the Marxian humor. For example, no two comic characters could be more out of place in the local speakeasy of the college town in *Horse Feathers* than Baravelli (Chico), who still curses under his breath in Italian (or faux Italian), and the manic dogcatcher played by Harpo who turns the telephone into a slot machine and violently disrupts the local card games. Again, they are funny because they do not belong in this stereotypical American locale. (As always Groucho is a partial exception: he has the gift of gab necessary to be a college president, although he is also occasionally strangely unfamiliar with American tastes and customs: he is blithely unaware of what an American football player would look like [he assumes Harpo and Chico qualify!].) Indeed, in the early days of the Marx's vaudeville act Groucho used a Yiddish accent. Of course much of vaudeville was based on ethnic humor, since the immigrant experience was becoming more and more typically American; the Marx Brothers were not anomalous in their Europeanness. However, by 1940 the time was ripe for a comedy team that didn't reflect the attitudes of those who had recently come to America, but those who were exporting inherent American attitudes instead.

The humor of the "Road" pictures could not be more different from that of the Marxes: Hope and Crosby bring American habits and attitudes with them wherever they go, and their determination to interpret exotic customs from their Main Street perspectives always has comic results. Significantly, when the Marx brothers are stowaways in *Monkey Business*, they are coming from Europe to a foreign America, whereas when Hope and Crosby play these roles in *Road to Rio*, they flee the country only to escape prosecution for having burned down a carnival. Invariably they interpret the exotic customs they encounter in terms of their own cultural biases. For example there are the shaving jokes they make in *Morocco* every time they speak to a man with a beard. This predilection for interpreting foreign cultures in terms of American customs reaches its apogee in the final picture, *Road to Hong Kong*. Here they visit the most remote locale in the entire series, a lamasery in Tibet, so that Hope's character can taste an exotic herb that will restore his memory. As they enter the monastery they are greeted by a thin, ascetic looking monk. When Hope informs the monk that he doesn't remember anything about money and girls, the monk intones that "in life money and girls are not important." Hope turns to Crosby and says, "He needs a couple of weeks in Las Vegas." Crosby asks, "Hey Slim . . . Who's the boss here? The number one fellow? Who pays the tab on the pad?" The monk replies solemnly, "the grand lama." Hope interjects, "so he's the pro," and Crosby mutters under his breath, "Jack Lama." Then, alluding to the staff with which Hope has been hiking the remote mountains, he tells Hope, "Bring your niblick" as they follow the monk inside. Instinctively they translate anything exotic into the terms of American popular culture and the assumed desires of out of work American males: dollars and dames. They are never interested in actually learning anything from these cultures: they are all merely way stations—and possible sources of a quick buck or a real "strike"—on their continual road to freedom from conventional expectations: marriage, a career, a family.

Of course, part of the appeal of the Americanness of the team had to do with the war: Two of the most successful films in the series were made at the height of this country's involvement, *Morocco* (1942) and *Utopia* (1944), while the first two were released as the country's entry seemed more and more imminent: *Singapore* in 1940 and *Zanzibar* in 1941. Although it would be misleading to attribute the series' popularity to patriotism, it is likely that the team's stubborn maintenance of distinctly American attitudes towards money, women, and class, as well as the national popular culture references in the nonstop wisecracking, endeared Hope and Crosby to an anxious audience. Certainly Abbott and Costello were appealing in the same way, especially in the films that featured military service (*Buck Privates* and *In the Navy*), but the first "Road" picture was released a year before these two films, and Hope and Crosby themselves became almost synonymous with the contributions of Hollywood to the war effort. This is not to deny that the most obvious appeal of the first few "Road" pictures was comic escapism from the deprivations of the late Depression years and the fears concerning the turmoil in Europe, but this escapism was particularly effective because of the readily identifiable attitudes and values of Hope's and Crosby's personae.

In retrospect, *Singapore* is a good introduction to both the Hope/Crosby persona nae in the series, as well as the range of characters that Crosby portrayed in the for ties, his greatest and most popular period as a screen actor. Whether it be the Father O'Malley pictures, the two Fred Astaire films, or the *Road* pictures, Crosby invari ably plays a man who is—or could be—successful in mainstream American pro fessions—business, the clergy, show business—but who either opts out of this predictable success or modifies the cultural expectations of such a position be cause of his need for more personal freedom, or because the elitist stuffiness of the position offends his desire to relate to people from every class or walk of life. For example, Father O'Malley is the forties version of the "hip" priest who respects rit ual and tradition, but who loves popular culture from baseball to hit songs and who wants to undercut all class divisions in his parish. In both of the films he made with Fred Astaire, Crosby endeavors to establish alternative paths to personal and pro fessional success. In *Holiday Inn* he wants to stay in show business, but only on terms that will allow him both personal freedom and artistic choice in the country inn, which is open only on holidays and is located physically and psychologically far from the routinized performance and publicity characteristic of Broadway and Hollywood. In *Blue Skies* he needs to close each of his clubs as soon as they have been established so he can take on the challenge of creating a new one. In each case Crosby's character is disillusioned by what has been considered successful in the past because of what he considers to be arbitrary cultural and/or personal restric tions. In effect, Crosby wanted to combat the conformity of mainstream culture.

In *Road to Singapore* the mainstream culture is his father's shipping company and the elitist social world it supports, complete with a desk job for life and mar riage to a girl he does not love. Hope's character represents the alternative to all this: rootlessness and freedom, "laughs" in place of "success." Crosby's Josh Mallon, like all of his characters in the forties, hates pomposity and stuffiness. Crosby's true spirit emerges early in the movie when he joins Hope (Ace) in a vaudeville routine during the party on his father's yacht, aligning himself with lower class tastes. When his fiancée's brother attempts to insult both Hope and Crosby for their crudity, the boys initiate the first of many brawls they are involved in throughout the series, horrifying his father and deeply antagonizing his prospec tive father-in-law. The boys are soon off on the road—which usually is never *to* anywhere in particular, despite the films' titles, but which definitely leads away from society's expectations of success and debilitating class consciousness.

Of course, the Dorothy Lamour character always provides an interesting dou ble-edged conflict. When she eventually enters the story, the Hope and Crosby characters have been introduced as out of work American carnies or vaudevillians who have somehow arrived in a confusingly foreign locale. When Lamour ap pears, she is first viewed by the boys as ravishingly exotic, someone unlike the girls from home in her "native" sensuality and erotic promise. Their friendship gives way to their lust as they proceed to fight over her. But eventually the exotic Lamour becomes another kind of threat to their bond: in order to win her, one of them would have to exchange his freedom for the domesticity she insists upon. This is all made quite clear immediately in *Singapore*: at first they throw her out of their bachelor hut when she begins to treat it as a home, but soon they are both competing to show her how domestic each can be. Thus, the pictures always end with Crosby presumably trading his "on the road" life for wedded bliss and the pleasures of pipe and slippers. But as Gary Giddins points out, this is merely a concession to Hollywood romance clichés, which the pictures are actually spoofing: "the audience knows who the real couple is . . . the movie fades as Bing and Bob go into their patty-cake crouch. . . ."[1]

Lamour's character is not easy to define in terms of gender roles in forties and fifties Hollywood. On the one hand she is a pure object of desire, fought over by the boys like any other potential possession. On the other hand, she often is portrayed as completely self-determined: she and her sister manipulate the boys throughout *Zanzibar*, as Lamour uses her sexuality to con Hope and Crosby to take her across Africa to her rich fiancé. In *Utopia* she is a resourceful dance hall singer who—as she does in many of the films—makes successive dates with the boys in order to seduce them to obtain a treasure map. She is never a passive object—her vulnerability is only revealed after she falls in love with Crosby's character—usually about halfway through each film. At this point many of her decisions are driven by her own desire. But she is never the passive, needy, sexually compliant woman: Hope and Crosby objectify her, but she refuses to conform to their fantasies.

Through the first third of the films they made together, Hope and Crosby seem to have an equal effect (or lack thereof) on Lamour as they connive to win her affections exclusively. The turning point comes when Crosby serenades Dorothy with a ballad; after having Crosby sing to her, Lamour is his forever. Crosby's ballads somehow function as metaphors for romantic sex: they appeal directly to her erotic desires, but they also assure her that sexual fulfillment will be intertwined with beauty, emotion, and respect. The promise inherent in Crosby's love songs contrasts dramatically with Hope's blatant urge for quick, non-committal sex. From the moment Crosby croons "Moonlight Becomes You" or "But Beautiful"—two Burke and Van Huesen classics that Crosby introduced in the series—the contest with Hope is over. This is particularly evident in *Utopia* when Sal (Lamour), who has shown an impartial lack of real interest in either of the boys after she meets them, suddenly falls for Crosby in the middle of his rendition of "Welcome to My Dream." A close shot reveals her almost instantaneous wide-eyed adoration; Crosby's ballad singing literally casts a spell over her. Of course, Hope's blatant egotism prevents him from grasping the fact that Lamour is in love with Crosby until the final scene of each film.

Much has been made of the "cruelty" and constant "betrayals" in the relationship between the Hope and Crosby characters. Typical is this quotation from a 1970s biography of Bob Hope: "Ostensibly buddies, the pair actually engage in fierce rivalry over money, sex and personal vanity. While competing for Lamour's affections, neither has any compunction about publicly disclosing the other's penchant for philandering. Hope alludes to Crosby's age with references to senility while Crosby dismisses Hope with the disclaiming, 'Junior.' "[2] However, I would argue that these tendencies result from the vaudeville roots of the literal and fictional partnership, for Hope and Crosby's relationship in the *Road* pictures is essentially an extended vaudeville routine in which exaggerations of a character's foibles are assumed. As a matter of fact, their performing partnership did begin as an actual vaudeville routine in the Capitol Theater in New York in 1932 when they decided to team up after a few weeks on the same bill. The put-downs and the rivalry for women started there and were an essential part of their vaudeville dynamic. All vaudeville acts needed to be defined by very broad, obvious character types in order for a short routine to be successful. That Crosby was crafty and Hope was gullible, that Crosby had the brains and Hope had the brawn (as Crosby's character puts it), and that women preferred Crosby to Hope were simply necessary differentiations that made them a complementary pair. But a subtext of all the conflicts and arguments between them was that they were inseparably drawn together by their shared values and wit. The fact is that Crosby would not have been with Hope if he had not preferred their partnership to the more socially accepted life he was clearly capable of having based on his articulateness, his manners, and his suave charm.

The *Road* series gave Crosby the best opportunity he ever had in his career to develop his comedic talents, the ones he had begun his film career with in the Mack Sennett shorts of the early thirties. It is sometimes assumed, as with most two-man comedy teams, that Hope was the comic and that Crosby was the straight man, but of course this assumption is inaccurate. Certainly differences in comedic approach are obvious: Hope's talent for physical comedy, particularly the hilarious use he made of his eyes and his genius for verbal double take, was unmatched in the sound era. In addition, his barely contained physical energy was counterpointed nicely by Crosby's relaxed coolness: thinking of a typical scene from the series, one pictures Crosby standing nonchalantly still while Hope shakes him or buzzes around him trying to get his attention or make a point. But the key to the distinctive humor of these films is that both actors can wisecrack equally well and equally fast, that together they create an unprecedented double volley of wit in which they seem to harmonize with each other's deliveries.

With Hope, Crosby allowed himself a silliness in his physical comedy, too, that he never exhibited anywhere else after the Sennett films. Throughout the thirties Crosby played stereotyped romantic leads in light musical comedies, though even here he managed to assert a definite Crosby presence: unpretentious, quick-witted, self-contained, and the object of women's pursuit. In films with such established or up-and-coming stars as Marion Davies (*Going Hollywood*), Carole Lombard (*We're Not Dressing*), Frances Farmer (*Rhythm on the Range*), and Shirley Ross (*Waikiki Wedding*), Crosby's charm and good looks are always accompanied by a cool reserve that simultaneously attracts and infuriates the women who fall for his romantic yet masculine singing, his relaxed, unthreatening sexuality, or both. With Hope he created a unique comic character: the clever con man who cannot refrain from duping his partner and who would rather bilk an audience than work for a living but who also possesses the subtle allure and unpretentious self-assurance that always wins the girl.

As for Bob Hope, biographer Charles Thompson points out that these films (he is talking in particular about *Zanzibar*) "firmly set the seal on the comic character

Bob had been gradually building over the years; from now on he would portray himself as the egoistic, excitable, fumbling, cowardly romantic who inevitably loses the girl—particularly if the suave, cool Bing was around. He became the butt of the biggest jokes and the world loved him for it. His *Road* persona was to dominate his film, radio, stage, and (in later years) television performances."[3] Prior to teaming with Crosby, Hope's two-year film career featured roles that capitalized on the fast delivery that he had honed in vaudeville, on Broadway, and on the radio, but which often found him a well-heeled entertainer or even a college tutor in *College Swing* (1938)—here Gracie Allen was the nitwit, not Hope—with none of the later uneducated, working class, traits that became dominant in his roles in the forties. Hope's first film, *The Big Broadcast of 1938*, is essentially a vehicle for W. C. Fields, though Hope and Shirley Ross steal the picture with their witty but poignant rendition of "Thanks for the Memory," which would of course become Hope's theme song. After a series of silly comedies in which he co-starred with other Paramount comics such as Martha Raye and Burns and Allen, Hope finally had the male lead in *The Cat and the Canary* (1939) with Paulette Goddard, and his ability to wisecrack in the midst of the scare effects in this famous haunted house story appealed to critics, audiences, and Paramount alike. At this point the studio brass decided to pair him with their biggest star, Bing Crosby. Through their teamwork, both Hope and Crosby found comic personae that best suited their abilities and personalities, and they were off on the *Road* journey that would end only with Crosby's death in 1977.

It is important for us to remember that Crosby was America's most famous singer in 1940 when the series began. Sinatra's career was in its infancy, and Crosby had left his competitors from the early thirties far behind—Al Jolson, Rudy Vallee, and Russ Columbo. Bing Crosby was then synonymous with American popular music. Audiences came to the *Road* pictures to laugh, but also to hear Crosby sing. His voice is certainly essential to the *Road* series, both in the ballads and in the patter songs he often performed with Bob. Without the songs the movies would still be very funny, but they would lose the emotion generated by the love songs and the camaraderie that emanates from the patter tunes. Indeed, we see Hope and Crosby most in synch when they are performing within the film, usually a vaudeville derived number that includes a few soft shoe steps and other snippets of early twentieth-century show dance. The most famous patter song (minus the dance steps) is "We're Off On the Road To Morocco," but the first song to be included in the series was *Singapore*'s "Captain Custard," which Hope begins but during which he is soon accompanied by Crosby, a number that functions in the diegesis as Crosby's pledge of allegiance to the friendship and his concomitant rejection of the rigid highbrow tastes of his father and his prospective in-laws. The final duet, "Teamwork" from *Hong Kong*, is a classic vaudeville number whose lyrics, interestingly, undermine the song's title by contrasting Crosby's singing with Hope's joke telling as their distinctive talents, just as Crosby's singing is contrasted with Astaire dancing in the opening number of *Holiday Inn*, "I'll Capture Her Heart." Ironically, "Teamwork" simultaneously reveals Crosby's humor and Hope's ability to handle this kind of up-tempo number quite well. Though they sing about contrast and rivalry, this final song together underscores the inimitable teamwork of these two inimitable performers.

As a comedy team, then, Hope and Crosby established a brand of wacky, self-re-flexive humor that built upon two particularly American comedic traditions: the wisecrack and the slapstick of the vaudeville team. They created personae that were recognizably American types, and they integrated the newly developed American popular song—both the romantic ballad and the jazz tinged patter song—into the spectacle and the narrative. Eschewing the straight man/stooge dichotomy, they developed a two-man rhythm based on one-liners and inevitable responses. (Martin and Lewis, the next great Paramount comedy success story, returned to the straight man/comic paradigm, though the musical numbers in the Martin/Lewis films, and in particular Dean's love ballads, are, of course, directly influenced by the *Road* formula and Crosby's singing.) The *Road* pictures represent one of the pinnacles of Crosby's career. In addition to being one of the greatest American popular singers, Bing Crosby was also half of America's greatest comedy team.

Notes

1. Gary Giddins, *Bing Crosby: A Pocketful of Dreams, The Early Years, 1903–1940* (Boston: Little, Brown and Company, 2001), 590.

2. Joseph Morella, Edward J. Epstein, and Eleanor Clark, *The Amazing Career of Bob Hope* (Carlstadt, NJ: Rainbow Books, 1973), 106.

3. J. Thompson, *Bob Hope: Portrait of a Superstar* (New York: St. Martin's Press, 1981), 58.

7

Crosby at Paramount: From Crooner to Actor

Bernard F. Dick

During Hollywood's Golden Age, the studios created, shaped, and promoted the personae of their contract players to such an extent that a Warner Bros. star like Bette Davis could never have achieved the same degree of stardom at another studio. Think of Gene Kelly and Judy Garland without MGM, and without directors on the order of George Sidney, Charles Walters, and Vincente Minnelli. Think of Rita Hayworth without Columbia, where she reigned without competition. And finally, think of Crosby without Paramount; or, rather, think of Crosby in the 1930s at any other studio. Warner Bros. had its resident crooner in Dick Powell. Universal and Columbia were courting sopranos—Deanna Durbin and Grace Moore, respectively. Fox was grooming Alice Faye, and MGM had a powerhouse team in Jeanette MacDonald and Nelson Eddy. Although Crosby put in two appearances at Universal (*East Side of Heaven* [1939] and *If I Had My Way* [1940]), that studio could never have become his home. Universal eventually found its own musical voice, which was not that different from Paramount's. The format was the same: comedy (romantic/farcical/slapstick) with musical interludes. Although Universal could claim to have its share of stars (e.g., Allan Jones, Donald O'Connor, Gloria Jean, Susanna Foster, Peggy Ryan), none of them ever became movie icons or international celebrities. Crosby, on the other hand, became both—and Paramount helped. If Crosby had never spent a quarter of a century at Paramount, he would still have been the recording artist, but never the Oscar-winning movie star.

With the coming of sound, Paramount embarked upon a new kind of movie that was neither a musical nor a straight film, but one with musical numbers that were rarely integrated with the plot and were, for the most part, diversions. In other words, these films were not musical comedies, but comedic musicals. That tradition lasted well into the 1950s and 1960s at Paramount; for example, the Dean Martin and Jerry Lewis films, which had to assume that form to show off Martin's voice; and Elvis Presley's films, which were intended to show off his, even when they were plot-driven (e.g., *Loving You* [1957], *King Creole* [1958], *Blue Hawaii* [1962]). *King Creole*, in fact, could have been a straight film, based as it was on Harold Robbins's *A Stone for Danny Fisher*. It was also directed by Michael Curtiz, whose forte was melodrama. Had Robbins's novel been filmed ten years earlier, it would have been a Warner Bros. release directed by Curtiz, with a musical score by Max Steiner, starring a non-singing "tough guy" like John Garfield. Revamped as a vehicle for Elvis, *King Creole* was *Danny Fisher* transplanted to New Orleans and embellished with songs; few 1958 moviegoers were interested in seeing Elvis in a straight dramatic role.

It was natural for this kind of movie—comedy (and on rare occasions, drama) *cum* music—to originate at Paramount. Adolph Zukor, but for whom there would have been no Paramount, began in exhibition with an arcade on Union Square. The arcade, known as the Automatic One-Cent Vaudeville, featured the usual coin-operated peep shows but also had an area where those who preferred sound to image could listen to records. And so the visual and the aural were housed under the same roof. That practice continued even after the formation of Paramount Pictures. In 1929, Zukor acquired a half interest in CBS, which he had to give up in the early 1930s when Paramount nearly went bankrupt.[1] But at the time, Zukor had been thinking of an alliance between film and radio, just as David Sarnoff had been a year earlier when he created that great misnomer, RKO Radio Pictures, envisioning a company that would combine film, live entertainment, radio, and even television, which was then in its embryonic form. Small wonder, then, that Paramount courted radio performers such as George Burns and Gracie Allen, Bob Hope, and of course, Crosby—all of whom had their own shows; and singers such as Martha Raye, Lanny Ross, and Shirley Ross, who appeared regularly on the air.

When Barney Balaban, later to become president of Paramount, went into exhibition in Chicago with Sam Katz to create the theater chain Balaban & Katz, they made vaudeville part of the bill at select theaters, specifically movie palaces. That tradition continued for many years at Paramount's flagship theater, appropriately called the Paramount, at 1501 Broadway, whose stage door was thronged in the 1940s by bobby-soxers waiting to get Frank Sinatra's autograph or a piece of his clothing.

Rather than make movie musicals, Paramount chose the reverse: the musical movie, which originated in 1929 with *Innocents of Paris* and the better known *The Cocoanuts*, the Marx Brothers's first film, based on George S. Kaufman's Broadway hit with songs by Irving Berlin. *The Cocoanuts* was no more a musical than the later Marx Brothers vehicle *A Night at the Opera* (1935) was, despite the excerpts from Verdi's *Il Trovatore* and the presence of Kitty Carlisle and Allan Jones in the latter. To paraphrase the title of Victor Borge's one-person show, this was comedy not so much in, as with, music.

That kind of film, with a structure loose enough to accommodate specialty numbers, prevailed at Paramount during the 1930s, the decade when Crosby arrived at the studio. Actually, if one looks at the body of Crosby's work, there is only a handful of films that qualify as musicals in the traditional sense—that being the MGM paradigm, which for better or worse, had become the norm, despite the fact that there had been more interesting variations on the musical format at other studios, such as Fox and Warner Bros. The closest Crosby came to making conventional musicals—that is, music-driven narratives with solos, duets, ensembles, and dance sequences—was in movies like *Dixie* (1943), *Blue Skies* (1946), and *White Christmas* (1954), all of which had to feature production numbers—some rather lavish—because they were about show business. It is even hard to think of *High Society* (1956) as a movie musical in the classic sense. An MGM release, *High Society* is Philip Barry's *The Philadelphia Story* (1939, filmed in 1940), with songs by Cole Porter that are more or less integrated with the action. Even so, *The Philadelphia Story* succeeded on its own, both as a play that enjoyed a successful Broadway engagement, and as a film that was honored with Oscars for best actor (James Stewart) and best adapted screenplay (Donald Ogden Stewart). *High Society*, which is an ensemble piece rather than a "Bing Crosby movie," was only nominated for best song and scoring, winning in neither category.

High Society represents the mature Crosby, the actor who knew that he was merely a member of a quartet (the others being Frank Sinatra, Grace Kelly, and Celeste Holm) and not the star. But Crosby's ability to see himself as a team player rather than the main attraction took him years to acquire. And it began at Paramount in 1932.

Although Crosby was ideal for the kind of musical movie that had become a Paramount staple, the studio at first had no idea how to market him. For his third film, *Too Much Harmony* (1933), exhibitors were encouraged to capitalize on his "tremendous reputation"; they could even receive a free copy of the press release "Bing Crosby Confesses: America's King of Crooners Now Reveals His Inmost Secrets of a 'Bad' Boy Who Made Good!"[2] Paramount obviously envisioned an audience familiar with Crosby's less than exemplary past, which included a jail sentence for reckless driving in 1929 that was a matter of common knowledge.[3]

The same exhibitors were offered another freebie: *Learn to Croon in Five Thrilling Lessons by Bing Crosby*. Here is an excerpt: "Learn to croon. It's simple. Just gaze up at the sky, roll your eyes dolefully like a dying calf in a snowstorm, warble a few bars, say boo-boo-boo, sing a bit more, add another dash of boo-boo-boo, and voilà! You're a crooner."[4]

It is impossible to imagine Crosby writing such drivel, yet the tone sounded flippant and irreverent enough to suggest that he had. That was the problem. Crosby may have been hip, but few knew what "hip" meant. Many thought "hip" meant "smart-alecky" rather than "being with it"—the art of knowing the score and sharing that knowledge with the public, hoping that audiences know the difference between a smart ass and a cool guy.

In 1944, when Paramount was about to release *Going My Way*, the studio took a different approach to Crosby. Although he had been at the studio for more than a decade, Paramount was concerned that Crosby was being perceived as lazy, probably because of the song by that name, which he introduced in *Holiday Inn* two years earlier. Ironically, in *Holiday Inn*, "Lazy" is part of a montage, in which the

Crosby character is working so hard to transform a farmhouse into an inn that he ends up being hospitalized, presumably for nervous exhaustion. Perhaps, also, the "lazy" epithet had to do with the fact that Crosby sang so effortlessly, as if natural-ness and laziness were the same. Dick Haymes, who had also mastered the art of the soft croon, was never categorized as lazy. Haymes's looks, of course, helped. Crosby, on the other hand, often appeared sleepy—sometimes with good reason. The Crosby sound, which had the sweetness of a lullaby, even in a love song, could easily have been mistaken for inertia. The pipe may have added to his laidback im-age, suggesting the academic with the pipe who always seemed more relaxed than his chain-smoking colleagues.

Paramount was never at a loss for tie-ins. Exhibitors were told to have their to-bacconists push Mastercraft pipes. As for Crosby's laziness, exhibitors were ad-vised to make sure that the local press and radio stations got Crosby's side of the story: "Sure I'm lazy, in an exhausting way."[5] The "exhaustion" was the result of "fathering a quartet of baritones."

It is understandable that Paramount was concerned about Crosby's image when the 1943–44 press book was being prepared. In *Going My Way*, Crosby would be playing a priest, Father O'Malley—a role that would win him his only Oscar. Since priests are not supposed to be lazy, Paramount was determined to convince the public that Crosby was not lazy, despite his persona.

The July 1945 *Modern Screen*, which reached the newsstands a few months af-ter Crosby won his Oscar, contained the first installment of a two-part biography that ignored neither his jail sentence nor his insouciance: "Bing has the reputation of being the laziest man in Hollywood. Bing is lazy like a bee in blossom time. But the false impression is understandable. He makes work look like play—and for Bing Crosby that's actually what it is. And always has been."[6] Crosby himself contributed to that perception. On Academy Awards night, March 15, 1945, at what was then known as Grauman's Chinese Theatre, Gary Cooper presented Crosby with the best actor Oscar for *Going My Way*. Despite his gratitude, Crosby could not help but engage in a bit of flippancy: "All I can say . . . is that it sure is a wonderful world when a tired old crooner like me can walk away with *this* hunk of crockery!"[7] "Crockery" was the right word. During World War II, the Oscars were made of plaster. The piece of crockery came from practicing the ancient principle of *ars artem celare*: "It is an art to conceal an art."

In his movies, Crosby never seemed to be doing what moviegoers would con-sider a day's work. In *Here Is My Heart* (1934), Crosby's character has apparently been able to retire in his thirties and play at being Huck Finn—not on a raft but on a luxury liner, where he becomes so enamored of Kitty Carlisle that he pretends to be a waiter. He has an ulterior motive, but that's secondary. In *Waikiki Wedding* (1937), Crosby played a publicist for a pineapple company but behaved more like a beachcomber. Paramount must have wondered how the public would accept Crosby with a Roman collar, despite the fact that he was a practicing Catholic—in the sense that he attended Sunday mass. Then, the typical movie priest was Charles Bickford in *The Song of Bernadette* (1943) or Gregory Peck in *The Keys of the Kingdom* (1944), both of whom looked too solemn (and in Peck's case, too saintly) to break into song. Long before there was the Singing Nun, as portrayed by Debbie Reynolds in the 1966 film of that name, there was Crosby, the singing priest, who looked as comfortable at the piano as he did at the altar.

Paramount need not have worried; *Going My Way* was a huge hit in addition to winning Oscars for best picture, actor, supporting actor (Barry Fitzgerald), director (Leo McCarey), original story (McCarey), original screenplay (Frank Butler and Frank Cavett), and song (the ever popular "Swinging on a Star" by James Van Heusen and Johnny Burke). The film, however, was not Crosby's best work as an actor. That came later.

It was not surprising that Paramount cared about Crosby's image in 1944. His first film for the studio, *The Big Broadcast* (1932), saddled him with a persona that would have consigned a less talented performer to oblivion. *The Big Broadcast* capitalized on Crosby's public and private selves, placing him in the position of playing himself (the character is known as Bing Crosby), who is both an irresponsible boozer and a ladies' man; the character is also suicidal. When "Bing Crosby" is ditched by his fiancée, he attempts suicide with Stuart Erwin, who had top billing in the film for no other reason than his having been in the business longer. Anyone watching *The Big Broadcast* and knowing nothing of the Crosby legacy would think that he or she was in the presence of a mediocre actor with a great voice, who, if he was to stay in pictures, should do something about his eye makeup.

Crosby started in movies at the right time: during the Great Depression. However, that was also the era of screwball comedy, with its variations on the princess and the commoner; heiresses hooking up with newspaper reporters (*It Happened One Night* [1934]); and rich kids taking jobs at an Automat to be independent of their wealthy fathers (*Easy Living* [1937]). Who cared, if in *Here Is My Heart*, Crosby's main problem was finding the mate to a pistol owned by a Russian princess? What mattered was that she was a white Russian; and with Kitty Carlisle in the role, no one would have mistaken her for a Bolshevik.

The *Modern Screen* article quoted an anonymous friend of Crosby as saying, "He was a natural, right from the start and that's what he is today."[8] The "start" was the 1930s. Although Crosby's films were not exactly screwball, they had the same kind of fairytale premise that love conquers all, including class—a theme that Paramount espoused during the period in such films as *Tonight Is Ours* (1933), *All of Me* (1934), *Bluebeard's Eighth Wife* (1938), *Café Society* (1939), and *Midnight* (1939); and that recurred in such Crosby films as *Here Is My Heart* (rich man/poor girl), *Waikiki Wedding* (deceiving male/gullible girl), and *Double or Nothing* (Cinderella from the working class).

The films of the 1930s may have established the various facets of Crosby's screen image—playboy, singer, songwriter, race track habitué; however, Crosby the actor was yet to emerge. It is impossible to pinpoint a year or a film during which one can say, "Behold the actor wriggling out of the crooner's cocoon." The trajectory of a career does not allow for such simplistic tracking. Although there are numerous examples of a breakthrough performance in film, the theatre offers better ones, mainly because the emergence of the butterfly is so palpably evident.

Skeptics questioned the casting of Dorothy Collins, known primarily as a singer on NBC-TV's *Your Hit Parade*, in Stephen Sondheim's *Follies* (1971) in which she introduced the classic torch song, "Losing My Mind." How could perky Dorothy Collins play a middle-aged housewife who tries to convince herself that her husband still finds her beautiful, yet knows intuitively that there is a void in her life? Collins's performance in *Follies* was a revelation, as was Ethel Merman's Mama Rose in *Gypsy* (1959). Although Merman could have turned Rose into the stage mother from hell, she channeled her own bitterness and frustration—feelings that are not restricted to show people—into the character's, so that it seemed that she and Rose shared the same nature, which in a sense they did. Were Collins and Merman waiting for the right vehicle to reveal an untapped talent? Was there a buildup of resentment over the years—for example, anger at being typecast or taken for granted—that found a release in a career-defining role? Did Collins and Merman finally have the script, the songs, and the part to which they could bring their emotional baggage? Were they reacting to the material with a burning conviction that they may not have understood themselves, but that spelled the difference between an empathetic performance and a perfunctory one? To quote the mantra of Sanford Meisner, who taught several generations of actors at the Neighborhood Playhouse School of the Theatre, "Acting is reacting." He also advised his students to act before they thought.

So when did Crosby the crooner become Crosby the actor? The answer is simple. The crooner was always an actor. Like every artist waiting for the right combination of script, costars, and director, Crosby needed a vehicle to reveal that talent. In the case of Humphrey Bogart, for example, the right combination comes with *High Sierra* and *The Maltese Falcon* in 1941, followed by his signature film *Casablanca* (1942); next, *Action in the North Atlantic* (1943), *Passage to Marseilles* (1944), *Conflict* (1945), and the abominable *The Two Mrs. Carrolls* (1947); then, a resurgence with *The Treasure of the Sierra Madre* (1948), followed by three years of servitude in B movies at Columbia until emancipation arrived with *The African Queen* (1951), resulting in Bogart's only Oscar. After that it was back to the Bs, until death came in 1957.

Bogart, however, never made a musical; thus it is easier to trace his evolution as an actor than it is that of a singer, who must act through song. Crosby, however, also made several films with crucial scenes that required pure acting (or better, reacting), notably the concluding moments of *The Bells of St. Mary's* (1945) and *Riding High* (1950).

Perhaps Crosby aficionados noticed that *The Bells of St. Mary's* was not a Paramount film but an RKO release—and even they probably had no idea that it had been co-financed by RKO and Rainbow, Leo McCarey's production company. The average 1945 moviegoer saw *The Bells of St. Mary's* as the sequel to Paramount's *Going My Way*, since the films both had the same star, as well as the same director, Leo McCarey. Like its predecessor, *Bells* was enormously popular, and became RKO's highest grossing film of 1945. Although *Bells* received just one Oscar (sound recording), Crosby, Ingrid Bergman, and McCarey were nominated for best actor, actress, and director, respectively; and the film was nominated for best picture. Crosby reprised his Father O'Malley character—a new pastor faced with a parish school in such a state of deferred maintenance that it is on the verge of being condemned, and a faculty of nuns whom he succeeds in charming, all except for Sister Benedict (Ingrid Bergman). Although Sister Benedict and Father O'Malley respect each other, their philosophies of education are radically different. At the end, Father O'Malley informs Sister Benedict that she must leave St. Mary's; he does not, however, explain the reason: her worsening tuberculosis, which requires a change of climate and recuperation in the Southwest. Assuming she is being transferred because of their disagreements, Sister Benedict, who intends to remain faithful to her vow of obedience, retires to the chapel and begs God to remove all bitterness from her heart. Finally, Father O'Malley realizes that she must hear the truth. After he explains the gravity of her condition, Sister Benedict, thanks to Bergman's artistry, looks transfigured, closing her eyes in an unspoken prayer of gratitude that nothing personal was involved in the decision. Whether it was McCarey's direction, the empathy that Crosby and Bergman felt for their characters, or the professional respect the two actors had for each other that turned a scene of leave-taking into an unspoken declaration of love, one will never know. But Crosby and Bergman were not so much acting as reacting to each other on two different levels: Crosby as a priest delivering a grim diagnosis to a nun; and Bergman as the nun welcoming the diagnosis as a godsend because it explained the reason for her having to leave; Crosby as a man saying goodbye to a woman, whom he may never see again but whom he loves for her transcendent spirituality—a quality that he knows is beyond him; and Bergman as a woman bidding farewell to a man on whom she can only bestow a radiant smile in lieu of the more traditional form of affection in which neither can engage.

Another extraordinary moment occurs at the end of *Riding High*, Frank Capra's remake of his earlier film, *Broadway Bill* (1934). Broadway Bill is a racehorse that Dan Brooks (Crosby) intends to make into a winner. He almost succeeds. However, at the end of the race, Bill finishes first and suddenly collapses. When Brooks sees what has happened, he pushes his way into the crowd until he reaches Bill and then drops to his knees. A veterinarian arrives and, after listening to Bill's heart, determines that the excitement was so intense that Bill's heart had literally burst. Stunned, Brooks walks away. In the next scene—one that is completely wordless—he is in the barn. Alice (Coleen Gray) enters, tears welling up in her eyes. There are no tears, however, in Brooks's. His face is a mask of grief and incomprehension, stopping short of despair. Alice, who loves Brooks even though he is engaged to her sister, does the crying for him. Not only is the scene a paradigm of grief purged of histrionics; it is also an example of one person's ability to feel the suffering of another who is too devastated to express it himself. Crosby proved, on these and other occasions (e.g., *Little Boy Lost* [1953] and *Man on Fire* [1957], not to mention *The Country Girl* [1954]), that he could do straight acting. Crosby was also a singing actor, able to act/react through song—a talent that even some of the greatest opera stars lacked. The problem is the format, whether it is opera, musical theatre, or the musical film. Ideally, musical numbers should be the equivalent of dialogue, advancing the plot or deepening the characterization through song and/or dance. However, the integrated musical is relatively rare in both the theatre and in film. For every *Singin' in the Rain* (1952), there's a *Coney Island* (1943), *Easter Parade* (1948), and *There's No Business Like Show Business* (1954), where the action is segmented to allow for a variety of musical numbers that bring the plot to a halt instead of driving it forward.

Arguably, Crosby revealed that he was a singing actor for the first time in *Waikiki Wedding* in the scene in which he helped Shirley Ross recall the lyrics to "Blue Hawaii," while at the same time courting her without her realizing it. Ross begins humming the song, but has trouble remembering the lyrics. Crosby joins in, as if he were her prompter. As they harmonize, the romantic lyrics begin to affect them. The scene then becomes something more than a man's jogging a woman's memory. What is impressive is the naturalness, the sincerity of Crosby's reacting to Ross's groping for the words, and her awed response to his mastery of them. Some credit for the scene's effectiveness should be given to Shirley Ross, who brought out something in Crosby that neither Kitty Carlisle nor Mary Carlisle had: a warmth that was both compassionate and amorous. Was it the scene? The context? The song? Ross? When Ross and Bob Hope sang "Thanks for the Memory" in *The Big Broadcast of 1938*, Ross emphasized the poignancy of the lyrics, which affected Hope, who looked reflective and even rueful. Perhaps Ross had the same effect on Crosby in *Waikiki Wedding*. At any rate, what would otherwise have been a wooing scene became an expression of tender longing, as two dreamers blended their voices in perfect harmony, prefiguring a happy ending for a romance that started with deception.

No one can make a case for *Welcome Stranger* (1947) as a major Crosby film, yet it offers a superb example of his ability to act solely through song. Paramount planned *Welcome Stranger* as a reunion for Crosby and Barry Fitzgerald, this time as doctors: Crosby played the big city medic with a ready quip and a worldly and often wicked sense of humor; Fitzgerald's part was the old geezer whom Crosby is supposed to assist and eventually replace. Crosby's urbanity has a chilling effect on the locals, who never seem to have journeyed out of their quaint New England town and who regard Fitzgerald as the quintessential doctor. Eventually, the town rallies around Crosby, but in the meantime, it is standoff time between the parochial community and the laid-back interloper.

On the evening of a square dance, the caller is detained, and a substitute is unavailable. Crosby, who supposedly has all kinds of talents, steps up to the mike, even though he is decidedly unwelcome. He begins on the stage, flawlessly lip-synching the number (prerecorded, as was customary) with its tricky lyrics. Spotting Joan Caulfield dancing with the stuffy Robert Shayne, Crosby slowly makes his way off the stage, singing all the time without missing a beat, until he cuts in, much to Shayne's annoyance. Crosby continues as caller while dancing with Caulfield, turning a square dance into one of courtship—or better, a mating dance. If one studies the sequence, it is obvious that Crosby is wooing Caulfield without her knowing it; and that she is responding in as discreet a way as possible on a crowded dance floor. The scene has charm, wit, and a cool sexiness, which Crosby had no difficulty exuding with the right actress—but not with the patrician

Joan Fontaine in *The Emperor Waltz* (1948), the marmoreal Rhonda Fleming in *A Connecticut Yankee in King Arthur's Court* (1949), or the bubbly Ann Blyth in what may have been Crosby's worst movie, *Top of the Morning* (1949). Not only did these films fail to challenge Crosby, but they also saddled him with scripts in which he was upstaged by dogs *(The Emperor Waltz)*, gadgetry *(A Connecticut Yankee)*, and scene-stealing character actors *(Top of the Morning)*.

To many, Crosby's best acting occurred in *The Country Girl* (1954), which brought him another Oscar nomination. The film, an adaptation of Clifford Odets's 1950 play of the same name, meant so much to Crosby that he asked director George Seaton, who had also written the screenplay, to compose a biographical sketch of his character, Frank Elgin—a stage actor battling alcoholism and his own personal demons, who is about to make a comeback. Seaton apparently did, as Crosby states in an essay that he claims to have written himself and that was picked up by various newspapers, including the *New York Times*, which ran it in Arts and Leisure on December 12, 1954; a headline writer at the *Times* gave the piece the bizarre title, "Bing Scans His Elgin," although the copy in the Bing Crosby file at the Fairbanks Center for Motion Picture Study (FCMPS) in Los Angeles is untitled. According to Crosby, the rehearsals were grueling, and Seaton was a taskmaster: "I must confess that there were times when I got a little impatient. There were times when it seemed to me that [Seaton] was picking lint, but I stayed in there and did it like a good boy." Crosby was justly proud of his performance; perhaps, if *On the Waterfront* had not been released that year, he might well have won a second Oscar. But there was no comparing Crosby's Frank Elgin with Brando's Terry Malloy. Still, Crosby could say with confidence, "No one can take away from me the warm realization that for once in my career I took hold of a challenge and gave it the full try."[9] Actually, he had done it more than once, but not with such brutal honesty.

Seaton revamped Odets's drama for Crosby, making Elgin not merely an actor but a singing actor. In fact, Bernie Dodd (William Holden), the director, makes much of the fact that Elgin could both act and sing. Elgin's return to the stage, then, is to be in a musical, *The Land Around Us*, which looks like a proletarian version of *Oklahoma!* with touches of *Paint Your Wagon*—something the Group Theatre would have produced if it staged musicals. Seaton, who was familiar with the Paramount product, knew that inserting musical numbers in what would otherwise have been straight comedies was typical of the studio; however, adding songs to dramatic films was not. On those few occasions when Crosby appeared in musicals with serious overtones (e.g., *Dixie, Blue Skies*), the setting was the world of popular entertainment (the minstrel show and the musical stage, respectively). However, those films were conceived as musicals from the outset, even though the heroine in *Dixie* was a paralytic; and the Fred Astaire character in *Blue Skies* was a performer who drank too much before going on stage and fell from a ledge during a dance sequence, thereby ending his career. Clifford Odets made no allowances for music of any sort in *The Country Girl*. The year before Crosby made *The Country Girl* he appeared in *Little Boy Lost,* playing a father searching for the son he had by a French woman who was killed by the Nazis during World War II. Crosby transcended the material, turning in an affecting performance that will never be more than a footnote in his career. *Little Boy Lost* was also directed by George Seaton, who wrote the screenplay as well. Although the story needed no songs, Seaton and Paramount realized that the public was not ready for Crosby in a straight part, particularly since the audience is kept wondering until the end if the boy Crosby has discovered in a French orphanage is really his son. Thus, songs by the familiar team of Johnny Burke and Jimmy Van Heusen were grafted onto the plot but did nothing to enhance the film's appeal, which proved to be limited.

It was Seaton who decided upon the form of *The Country Girl*: a drama in which music is wedded to the action, so that there is no confusion between music as diversion and the music-as-plot device. The former was the case in *Little Boy Lost* in which the songs were more decorative than integral. That need not have occurred if Seaton had had more faith in Crosby, who apparently felt such a strong connection with the subject matter that he could have played the role convincingly without singing a note, doing *The Country Girl* as Odets had written it. However, Seaton and Paramount took no chances. When it came to Bing Crosby, music was not the food of love; it was the sound of box office success.

At least the Harold Arlen/Ira Gershwin songs in *The Country Girl* are plot related, consisting of two kinds: the title song from Elgin's comeback show, "The Land Around Us," and two others: "You've Got What It Takes," which Elgin cannot bear to hear, since it was recorded on the day his young son was fatally struck by a car; and "Love and Learn," a duet with a lounge singer that is irrefutable proof of Crosby's ability to act out a song, in this case while drunk—the result of a disastrous tryout that has shattered Elgin's self-confidence and driven him back to the bottle. In the two sequences from *The Land around Us*, we see little evidence of Frank Elgin, the great singing actor that his director insists he is; however, in a scene totally unrelated to the musical, Crosby proved unequivocally that he was a singing actor in the true sense of the term: a singer who acts out a song as if it were dialogue.

The Boston tryout has taken its toll on Elgin. The brutal reviews have caused him to buy alcohol-laced cough syrup; when that fails to work, he drops in at a bar. A blowzy performer is working the lounge as she sings "Love and Learn." She makes her way into the bar area, sidling up to Crosby, singing all the time. Visibly drunk but still able to remember the lyrics (which Elgin has always been able to do), Crosby turns away from the bar and joins in—but in character, never losing his boozy look, with his eyelids half shuttered, and his face suffused with a smile coming from the tranquilizing effect of alcohol.

Crosby had sung duets in the past—some motivated, such as the "White Christmas" scene in *Holiday Inn*, when he teaches the lyrics to Marjorie Reynolds, and each grows lost in thought, feeling the interplay of the nostalgic words and wistful music; others unmotivated, such as in the opening of *Dixie*, when Crosby romances Reynolds with "Sunday, Monday, and Always" for no other reason than that Burke and Van Heusen composed the song for the movie. That *Dixie* begins with "Sunday, Monday, and Always" is unimportant; it could have ended with the song as well—its placement having nothing to do with the plot.

In *The Country Girl*, after the alcohol-fueled duet is over, Crosby turns around and sees his reflection in the mirror behind the bar. Suddenly, he hears "You've

Got What It Takes," the song that he recorded on the day his young son was killed and for whose death he holds himself responsible. Unable to bear the sight of his face or the sound of the music that reverberates in his consciousness, he hurls his whiskey glass at the mirror. Although it may seem that there are two sequences, there is only one. While Crosby is harmonizing with the lounge singer, he has his back to the bar; when the number is over, he turns around, and seeing his reflection, changes from an amiable boozer to a destructive drunk; and, for the skeptics, from a crooning actor to a singing actor.

Crosby's face has never looked so introspectively sad as it did in *The Country Girl*. Was this Crosby or Frank Elgin? In his autobiography, Adolph Zukor has written: "Many who know Crosby intimately think of him, despite his affability, as a lonely man. He will be found late at night in some little hamburger joint, reading his paper, sipping coffee. . . . For a man with a famous face he has an amazing ability to conceal himself."[10] That may be true; but what Crosby never concealed was his art.

Notes

1. Bernard F. Dick, *Engulfed: The Death of Paramount Pictures and the Birth of Corporate Hollywood* (Lexington: University Press of Kentucky, 2002), 18–19.

2. Paramount Press Book 1933–34, 7.

3. Gary Giddins, *Bing Crosby: A Pocketful of Dreams, The Early Years, 1903–1940* (Boston: Little, Brown and Company, 2001), 208–11.

4. Paramount Press Book 1933–34, 11.

5. Paramount Press Book 1943–44, 6.

6. Kirtley Baskette, "Pennies from Heaven," *Modern Screen* (July 1945): 85.

7. Baskette, 48.

8. Baskette, 85.

9. Bing Crosby, "Bing Scans His Elgin," *New York Times*, 12 December 1954, X 7.

10. Adolph Zukor, *The Public Is Never Wrong: My Fifty Years in Motion Pictures* (New York: Putnam's, 1953), 2.

8

Bing Crosby, Walt Disney, and Ichabod Crane

M. Thomas Inge

From the very beginning of his career as a producer, Walt Disney turned to fairy tales, folklore, and children's literature as a source of inspiration and adaptation for his animated films. When he determined to produce a feature-length animated film in 1935, among the works he considered, before settling on the Grimm Brothers' story "Snow White and the Seven Dwarfs," was Washington Irving's "Rip Van Winkle." From the time of its publication in 1819, the story had inspired hundreds of dramatic versions, as well as operas, stage musicals, and ultimately films. At the time, however, the film rights were held by Paramount Studios, which refused to release them to Disney.[1] Some fourteen years later, Irving would again come to mind, but this time the story would be "The Legend of Sleepy Hollow" (1820), probably his second most widely known and popular short story.

The adaptation would constitute one-half of a double-bill feature, the first half based on the British classic *The Wind in the Willows* (1908) by Kenneth Grahame. It was released on October 5, 1949, under the title *The Adventures of Ichabod and Mr. Toad,* and despite an uneasy marriage of mood and subject matter, the critics welcomed the film as a return to the classic animation the Disney Studios had largely abandoned in the late 1940s for combined live-action and animation anthologies, such as *The Three Cabelleros* (1945) and *Song of the South* (1946). The two parts would have a longer life when released separately for television and theatrical showings and as videotape reissues.

Disney had learned by then the value of using well-known personalities to provide easily-identifiable voices for the characters and narrators in his films, especially singers like Nelson Eddy, Dinah Shore, Dennis Day, Francis Langford, the Andrews Sisters, and even Roy Rogers and the Sons of the Pioneers. Having selected the ultimate British accent of Basil Rathbone to narrate the adventures of Mr. Toad and the denizens of Toad Hall, he would naturally turn to a quintessentially American voice to narrate the second half of the film. He could have done no better than to select Bing Crosby, who by then, in the eyes and ears of the public, had come to define, more than anyone else according to his biographer Gary Giddins, "what it meant to be American" since "his was the voice of the nation, the cannily informal personification of hometown decency—friendly, unassuming, melodious, irrefutably American."[2] It was, no doubt, this same identification that had led to his being cast, at about the same time, as that classic American literary figure Hank Morgan in the Paramount Pictures musical adaptation of Mark Twain's satiric novel *A Connecticut Yankee in King Arthur's Court* released early in 1949. It was, in fact, Crosby's standing as perhaps the most successful and widely-loved performer in the first half of the twentieth century that would create a problem for Disney's film and entirely subvert the meaning of the original story on which it was based.

Three songs were written especially for the film by Don Raye and Gene DePaul, who also contributed songs to *So Dear to My Heart* (1948) and later *Alice in Wonderland* (1951): "Katrina," "Ichabod," and "The Headless Horseman." As their titles imply, all are closely tied lyrically to the plot of the story, so no one song would have any life beyond the film as single recordings or as part of Crosby's repertoire. His easygoing, smooth, and laid-back delivery made the songs and narration seamless and gave to the entire film a mood and tone suitable to the basic folkloric material with which both Irving and Disney were working. The older oral tradition of tale telling and the modern tradition of the crooner seemed to blend and lend authenticity to each other.

That Crosby had become a national touchstone for friendly persuasion and nonaggressive sex appeal is indicated by his appearance, at least in caricature, in an earlier animated film short from Warner Bros., Frank Tashlin's *Swooner Crooner* of 1944, which has the following plot line:

Porky is a chicken-farmer doing his bit for the war effort. His egg "factory" is a highly structured system of conveyor belt assembly lines, punch clocks, and Rube Goldberg contraptions for extracting maximum production from the beleaguered hen employees. Production is interrupted, however, when Frankie, a Sinatralike cockerel, appears on the scene and reduces the hens to screaming, wilting, and—most important—nonegg-laying bobby-soxers. Porky retaliates by advertising for a rooster that will make his hens productive again. The applicants include fowl-caricatures of Al Jolson, Jimmy Durante, Nelson Eddy, and Cab Calloway. Porky settles on a Bing Crosby rooster whose soothing voice magically induces voluminous egg-laying in the hens, restoring a kind of order on the farm. When Porky asks how he does it, both roosters serenade him and he too produces a mountain of eggs.[3]

Donald Crafton reads the film as a patriotic wartime message designed to suggest "that entertainers can serve the war effort by relieving workers of stress, thereby making them more productive,"[4] but not if the entertainer merely encourages self-gratification and passive, nonproductive distraction.

This is accomplished by the frankly sexual nature of the conflict. Sinatra's voice urges the women toward unproductive release, evoked in images of masturbatory gratification. One hen shoots upright, revealing a "bra" under her feathers, then collapses with a dull thud. Another melts into a creamy puddle. The ultimate image of Frankie's power of mass sex appeal is when the swooning hens are framed between his legs and, as he rises to his toes to hit a high note, his heel spurs elevate to rigid points. It's more than the hens can take.

Crosby, on the other hand, provides erotic distraction, but its effects are channeled into egg-making. The hens' gargantuan achievements are accompanied by their clucks and sighs of orgasmic pleasure. The story seems to make a point about the social and military risks of excessive phallic power, represented by Frankie, on women. Crosby's fatherly, nonaggressive sexuality is preferable because it results in a socially tolerated sexual outlet for women: reproduction. But, disturbingly, the film leaves unresolved the problem of reproduction in a society with a diminished number of males, and then there's the question of how a porcine male mammal could lay eggs anyway.[5]

Here it seems Crosby's gentle seduction serves to displace the decidedly masculine aggression of Frank Sinatra's sexual power and frees the women from being helpless, passive victims of male authority.[6] A somewhat similar transition occurs in the Disney film, but the result runs contrary to the narrative intention of Irving's tale, and perhaps even the intentions of the Disney writers and animators. But we need first to examine Irving's classic story to understand what happens.

"The Legend of Sleepy Hollow" appeared in a volume entitled *The Sketch Book of Geoffrey Crayon, Gent.* in 1820. Drawing on German legends, local folk tales and ghost stories, as well as several real-life models, Irving also invested the characters and their actions with the symbolic weight of a set of economic and cultural tensions that were developing in the United States at that particular historic moment. In the first decades of the nineteenth century, the recently established United States was beginning to feel the impact of European progress and technology in the wake of the Industrial Revolution. New York had become the commercial capital of the nation and the state's economic power had passed from the Dutch farmers and land holders of the Hudson Valley to the capitalists and self-made entrepreneurs of the rapidly developing metropolis of New York City. Although Irving nominally supported the New York Federalists and their principles of class interests, economic stability, and centrality of governmental power, he disliked the capitalistic pursuit of money and materialism and its influence on the character and quality of life and culture. Money, privilege, and power, it appeared, were becoming more important than gracious living and the appreciation of nature. Thus in the very opening of the story, after a paragraph describing the natural beauty and tranquility of the area near Tarry Town, a peaceful valley interrupted only by "the occasional whistle of a quail, or tapping of a woodpecker," the narrator relates:

I recollect that, when a stripling, my first exploit in squirrel-shooting was in a grove of tall walnut-trees that shades one side of the valley. I had wandered into it at noontime, when all nature is peculiarly quiet, and was startled by the roar of my own gun, as it broke the Sabbath stillness around and was prolonged and reverberated by the angry echoes.[7]

This passage establishes at the start a contrast between natural tranquility and rude commotion, between peaceful quiet and violent activity, which is developed and counterpointed at various places in the story, climaxing in the calamitous motion surrounding the midnight encounter with the headless horseman and the "tremendous crash" of the pumpkin against Ichabod's head.[8] But there is thematic significance in using a gun as the violator of the peace in this beginning passage, a perfect symbol of the destructive nature of technology. Irving may be suggesting that the story to follow is about other intrusions on the old fashioned way of life in the valley, and about new forces being unleashed in this Edenic society through the character of Ichabod Crane.

Sleepy Hollow, we are told, is just the sort of retreat to which the narrator would retire should he wish to permanently escape "the world and its distractions, and dream quietly away the remnant of a troubled life."[9] Here, he reports, the "population, manners, and customs remain fixed; while the great torrent of migration and improvement, which is making such incessant changes in other parts of this restless country, sweeps by them unobserved."[10] In such a stable, settled community, he says, legends, tales, and superstitions—tradition, in other words—can thrive, while they are "trampled under foot by the shifting throng that forms the population" of the progressive communities.[11] The young people of Sleepy Hollow are already beginning to show what the narrator calls "the symptoms of city innovation"[12] through the wearing of straw hats, fine ribbons, and white frocks by the girls, and the short, square-skirted coats with big brass buttons and the queued hair by the boys (even in those days, it seems, youngsters showed their rebellion through a change in dress). It is Katrina's father who best symbolizes the comfort and security of the agrarian way of life that characterizes his community. "Old Baltus Van Tassel," says the tale teller, "was a perfect picture of a thriving, contented, liberal-hearted farmer. He seldom, it is true, sent either his eyes or his thoughts beyond the boundaries of his own farm; but within those every thing was snug, happy, and well-conditioned. He was satisfied with his wealth, but not proud of it; and piqued himself upon the hearty abundance, rather than the style in which he lived."[13]

What is there about Ichabod Crane, the ungainly schoolmaster and singing teacher, that could threaten this idyllic Arcadia? Ichabod, a Hebrew name which means "inglorious" or "without honor," is an opportunistic Connecticut Yankee, not too different from the kind that Mark Twain would write about exactly seventy years later. Although he pretends to be a man of letters who brings with him all the enlightenment and cultural savoir faire of the Eastern centers of education and urban sophistication, in the classroom he maintains authority not by intellect but by the switch, called "that scepter of despotic power" and "the birch of justice."[14] Unlike Chaucer's clerk, about whom it was said, "gladly would he learn and gladly teach," Ichabod has no professional or scholarly dedication, and should he rise in life, he thinks, he would turn his back on the schoolhouse, snap his fingers in the faces of his patrons, and "kick any itinerant pedagogue out of doors that should dare to call him comrade!"[15] His lack of enlightenment and liberality is indicated by his worship of Cotton Mather, that narrow-minded, dogma-bound old Puritan witch hunter.

This is not to imply that he has any firm principles, theological or otherwise, because he is highly flexible, deferential, and willing to be of use—to rock the cradle or mend the fences—if it means bed or board, or a chance to spark the ladies. His values are all clearly those of a materialist and hedonist. When he observes nature, it is not with appreciation for the beauty of the season but with an appetite for the food it will yield, as this passage makes clear:

As Ichabod jogged slowly on his way, his eye, ever open to every symptom of culinary abundance, ranged with delight over the treasures of jolly autumn. On all sides he beheld vast stores of apples; some hanging in oppressive opulence on the trees; some gathered into baskets and barrels for the market; others heaped up in rich piles for the cider-press. Farther on he beheld great fields of Indian corn, with its golden ears peeping from their leafy coverts, and holding out the promise of cakes and hasty pudding; and the yellow pumpkins lying beneath them, turning up their fair round bellies to the sun, and giving ample prospects of the most luxurious of pies; and anon he passed the fragrant buckwheat fields, breathing the odor of the bee-hive, and as he beheld them, soft anticipations stole over his mind of dainty slapjacks, well buttered, and garnished with honey or treacle, by the delicate little dimpled hand of Katrina Van Tassel.[16]

Katrina is described as "plump as a partridge" and as "ripe and melting and rosy-cheeked as one of her father's peaches."[17] When Ichabod surveys the natural bounty and livestock of her father's farm, he is excited to lustful visions of culinary delight in another passage:

The pedagogue's mouth watered, as he looked upon this sumptuous promise of luxurious winter fare. In his devouring mind's eye, he pictured to himself every roasting-pig running about with a pudding in his belly, and an apple in his mouth; the pigeons were snugly put to bed in a comfortable pie, and tucked in with a coverlet of crust; the geese were swimming in their own gravy; and the ducks pairing cosily in dishes, like snug married couples with a decent competency of onion sauce. In the porkers he saw carved out the future sleek side of bacon, and juicy relishing ham; not a turkey but he beheld daintily trussed up, with its gizzard under its wing, and, peradventure, a necklace of savory sausages; and even bright chanticleer himself lay sprawling on his back, in a side-dish, with uplifted claws, as if craving that quarter which his chivalrous spirit disdained to ask while living.[18]

Ichabod's pursuit and courtship, then, is purely a pursuit of materialism. He has no wish to marry Katrina in order to settle down and emulate her father's agrarian existence. Instead, he wants the property she will inherit to sell in order to invest in greater projects in the name of progress and advancement. We find this out in the next paragraph:

As the enraptured Ichabod fancied all this, and as he rolled his great green eyes over the fat meadow-lands, the rich fields of wheat, of rye, of buckwheat, and Indian corn, and the orchards burthened with ruddy fruit, which surrounded the warm tenement of Van Tassel, his heart yearned after the damsel who was to inherit these domains, and his imagination expanded with the idea, how they might be readily turned into cash, and the money invested in immense tracts of wild land, and shingle palaces in the wilderness. Nay, his busy fancy already realized his hopes, and presented to him the blooming Katrina, with a whole family of children, mounted on the top of a wagon loaded with household trumpery, with pots and kettles dangling beneath; and he beheld himself bestriding a pacing mare, with a colt at her heels, setting out for Kentucky, Tennessee, or the Lord knows where![19]

That last sentence is revealing. It demonstrates that Ichabod believes in motion for the sake of motion. Progress projects man into a series of actions with no particular end in mind, because the goals are never defined. Any kind of change is improvement and any improvement is bound to mean progress. Progress is the most important product of progress. Thus Ichabod is the embodiment of the social and cultural forces that will sweep away the agrarian way of life in the century to come. He is not the hardy pioneer but the drummer, the shopkeeper, the politician who would come after him. He is the city slicker out to fleece the country yokel and bed down with the farmer's daughter.

It is only natural, then, that his antagonist, the man who will challenge his efforts to undermine the community's mores, will be his opposite in every way. Brom Bones is a virile, hardy product of the rural environment. He is described in this way:

Among these [competitors for Katrina], the most formidable was a burly, roaring, roystering blade, of the name of Abraham, or, according to the Dutch abbreviation, Brom Van Brunt, the hero of the country round, which rang with his feats of strength and hardihood. He was broad-shouldered and double-jointed, with short curly black hair, and a bluff, but not unpleasant countenance, having a mingled air of fun and arrogance. From his Herculean frame and great powers of limb, he had received the nickname of Brom Bones, by which he was universally known. He was famed for great knowledge and skill in horsemanship, being as dexterous on horse-back as a Tartar. He was foremost at all races and cock-fights; and, with the ascendancy which bodily strength acquires in rustic life, was the umpire in all disputes, setting his hat on one side, and giving his decisions with an air and tone admitting of no gainsay or appeal. He was always ready for either a fight or a frolic; but had more mischief than ill-will in his composition; and, with all his overbearing roughness, there was a strong dash of waggish good humor at bottom. . . . The neighbors looked upon him with a mixture of awe, admiration, and good will; and when any madcap prank, or rustic brawl, occurred in the vicinity, always shook their heads, and warranted Brom Bones was at the bottom of it.[20]

Brom is a "natural" who delights in physical strength and crude humor. He is an early example of the gamecock of the wilderness, a figure who will appear frequently in frontier humor and give birth to the legends of Davy Crockett, Daniel Boone, and the Big Bear of Arkansas. When he courts Katrina, his attentions are compared with the "gentle caresses and endearments of a bear."[21]

We are also told, however, that Brom "had a degree of rough chivalry in his nature,"[22] and although it would be easier and more manly to meet Ichabod in open combat, he realizes that the schoolmaster would be no physical match for him. Thus he decides to defeat Ichabod on his own terms. Since Ichabod lives by his wits, Brom will devise a scheme that requires ingenuity and takes advantage of the outlander's major weakness—his superstitious nature. The device of the headless horseman works as planned and rids the community, at least for a while, of the threat Ichabod had posed. Brom wins his bride and settles down to the traditional way of life before the materialistic entrepreneurs and money-grubbing capitalists arrive in greater numbers and pollute the fresh air of Sleepy Hollow with factory smoke. Once again, as in so much of American culture, brawn prevails over brain and common sense over romantic idealism.[23]

Disney's adaptation starts off in much the same spirit as Irving's story, depicting the peaceful tranquility of Sleepy Hollow, soon to be disturbed by the lanky, bird-like Ichabod striding down the road towards the village as Crosby's melodious voice sets the mood through narration. While this should have caused Crosby to identify with the community, or at least render him a neutral influence on the story, something happens early on to bring a closer identification with the enemy, the spindly schoolmaster.

After Ichabod has established his iron rule at the schoolhouse, tempered only by his awareness of which children have homes where the most abundant dinner tables are set, he turns to one of his additional tasks of conducting a singing school for young ladies. When Ichabod begins to sing for his voice students as a model and example, it is of course Crosby who provides the voice, not only the standard mellow phrasing but even the trademark "Bu-bu-ba-boo." Despite the howling distraction of Bron Bones's dog that coalesces with Ichabod's voice, the girls swoon over him, and the audience too is so charmed that Crosby and Ichabod become inextricably associated for the rest of the film. We first see Katrina Van Tassel through the eyes of Ichabod, and while the beauty, money, and property she represents are a part of his vision, we tend to identify with his sensibility and understanding of things. We are inclined to root for his suit in the courtship that follows.

A good many other changes by the Disney plotters and artists also tend to further a shift in sympathy. Brom Bones is shown to be an intrusive bully, usually outwitted in courtesy and courtship by the cleverer schoolmaster. The early efforts of Brom to attack Ichabod are thwarted by a series of chance missteps and moves by his opponent as he walks on his way, unconscious of the threats and near-blows. At the big party that serves as a climax for the events, while dancing with Katrina, Ichabod at the same time manages to light the pipe of old man Tassell and secretly consume a slice of cake. He expertly outmaneuvers Brom on the dance floor, sending the burly rustic into the arms of less attractive women. All the women at the dance clearly admire Ichabod, while Brom sulks in a corner, plotting his revenge.

Unable to beat his opponent in the arena of social graces and deportment, Brom turns to a scare tactic. While Ichabod enjoys his well-earned repast, Brom tells a ghost story as a prelude to his elaborate hoax of playing the headless horseman. While Crosby sings in this scene for Brom, it is a song of ghosts and terror, not romance and courtship, and we have already merged Crosby and Ichabod in our minds and sympathies anyway.

Ichabod leaves the party triumphant rather than rejected as in Irving's story, which makes Brom's actions more urgent. As he ambles home in a romantic stupor, Ichabod is suddenly surrounded with genuinely frightening sounds and objects, and even though they are exaggerated by his own sensibilities, it is less his superstitious nature than normal fear that besets him. The headless horseman, then, is a genuine, tangible threat. The Disney version undercuts some of the satire of

Irving's conclusion by having Ichabod happily married to a widow at the end rather than enter the aggressive and materialistic professions of law and politics.

In the original story, then, Ichabod Crane is an intruder, a crass outsider who represents the encroachment of industrialism and technology and their attendant rootlessness on the idyllic agrarian way of life in the Hudson Valley. He must be expelled from the community by the superior native wisdom of a Brom Bones. But the popularity of Crosby and his universally loved voice led viewers to identify more with Ichabod than with Brom, as did the subtle changes made by the Disney staff as well. The consequence of this is that the story was turned inside out. While rural brawn still prevails over rationalism and enlightenment, Ichabod's fall brings disappointment over the betrayal of romantic idealism. No one wanted to see Bing Crosby lose the girl.

Notes

1. Richard Hollis and Brian Sibley, *Walt Disney's Snow White and the Seven Dwarfs and the Making of the Classic Film* (New York: Simon & Schuster, 1987), 5.

2. Gary Giddins, *Bing Crosby: A Pocketful of Dreams, The Early Years, 1903–1940* (Boston: Little, Brown and Company, 2001), 4.

3. Donald Crafton, "The View from Termite Terrace: Caricature and Parody in Warner Bros. Animation," in *Reading the Rabbit: Explorations in Warner Bros. Animation,* ed. Kevin S. Sandler (New Brunswick, NJ: Rutgers University Press, 1998), 105.

4. Ibid., 106.

5. Ibid., 107.

6. Crosby himself was not always pleased or flattered by his frequent appearances in caricature in many of the celebrity cartoons of the time. Donald Crafton reports that on one occasion,

After the release of *Bingo Crosbyana* in May 1936 [from Warner Bros. under the direction of Frank Tashlin], the crooner tried unsuccessfully to have the film pulled, his lawyer stating, "The Crosby voice is imitated and the character of Bingo Crosbyana is shown as a 'vainglorious coward.' " (Ibid., 106).

7. Washington Irving, "The Legend of Sleepy Hollow," in *History, Tales, and Sketches* (New York: Library of America, 1983), 1058.

8. Ibid., 1085.

9. Ibid., 1058–59.

10. Ibid., 1060.

11. Ibid., 1078.

12. Ibid., 1075.

13. Ibid., 1066.

14. Ibid., 1072.

15. Ibid., 1076.

16. Ibid., 1074–75.

17. Ibid., 1065.

18. Ibid., 1067.

19. Ibid.

20. Ibid., 1069.

21. Ibid., 1070.

22. Ibid., 1071.

23. This discussion draws on material previously published in my essay "Washington Irving's Agrarian Fable," in *Perspectives on American Culture* (West Cornwall, CT: Locust Hill Press, 1994), 17–27.

9

A Couple of Song and Dance Men: Bing Crosby and Fred Astaire

Jeanne Fuchs

By the time Bing Crosby and Fred Astaire made *Holiday Inn* (1942), they were already stars of the first magnitude. Crosby had been in films since 1930[1] and was the top-ranked player at Paramount.[2] Astaire had been in films since 1933.[3] Prior to their film careers, they both had extensive experience in other media: vaudeville, recordings, radio, concerts, and musical theater. When recruited by Hollywood, Astaire was a star of the Broadway and London stage. By 1942, all but one of his movies with Ginger Rogers had been completed. Crosby had already appeared in numerous important films in which he sang and acted, including two of the "Road" pictures, *The Road to Singapore* (1940) and *The Road to Zanzibar* (1941). *The Road to Morocco* (1942) would be released the same year as *Holiday Inn*. Total triumph was still to come with *Going My Way* (1944) and *The Bells of St. Mary's* (1945*)*.

By the time *Blue Skies* (1946) was released, canonization had been bestowed on Crosby. Both stars were, in fact, so successful and so sought after that they commanded substantial salaries, which accounts for the two relatively unknown female leads in *Holiday Inn*.[4] The studio could not have afforded equivalent price tags for the stars' love interests played by Virginia Dale and Marjorie Reynolds.

Because *Holiday Inn* was such an enormous hit, Paramount pulled out all the stops with *Blue Skies*: Technicolor, lavish sets and costumes, production numbers and considerably more backup in terms of supporting cast. Olga San Juan is a case in point; she adds a decent dash of sex appeal in her singing, dancing, and acting assignments. She performs with what one critic calls "sassy suggestiveness."[5] San Juan provides a particularly effective addition since her spicy performance contrasts sharply with the vapid one given by the leading lady, Joan Caulfield. All in all, because of its lugubrious plot, the film lacks spark and interest. Crosby's singing and two great Astaire numbers save it: "Puttin' on the Ritz" and "Heat Wave." Otherwise it remains, as critic John Mueller labels it, "a dispirited and dispiriting film."[6]

Heightening interest in the film, however, was Astaire's announcement that *Blue Skies* would be his last movie. Fortunately, he didn't follow through on the threat. He joined the *Easter Parade* and his retirement was deferred for quite a long time.

So what did the two films in which the great stars appeared together amount to? The answer is a bit uneven: the dancing and the singing were sublime, as one would expect, but the greatest weakness in both films, especially *Blue Skies*, was the plot. Silly, bordering on ridiculous, it maddeningly lacked verisimilitude. It was based on an "idea" of Irving Berlin's, but was not well developed by the writers assigned to it. Similarly, *Holiday Inn* had as its genesis a concept that Berlin dreamed up for a Broadway revue that never materialized. The finished product, however, became one of the most popular musicals of the 1940s. Intimate and comfortable, with a gorgeous set—the inn—it remains a charming vehicle for Astaire and Crosby despite its somewhat hare-brained plot. In addition, the film immortalized Berlin's "White Christmas," which has sold the most records ever of any popular song.[7] Crosby's version alone sold over twenty-five million records.[8] (That was for eighteen minutes of work.)

In each film, the triangle remains the focal point: Astaire and Crosby vie for the same woman's favors, she chooses one of them, changes her mind, and changes her mind again, and in each case ends up with Crosby. In both films, Astaire "plays the romantic also ran."[9] It should be noted that the repentant Virginia Dale, "Miss Hit and Run" as Astaire calls her, returns to become his partner again at the end of the film.

In both *Holiday Inn* and *Blue Skies,* Crosby and Astaire have a number that they sing and dance together. These segments underscore the competitive nature of their characters in the film and are witty and humorous. The numbers rest squarely in the vaudeville tradition and give each actor the opportunity to display his special gifts and then some. In *Holiday Inn,* the tune is "I'll Capture Her Heart" (singing for Crosby, dancing for Astaire). At the end of the number, they end up together since during the "competition," their "prey" has eluded both of them. Undaunted, they dance off together.

While not much of a dancer, Crosby remains cool and confident; he projects such a positive image that he seems a better dancer than he is. He is actually graceful (he was very athletic in high school and college) and exudes an understated assurance that is most winning. Part of Crosby's success in the number can be attributed to his charm; he remains unpretentious and natural. Of course, his musicality and sense of rhythm also play a role in the overall quality of his performance. Astaire admired Crosby's dancing. He once said, "He's a wonderful performer. His dancing tickles me to death. But if I said he was a good dancer, it would be the same if Bing called me a good singer."[10]

Now Astaire is a better singer than Crosby is a dancer. In the above scene, he remains poised and undaunted by the Crosby charisma and stubbornly sticks to his strategy to win the woman by dancing. Actually, Astaire never liked his own voice much. He said it was "lousy" and that he could never make a living only singing.[11] Clearly, the greatest composers of Tin Pan Alley (with the possible exception of George Gershwin) did not agree with his evaluation of his own voice.[12] Oscar Levant, in a manic mood, went so far as to say that Astaire was "the greatest singer of songs the movie world has ever known."[13] Levant put Crosby in as "runner up" because he lacked Astaire's "unstressed elegance."[14] Crosby himself admired Astaire's singing and said, "He has a remarkable ear for intonation, a great sense of rhythm, and what is most important, he has great style."[15]

In the "Couple of Song and Dance Men" number in *Blue Skies,* there are heavier demands placed on Crosby's dance vocabulary. Nonetheless, he acquits himself well and shows a particular kind of attack and exuberance, especially at the beginning of the dance, that are uncharacteristic of his usual relaxed style. The number is rather long and contains some "impersonations" that today would be considered controversial or, at the very least, in poor taste (e.g. Crosby imitating a porter).

Despite the competition between the two men in each film to win the woman and the constant jockeying for a better position with their object of desire, neither of them presents himself as a convincing suitor. Neither one is ever passionate—never "hot." They lack erotic energy. On the contrary, they act totally "cool"—not necessarily in the jazz sense of the term. Maybe "tepid" or "lukewarm" are better words here. They remain distant and detached—much more like husbands than suitors. In addition, their goal is not so much conquest but marriage. No darker side is revealed or lies beneath the surface. Neither of them ever appears as sexually dangerous in the way, for instance later, Frank Sinatra and Gene Kelly were perceived in their films together. Even in the wonderful number with Virginia Dale, "You're Easy to Dance With," no real sense of possession is apparent and, at this point in the film, Astaire has won the woman, however fleetingly.

In 1870, Dostoevsky wrote an intriguing novella entitled *The Eternal Husband.* While it portrays a complex psychological situation of a husband who pursues his wife's former lover *after* the wife has died, the author makes the point clearly that some men are destined to be husbands and others lovers. As presented, the idea is not in the least banal, but rather riveting, and it explored in a profound and serious manner the many ironic twists and turns that the Russian author could devise.

There exists a correlation between Crosby and Astaire's characterizations, especially in the two films under discussion, and Dostoevsky's observations. Whatever Crosby's and Astaire's personal lives entailed, and that is of little importance here, their screen personae were quite similar. They represent the "eternal husband" just as Kelly and Sinatra represent the other side of that coin, the "eternal lover." To pursue the notion of the "eternal husband" further, it will be useful to examine a few films of these two stars in which they do not appear together.

A quick look at some of the "Road" movies, zany and chaotic as they are, reveals a pattern that bears out my premise. Bob Hope, cast as the "also ran" in both *The Road to Zanzibar* and *The Road to Morocco* (and actually all of the others), never gets the girl. While more handsome, funnier, and often more resourceful than Crosby, Hope remains the bachelor, whereas Crosby consistently wins Dorothy Lamour's heart. His goal in both films remains marriage. Hope remains the "eternal dupe" destined to be hoodwinked and out-conned by Crosby at every turn. He takes all the risks and miraculously survives. In a particularly odd scene, Crosby serenades Lamour (in *Zanzibar*) with "It's Always You" while he relaxes and *she* rows him around in a boat.

In *The Road to Morocco,* Crosby sells Hope as a slave in the palace to save his own neck. After an attack of guilt, Crosby discovers that Hope is being treated royally by the Princess (Lamour). It seems that Hope is scheduled to become the *first* husband of the Princess Shalimar. Crosby woos her right under Hope's nose. Once again, after many bizarre twists in the plot, Crosby wins the woman.

It may seem odd to mention *Going My Way* and *The Bells of St. Mary's* in the "eternal husband" context but in fact it supports my argument and advances it. On the metaphysical level, Father O'Malley is married to the Church. He becomes the universal father as well as the celibate "husband." When Super Priest meets Joan of Arc, the air becomes tinged with purity and love. Ingrid Bergman as a "bride of Christ" is also married to the Church; marriage in the ordinary sense is not an option for either character. It can, however, be postulated that the relationship between the two stars, while chaste, possesses many magical moments of great restraint.

More to the point of the argument is *The Country Girl*. From the pen of that most realistic of playwrights, Clifford Odets, comes a match with a theme that absorbed Dostoevsky, whose theory is under discussion: *the eternal triangle*. In effect, the comedies as well as the serious films share that common ground: Crosby-Dale-Astaire, Crosby-Caulfield-Astaire, Crosby-Lamour-Hope, Crosby-Kelly-Holden, and Crosby-Kelly-Sinatra (in *High Society*).

As the translators and annotators of *The Eternal Husband* have noted in the preface, "Dostoevsky's work represents a lifelong meditation on the same few themes, motifs, and figures. The love triangle, for instance, with all its ambiguities of pride and humiliation, outward magnanimity, inner rivalry, entered his work with his very first book."[16] It is through his profound exploration of the love triangle that the Russian writer arrived at his ideas of the "eternal husband" and "the eternal lover."

Odets's *The Country Girl* provides all the elements of the triangle and an extraordinary vehicle for its stars to act out the drama, a variation on the theme of the eternal triangle. Crosby begins as the husband and ends as the husband; he prevails as the husband. In many ways and for obvious reasons, he comes closer to the portrayal of Dostoevsky's husband in *The Country Girl* than in any other film. Frank Elgin (Crosby) has sunk very low; he is an alcoholic, a liar, and a helpless and hopeless person. Unlike Dostoevsky's wife, who represents the unfaithful spouse, Georgie Elgin (Grace Kelly) as the maligned, long-suffering wife presents a convincing portrait of the woman who absorbs abuse and appears trapped in an infernal situation.

Enter the "eternal lover" William Holden—younger, more handsome, decisive, and talented. Despite all these qualities, in the end Georgie remains faithful to her dissolute husband. Similar to the Russian husband, Crosby is ready to allow his wife to succumb to the lover, but *she* does not allow herself to do so. On a dark and more mysterious level, Crosby remains the "eternal husband" and actually defeats the "eternal lover."

An examination of four Astaire films will show how the persona of the "eternal husband" adheres to him throughout his career. Since most of his major work was in light-hearted, sophisticated musicals, the breadth of performance is not the same as Crosby's. Many of his films begin with what is called in Molière "le dépit amoureux," a kind of spiteful sulking or anger on the part of one character (usually a female), based on a misunderstanding, a mistake and, in most cases, mistaken identity. ("Le dépit amoureux" can only occur between those who are attracted to one another.)

The entire plot of *Top Hat* (1935) relies precisely on this ploy. Ginger Rogers believes that Astaire is married; Astaire believes that she, Ginger, is the mistress of an overbearing, foppish designer. The two main characters are attracted to one another but keep irritating one another because of the circumstances. Their mutual antagonism propels the film from the start. The whole mix up concerning who is married to whom, combined with the availability of only the bridal suite in Venice, along with a series of misunderstandings become the underpinnings of the movie, which ends with Ginger and Fred as a couple headed for the altar.

Similarly, in the two films with Rita Hayworth, *You'll Never Get Rich* (1941) and *You Were Never Lovelier* (1942), the plots revolve around mistaken identity and/or a misconception on the part of one of the characters (in both cases, the woman). As a beautiful chorus girl trying to ward off the advances of a married producer, Hayworth believes that Astaire is in league with the producer to help him to deceive his wife and obtain a diamond bracelet for Hayworth under the pretext that Astaire has purchased it for her. Pertinent plot shifts occur when a photo of Astaire and Hayworth appears in a gossip column item, saying they are engaged. Astaire joins the army to extricate himself from the producer-wife-chorus-girl mess and then puts on a show for the army with a production number in which all the chorines are dressed as brides (including Rita)—Hayworth is tricked into marrying Astaire on stage! Once again, the goal is marriage.

In *You Were Never Lovelier,* the ploy of mistaken identity takes on a Freudian twist. As the eldest daughter in an Argentinean family, Hayworth has the reputation of being an "ice princess" because no suitor appeals to her. Unfortunately, her two younger sisters cannot marry until she does. Her father, Adolph Menjou, decides to melt the princess by writing love letters to her from a secret admirer. Menjou even begins to have orchids sent to his daughter every day at a given hour. She is fascinated and begins to fall for her romantic "Lochinvar." By mistake, one day Astaire delivers the orchids and is seen. She believes that Astaire is the admirer. After many twists and turns, they realize that they are in love and will marry. Comedies are supposed to end in marriage, and this one suits Astaire (and Hayworth) perfectly.

In *Easter Parade* (1948), the situation has a variation. The age difference between Judy Garland and Astaire, while not stressed in the plot, forms the basis for a relationship in a Pygmalion mode. Having been abandoned by his long-time partner, Ann Miller, Astaire finds himself in need of creating a new one. He acts as mentor to Garland as he begins teaching her how to walk, talk, dress, and dance. After trying to make his new partner into a replica of the former one with poor results, Astaire realizes that he needs to build on her own specific strengths and talent. In the process, he falls in love with her. Thinking that Garland is in love with Peter Lawford, Astaire remains home and dejected on Easter. Garland assumes the aggressive role, buys him an "Easter bonnet" and drags him with her to participate in the Easter parade. As they stroll down Fifth Avenue, wedding bells are definitely ringing.

There is a parallel between Garland's "masculine" behavior in *Easter Parade* and Lamour's boat rowing in *The Road to Zanzibar* (with both men in passive mode), and Grace Kelly's wife in *The Country Girl* can also be added to this group. The strong woman dominates while the man becomes "feminized." Dostoevsky carries this notion very far in his novella; the husband character becomes obsessed with the lover, pursues him, and actually kisses him on the lips at one point in the story. That is not to suggest homosexual desire as a subtext in any of the above films, but rather to point up a psychological element that cannot be ignored: Some aspects of the eternal triangle and the challenges it presents contain homoerotic overtones.

A glimpse at a highly successful film not discussed as yet can shed further light on the eternal husband/eternal lover question. *High Society* (1956) fits the bill perfectly. Crosby goes from husband, to ex-husband, to husband again. John Lund, as the would-be husband, incarnates the consummate bore. What Tracy (Kelly) sees in him (other than that he is the opposite of her first husband) is unclear.

The triangle emerges again as a pivotal plot point in the person of Frank Sinatra, cast in the "lover" role. The pairing of Crosby and Sinatra as foils for one another is brilliant. Both men turn in spectacular performances; in particular, their duet "Well, Did You Evah!" represents a kind of virtuoso vying for position (the winning one). Crosby cited the duet with Sinatra as his favorite scene in any of his films.[17] The character comes face to face with his opposite, and once again he prevails, a point that is clear in the body language at the conclusion of the number. As they exit the room, Crosby, in a seemingly magnanimous gesture, seems to be dismissing Sinatra. The "eternal husband" faces off with "the eternal lover" and the former dominates. The younger, sexier, and worthy opponent does not prevail. The prey or the prize may be Grace Kelly but the real challenge exists between the two men. Crosby was probably the only person in the entertainment industry able to carry off such a coup. To be able to challenge Sinatra on his own turf and win while remaining totally poised and charming in doing so represents a major triumph. (Yes, it happens in the script, but the underlying competition, given the nature of the two stars, possesses meta-text symbolism.)

Astaire remains the archetype of the sophisticated, witty, and urbane man. He's the Mozart of dance. It is not in his repertoire to be mysterious or sexually aggressive. Furthermore, since his exclusive partner from age four to thirty-two was his sister, Adele, it is not difficult to see how his basic style developed as a partner who remains cool, considerate, and somewhat detached (perhaps even the "eternal brother"). He complements the woman at all times; he made all of his partners glow; they looked gorgeous, graceful, and talented even when, in some cases, they were not (Virginia Dale being a case in point). Yes, metaphorically the duets represent stages in lovemaking, many of them are seductive and often underscore the "surrender" by the woman at the end of the dance.[18] Once the music stops, however, these moments of sexuality evaporate.

Crosby, by the same token, possessed a nonchalant attitude from the beginning of his career. Rarely intense or overly serious, nonaggressive sexually, he projected an aloofness and detachment that were extraordinary for a screen idol. Perhaps that is one of the reasons why he was so convincing in his portrayal of priests. In *Holiday Inn* and *Blue Skies*, he remains maddeningly passive, almost indifferent to the women, even when they leave him. There are no wrenching scenes of protracted *adieux*. He betrays no sense of urgency, no passion, no sexual coaxing to persuade them to remain.

Both Astaire and Crosby disliked "mushy" love scenes and really had none in their films.[19] By the same token, neither fits into the Hollywood mold of the matinee idol. They each capitalized on their innate charm, their elegance, and their unparalleled talent to win over the audience (including *both* sexes). It worked. The two have undeniable appeal, which the whole world acknowledges. They represent in no small way the triumph of the Apollonian, which was particularly true of movies from the period. The ordered, the serene, the balanced, and the aesthetically pleasing are all present in their films. Despite their weak plots, the two films in which Crosby and Astaire appear together instill a fine sense of well being (after all they are musicals) as opposed to the Dionysiac frenzy that most recent films explore. *Holiday Inn* and *Blue Skies* offer a kind of musical "comfort food."

Even in the two pseudo-Dionysiac scenes in which Astaire is supposed to be drunk, there is almost nothing of excess in them. He looks as graceful as ever. The most convincing moment is perhaps in *Blue Skies,* the scene in the dressing room with Joan Caulfield when Astaire is quite drunk. In the "Heat Wave" number, however, which immediately follows, his drunkenness almost completely disappears until the moment when he falls from the bridge. In *Holiday Inn*, the drunken dance scene is much more in the Nick-and-Nora style than in the Ray Milland vein. It's comic and extremely well done—never dark or unsettling.

When Pete Hamill spoke at the Sinatra Conference in 1998, he referred to Sinatra as the first "urban singer," and in the next breath, by way of comparison, said that he always considered Crosby an "area code 800 singer." He meant this not as a criticism of Crosby, but rather as a way of situating Sinatra. Hamill had nothing but praise for Crosby and said that he loved listening to him. Part of the distinction Hamill made about Crosby underscores a vital clue to his universal popularity. Crosby made people, both men and women, feel comfortable and at home. He was neither threatening nor unsettling, especially to men. His audiences over the years not only responded positively to his unique ability to soothe them but also came to expect the familiar lulling effect he was able to achieve.

When we examine Astaire's and Crosby's screen personalities, and the personae created by them, what remains clear is that they complemented one another in every way; they were on the same wavelength and their partnership rescued Fred Astaire from ever having to name one of his female partners as the favorite.

Forever after their collaboration, when he was asked the perennial question, "Who was your favorite partner?" Astaire replied, "Bing Crosby."[20]

Notes

1. Gary Giddins, *Bing Crosby: A Pocketful of Dreams, The Early Years, 1903–1940* (Boston: Little, Brown and Company, 2001), 607–13.

2. Ibid., 504.

3. Bill Adler, *Fred Astaire, A Wonderful Life* (New York: Carroll and Graf Publishers, Inc., 1987), 181–82.

4. John Mueller, *Astaire Dancing: The Musical Films* (New York: Alfred A. Knopf, 1985), 200.

5. Ibid., 266.

6. Ibid., 263.

7. Giddins, *Bing Crosby: A Pocketful of Dreams*, 9.

8. Mueller, *Astaire Dancing*, 204.

9. Ibid., 11.

10. Adler, *Fred Astaire, A Wonderful Life*, 157.

11. Ibid., 169.

12. Ibid., 169.

13. Mueller, *Astaire Dancing*, 21.

14. Ibid.

15. Ibid.

16. Fyodor Dostoevsky, *The Eternal Husband and Other Stories* (New York: Bantam Books, 1997), X.

17. Giddins, *Bing Crosby: A Pocketful of Dreams*, 513.

18. Jerome Delamater, *Dance in the Hollywood Musical* (Ann Arbor: UMI Research Press, 1981), 109.

19. Mueller, *Astaire Dancing*, 199.

20. Ibid., 20; Fred Astaire's daughter, Ava Astaire, speaking at the Crosby Conference, revealed that her father's favorite partner was Rita Hayworth.

10

Rivalries: The Mutual Mentoring of Bing Crosby and Frank Sinatra

Samuel L. Chell

The joint radio appearances of Crosby and Sinatra between 1944 and 1954 reveal an extraordinary personal and musical rivalry, with the competition between the two singers providing the premise as well as the substance of their airtime together. In their scripted roles as father figure and upstart son, Crosby and Sinatra move from ad hominem insults to vocal "cutting contests" to sparkling duets in which they harmonize and take turns singing lead. Initially, their relationship, to borrow from literary critic Harold Bloom's work on poetic influence, might be described as manifestly Oedipal—a tension between the masterful predecessor and his resistant or strong successor. Yet the interaction between the two is so complete and reciprocal that it is easy to downplay the importance of their musical differences. Because the ground rules, along with the songs themselves, were shared, their rivalry might more accurately be described as a continuing, highly visible, public conversation, the sort of dialogue necessary to construct, then confirm a tradition. In short, Crosby and Sinatra are the primary shapers of the only body of musical literature sufficiently coherent to be considered an American canon of popular song.

Certainly any attempt to account for the enduring collection commonly designated "The American Songbook" requires an understanding of the different musical values of its two most prominent performers. Gary Giddins, Will Friedwald, and numerous other critics have established Crosby's importance as the first major white singer to assimilate the music of Louis Armstrong and, for that matter, the language of jazz. Yet, in approaching the Crosby-Sinatra encounters, the present-day listener will find it hard to ignore Crosby's other primary function: the maker and caretaker of melody. Friedwald calls Crosby "the first singer to truly glorify and exalt the American popular melody"[1] and emphasizes the musical diversity separating him from Sinatra.[2] And it is the vast range, as well as the quality, of Crosby's song choices that leads Giddins to observe, "the romantic vulnerability of a Sinatra is unsuited to these elemental melodies."[3]

While the contrast between Crosby's everyman and Sinatra's romantic hero has been widely acknowledged, there still remains the question of how these personal differences fit within the larger context of a musical tradition. Understanding the differences between Crosby's and Sinatra's relation to popular music, and above all to melody, requires resurrecting a term, which, through misunderstanding and irresponsible use, has heretofore been largely avoided in discussions of their music: melodrama. Peter Brooks, in his influential work, *The Melodramatic Imagination*, restores to the word its original meaning, "drama accompanied by music," as verbal text relying on musical language to acquire "inexorability and necessity."[4] More recently, Ben Singer has argued that melodrama, with its heightening of sensation, is both an expression of the inventions of modernity and a response to the insecurities and anxieties attendant upon these same changes.[5] The melodramatic, in other words, exposes deep-seated personal conflict and unrest, yet can be trusted to provide a sense of comfort to an audience recently made aware of threats to its security and well-being.

To these definitions, I propose to add three further features of the melodramatic. Firstly, its dominant theme is loss and recovery, which plays itself out equally in a stable text, in the performance of that text, and in the effect of the text on the listener. Because of this preoccupation with loss, melodrama makes us aware not only of the past, but also of the "past as past," the slipping away of life's precious moments. The best melodramatic artists simultaneously evoke conscious awareness of the past and ameliorate our fears concerning its loss, recovering from the transient texts of human experience the ones that deserve to be saved. Moreover, the melodramatic artist makes us feel as if we are returning to a cherished place or cultural landmark, even when we are visiting it for the first time. Melodrama covers the uncertain and the unknown with the caste of the familiar.

Secondly, the melodramatic artist is concerned with an expression that is direct and full, free of undercutting ironies and connotations. His primary emphasis in the interpretation of a song is always on its most accessible and universally understood musical meanings, especially melody, which he does not hesitate to foreground and display. By contrast, the artist whom we might think of as a modernist relies more heavily on indirect or ironic expression, frequently using the tension between verbal and musical meanings to dramatize the personal struggle that characterizes his own separateness from the cultural mainstream. Giddins makes this distinction between the melodramatic and the modernist artist clear with the following appraisal of Crosby's relation to melody and to the American public: "Bing had a genius for popularity. His major achievement was to plait the many threads of American music into a central style of universal appeal. But the price was exorbitant. To achieve universality, he had to dilute individuality."[6] Curiously, by placing a price tag on Crosby's wide appeal, the statement devalues the melodramatic while reflecting a modernist bias.

Thirdly, the final feature of the melodramatic concerns the audience. The melodramatic artist selects his texts as much from public as from private domains, since he conceives of his primary audience not as a single individual but as the community as a whole. By contrast, the modernist aims his performance at an individual, someone who is likely to share the private obsessions and internal conflicts that separate the self from the social macrocosm. As a result of targeting the broadest audience, the melodramatic artist can be expected to favor an inclusive repertory: folk tunes and nostalgic period pieces will take their places alongside songs of the day, a juxtaposition that in itself offers assurance to an audience trying to remain in touch with the present while not letting go of the past.

The foregoing definition of the melodramatic in modern popular culture offers a useful, if neglected, cultural model for distinguishing Crosby's stylistics from Sinatra's. Usually overlooked in discussions of Crosby's jazz singing and indebtedness to Louis Armstrong[7] is his equally important affinity with a type of song and style of singing stemming from this melodramatic tradition. Often, the primary feature distinguishing a 1930s Crosby recording from the sentimental but theatrical urgency in a Jolson performance is the closing of the space between performer and listener. Because of the microphone, Crosby was able to infuse the primary text of melody and words with a personal, intimate subtext based on vocal ornamentation and nuanced inflection. Every bit as engaging as his whistling, scatting, and vocalese on the hot second choruses of the jazz tunes was his creative crooning on the second choruses of the ballads and love songs. Whether the emphasis was placed on falsetto and rubato ("Just One More Chance"), sotto voce dynamic effects ("Out of Nowhere"), or heightened dramatic rhetoric ("Brother, Can You Spare a Dime?"), Crosby frequently managed to transform the second chorus into an emotive experience, a kind of operatic aria in miniature.

That this style of performance fell out of favor with the arrival of Sinatra and the big bands is reflective of changing conventions and tastes but certainly should not detract from Crosby's achievement. Bing Crosby showed that popular music could be bold without being brash, that it could sell through its own seductive charms, and most importantly, that it could be a specialized, sophisticated art without apparent effort. No doubt it was primarily because of Crosby that Billie Holiday learned the art of artlessness, acquiring a more natural elocution, just as songwriters were inspired by his understated approach to expand the expressive range of pop tunes beyond the blatancy of "Some of These Days" to the poignancy of "But Beautiful."

Listeners who are familiar with the ballads and love songs on the 1930s Brunswick recordings cannot fail to notice the use of vocal and declamatory effects, including the frequent swelling of the voice as a device for heightening drama and emotion. Even Crosby's pure jazz performances on songs such as "Mississippi Mud" and "Sweet Georgia Brown" can be seen as having aligned him with a vital folk tradition, much as the melodramatic writer Edna Ferber invoked African American music to separate her "living" characters from her "lifeless" characters in the classic, popular American novel *Showboat*. And when Crosby later returned to his Dixieland jazz roots, especially in his appearances with Louis Armstrong, he was never reluctant to express a preference for this tried and true music over contemporary trends.

By contrast, Sinatra would appear to have been the modernist, eschewing overt vocal techniques and devices such as the swoop or the trill in favor of an approach emphasizing the highly personal, complex drama inherent within the ironical meanings of his material. Yet the Crosby-Sinatra radio rivalry, while unique in American popular music, was anything but a conflict between disparate traditions. As an examination of their mutual radio appearances demonstrates, their rivalry concerns a disagreement about what belongs in that tradition and how best to interpret its accepted texts; it represents the kind of generational struggle that proves, as well as sustains, the existence of a single, developing tradition.

On the radio show aired February 1, 1944 ("Command Performance"), Sinatra's role called for him to play Crosby's singing instructor, as Sinatra performed "Learn to Croon," recorded by Crosby in 1933. The show's premise is a singing contest between the progenitor and the upstart for the hand of Dinah Shore, who chooses between the "crooner" and the "swooner." As the patriarch of the old order, Crosby expresses disdain for someone whose style is less than "easy and graceful." Sinatra counters by referring to Crosby as the has-been who needs some lessons, then appears to meet Crosby in the latter's territory by singing the refrain to the 1927 "Stardust" (later in his career Sinatra returned to the song but made it his own by singing only the verse). Finally, the two contestants locate common ground, harmonizing on the more contemporary "People Will Say We're in Love." If a winner must be selected in the first round, score a solid victory for Crosby, who demonstrates why he remains the reigning champ and voice of experience.

Later in the same year, on November 16, 1944 ("Kraft Music Hall"), the two went after each other once again with Sinatra cast in the role of "the voice" and Crosby as "the brow." As the voice of experience, Crosby dispenses fatherly advice to the new voice on the eve of Sinatra's own radio show, counseling him to include "good music" and some "older people too." The sage advice is apparently not taken seriously by the young upstart. Ten months later, on September 6, 1945 ("Command Performance"), the competing singers staged another battle of musical heavyweights, each determined to be lead man to Judy Garland, with Bob Hope acting as judge. Caricature and personal insults are more pronounced than in previous radio encounters, as the combatants are described as "Fatty vs. Atlas," "flesh vs. fancy," and "hairless vs. breathless." After Crosby auditions with high trills and grace notes, Sinatra refers to him as a "dead battery" and as a singer "in the twilight of his career." Sinatra then sings a striking modern version of a vintage tune—Jerome Kern's "All the Things You Are"—culminating on a powerful, falsetto-free, high G-flat. After the solo, Garland chooses Sinatra over Crosby, but Sinatra gallantly and patronizingly refuses the honor because "nobody's better than Crosby." Sinatra as "dad" then sings "Bingy Boy" (to the melody of "Sonny Boy") in a role reversal that acknowledges the early singer's voice of "ease and smoothness" but makes the voice of the latecomer dominant. The boys end by harmonizing on a tune that is once again more in Crosby's than Sinatra's territory—"You Are My Sunshine"—meeting the precursor's criteria for tones that are "real silky, real smooth." But on this occasion the new singer can afford to be conciliatory: he has scored a conclusive victory on behalf of a more modern, consciously artistic, and sophisticated music.

The next meeting, March 21, 1954 ("The Bing Crosby Show"), was on the eve of the Academy Awards and pitted not only the two song stylists against each other, but the actors as well. Sinatra was the aspiring Hamlet, but Crosby was the reigning Player-King with one Oscar in the bank already. As usual, Crosby insists on music that is "easy and smooth," and together they execute three of pop music's most enduring expressions of the elegiac: "Among My Souvenirs," "September Song," and "As Time Goes By." The songs, at once sentimental and complex, bring out the contrasting interpretive approaches of the two—Crosby sounds nostalgic, reminding listeners of a time when life was calmer and simpler; Sinatra, on the other hand, evokes personal loss, using his new persona as "serious dramatic actor" to inject a sense of living drama in these familiar lyrics from the past. And yet the two stylists complement each other to a remarkable degree. Crosby sounds perfectly comfortable with the virtually meter-less slow tempo established by Sinatra, and Frank in turn begins to acquire some of the smooth richness of the Crosby timbre. The performance may represent as satisfying a duet by two baritones as any on record. If the listener is still keeping score, this encounter must be judged a draw.

Even when the radio arena became largely displaced by movies and television in the 1950s, the rivalry had become so well established in listeners' minds that it continues, if at a coded, sub-textual level. The spectator who recalls the radio contests cannot help but respond to a palpable, similar rivalry between Crosby and Sinatra in their shared screen appearances in *High Society* (1956) and in *Robin and the Seven Hoods* (1964). Both films cast Frank as the smart-talking, "with-it" character playing off of Crosby's stodgy persona, a contrast that is especially exploited during the musical numbers. During the drunken bonding between the two on Cole Porter's "Well, Did You Evah!," Crosby's insertion of a retro, un-chic "boo-boo-boo" occasions from Sinatra a quick rejoinder: "Don't dig that kind of croonin', chum." Although the comment called attention to the generational and stylistic divide between the old pro and the contemporary king of pop, Crosby always singled out this number as his favorite musical performance captured on film. It is not hard to understand why. While referring to himself as "the forgotten man," Crosby simply lights up the screen, commanding the spatial field. Sinatra, listed at 5 feet 8 inches, may have had the advantage by an inch, but it is Crosby who appears to stand taller in their musical numbers. The graceful agility and resourceful economy of his physical movement match the unerring smoothness of his elocution. Chest and chin out, shoulders level and still, and weight back on his heels, Crosby's visual persona welcomes us into its field more so than does the somewhat ungainly, less polished character played by Sinatra.

Crosby clearly has no less a swell party during "Style," the Cahn-Van Heusen number that joined him with Sinatra and Dean Martin in the rat pack musical, *Robin and the Seven Hoods*. Neither a Robin nor a hood, Crosby was once again cast as an anachronism, a hopelessly square pedant at the mercy of the wisecracks and insults of "in style" insiders. But once again it is the old hat that steals the scene, as Crosby not only eventually dons stylish threads but also takes his place in the middle of the trio, singing and dancing on behalf of being in fashion. Here, Crosby is anything but yesterday's venerable star framed between two current favorites. Rather, he centers our attention on the more accomplished dancer, the experienced pro, capable of whipping individual media personalities into some semblance of a coherent dance team.

Crosby's settling and salutary effect on Sinatra is especially evident in the stars' joint televised appearances. Although Sinatra's edgy persona and dramatic electricity could serve him well on large movie screens, his problems with television ratings have been widely acknowledged.[8] In fact, it is somewhat ironic that footage from Sinatra's short-lived and largely unsuccessful series has recently been mass-marketed on DVD to the same cross-section of the public that once chose to tune him out.

A collection being marketed as *The Classic Duets* includes two Crosby appearances. The first, from the Edsel Show special of October 13, 1957, reunites Sinatra and Crosby after their *High Society* collaboration, but also recalls their radio meetings with a revival of "September Song," undoubtedly the musical highlight of the disc. The second, from the Timex Show series of October 19, 1959, places Crosby in the company of Frank Sinatra and Dean Martin, this time for a vocal-dance performance of "Together Wherever We Go." The number clearly anticipates the trio's work in *Robin and the Seven Hoods*, with Crosby providing the necessary glue. His crisp and economical movements contrast with the gangling mannerisms of his younger companions, even when he is serving as one of the bookends framing the host. At the song's midpoint, Crosby sings the line "Our singing wins us medallions" and then, as if to make good on his boast, claims the middle position in the visual choreography while leading the ensemble to a winning finish.

Sinatra's turning back to his old radio mentor for help in conquering the new medium is made explicit in another recent DVD release, *Happy Holidays with Bing and Frank*, with Sinatra and Crosby and a restoration of a Sinatra Christmas show telecast December 20, 1957. The modest production values of the show, set in a sort of domesticated bachelor pad, and its minimal cast of two middle-aged Catholic males, might easily disguise its uniqueness and daring. Determined to bolster his ratings, Sinatra installed himself as the show's director and immediately insisted on Bing Crosby as his sole guest star. The Sinatra style had proven successful at luring large numbers of responsive listeners to cabarets and concert halls, but getting invited into American living rooms to share the family hearth at Christmastime would require a different strategy, if not a makeover. It would not work for Frank to bring his family on board, especially with the public's memory of Ava Gardner still in his wake. Nor could he afford to draw undue attention to the irreverent swinger and outcast loner of the Capitol theme albums. He needed an everyman, not merely as a buffer and genial co-host, but as a complementary soloist and chorus. But would it prove wise to base the entire show on the vocalizations of its two baritone superstars, a premise without precedent and with few imitations?[9]

The results unmistakably support Sinatra's judgment. Frank begins the show on a faltering note, dropping a tree ornament while sounding uncharacteristically tired and hoarse on "Mistletoe and Holly." At this early point, but perhaps none too soon, Crosby arrives on the spartan set and remains for the show's duration, singing flawlessly and radiating infectious comfort and joy (even while wearing a grotesquely oversized Victorian top hat). Solo spots are few: the emphasis is not on the individual stars, but on the felicitous effects of their musical interaction. When Crosby tells Sinatra "that kind of singing will go on forever," we can only wholeheartedly second the sentiment. And when he encourages Sinatra to join him in singing "White Christmas," our response is not merely to the making of music but to the creation of a legacy.

The influence of Crosby on Sinatra and, for that matter, virtually all other popular singers, can never be understated. Few Sinatra followers would deny that his greatest musical legacy is the Capitol concept albums of the 1950s, a period during which the singer's choice of repertory took a decidedly reactionary turn toward the best songs of the prewar years. Without the influence of Crosby, Sinatra would have had to look elsewhere for material no less than for inspiration. As the matrix of American popular singing, Crosby not only supplied the sound, the style, and the instrument—the microphone—but because of his sheer weight and magnitude, in effect, he dictated the musical texts worthy of inclusion in the Songbook. On the other hand, the direction of influence was not all one-way: the difference that Sinatra, the latecomer, made in the art of the forerunner must equally be taken into account.

On March 28, 1954 ("The Bing Crosby Show"), the boys reunited to celebrate Frank's Oscar for *From Here to Eternity*. While the newly triumphant thespian chose repertory more characteristic of Sinatra the swinger, Crosby delivered an especially slow, expressive "Imagination" that showed the unmistakable influences of the Sinatra dramatic style. Although Sinatra and Crosby had each previously recorded the Burke-Van Heusen song, this 1954 Crosby performance is particularly stunning in its reflective naturalness and direct, highly personal manner of delivery. Normally, it was Sinatra who took the dance step, if not the beat out of Crosby's lilting ballads, transforming them into poignant soliloquies of the modern psyche. This time it was Crosby's turn to drop all reminders of the various charms at the crooner's disposal, and submit a reading that placed the listener completely within the world of the song. There are no reminders of the singer's vocal technique, no heightening or expressive devices other than the breath required to bring a familiar song to life. It is unlikely that an interpretation this singularly transparent and compelling would have been possible without the descendant's influence on the progenitor. Finally, in response to Crosby's call for something "real silky, real smooth," Sinatra joined Crosby for a sentimental, nostalgic duet of baritones on "There's a Long, Long Trail," which wound comfortably through familiar public domain territory.

Through the course of the Crosby–Sinatra meetings, the listener becomes increasingly aware of the singers' contrasting yet complementary musical values. For Crosby, the founder of a tradition and its overseeing patriarch, a song's meaning was as much a function of the melodic as it was the dramatic; for Sinatra, the latecomer anxious not simply about his own unique identity but about the vulnerability of a musical tradition dating back to the time of the founding father, it was not the recalling of but the re-creation of the dramatic moment that was paramount. But in the end, their duels yielded to duets, in effect making the case that the contrast between the two chief representatives of a great tradition was possible only because of their shared musical values.

Notes

1. Will Friedwald, *Jazz Singing: America's Great Voices from Bessie Smith to Bebop* (New York: Da Capo, 1996), 31.
2. Friedwald, "Bing: His Legendary Years—An Appreciation," liner notes on the recording 1993, CD, MCAD4/C4-10886.
3. Gary Giddins, *Bing Crosby: A Pocketful of Dreams, The Early Years, 1903–1940* (Boston: Little, Brown and Company, 2001), 546.
4. Peter Brooks, *The Melodramatic Imagination* (New York: Oxford University Press, 1976), 14.
5. Ben Singer, *Melodrama and Modernity* (New York: Columbia University Press, 2001), 11, 133.
6. Giddins, 517.
7. See, for example, Friedwald: "Crosby's greatest accomplishment—the result of all his alchemy—was the application of jazz to the music of Tin Pan Alley" (*Jazz Singing*, 32).
8. In a question-and-answer session following the initial screening of the restored *Happy Holidays with Bing and Frank* and included with the DVD, Nancy Sinatra acknowledges, "Dad didn't do well on television"—to which Tina Sinatra adds, "He had to fail somewhere."
9. The "Little Drummer Boy" duet with David Bowie on Crosby's 1977 Christmas Show bears resemblance to the Crosby-Sinatra Christmas encounter, especially in its intergenerational implications. But it is only one of the show's moments, as Bowie shares considerable screen time with other guests, ranging from Crosby's family to Twiggy.

11

From Crooner to American Icon: Caricatures of Bing Crosby in American Cartoons from the 1930s to the 1950s

Stephen C. Shafer

In the world of cartooning, the tradition of caricature has always been an important part of the artist's assortment of ways to make a point or to gain a laugh. In animated cartoons, this element has enhanced many short subjects. Whether traditional cartoon characters were imitating popular individuals or whether the characters themselves were recreations of celebrities or public figures, seeing the caricature helped the audience members feel that they were part of an inside joke.

It is a measure of the universality and the importance and pervasiveness of Bing Crosby's image in American culture that his caricature and specific references to his persona can be found relatively frequently in cartoon releases during the golden age of Hollywood animation from the 1930s to 1950. A quick glance at The Big Cartoon DataBase on the Internet (www.bcdb.com) turns up no less than twelve references to Bing Crosby, and my limited research in this area shows that the database, though very helpful, is by no means complete, at least in this specific case. I have examined as many of these cartoons as I could locate, and there were several additions that I discovered that had not been referenced on the database. Therefore, this study is centered primarily on short subjects I could track down and accordingly it is limited by the gaps currently present in the availability of American cartoons in this period. Since the wisecracking, more contemporary-sounding, show business savvy cartoons during the period from the 1930s to the 1950s invariably were those from Warner Bros., it should come as no surprise that references to Looney Tunes and Merrie Melodies are sprinkled throughout the text as examples, and likewise, since they were the short subjects that seemed more likely to make show business references, it is perhaps to be expected that they predominate, in spite of the fact that Crosby was under contract to Paramount, not Warner

Bros. However, other references to Bing Crosby may be present among the cartoons released by other studios whose work I was unable to examine.

Still, what I find interesting is the fact that the representation of Bing Crosby, more than other celebrities whose image is depicted in American cartoons, to me seems unique in that it changed significantly over the course of time. Other caricatures of show business celebrities tended to remain constant in cartoons. For instance, cartoon portrayals of Edward G. Robinson always centered on short, squat, violent gangsters with thick lips and squinting eyes. Likewise, drawings and caricatures of Jerry Colonna always had the big eyes, the handlebar moustache, and the wisecracking barbershop tenor voice. But Bing Crosby in cartoons was different. He changed. And that evolution, perhaps not surprisingly, corresponded to the changing public persona of Bing Crosby. It is that transformation that I find fascinating because I am not aware of any similar shift in the image of an animated cartoon caricature of any other major public figure, and it is that changing image that this paper will attempt to demonstrate in references to selected cartoons.

The first connection I could find between Bing Crosby and a cartoon is not really a depiction of Crosby at all. In fact it is not really a short subject, and Crosby is not even portrayed. The cartoon is a portion of the 1930 Universal revue, *The King of Jazz,* which centered on Paul Whiteman. Early in the program, the explanation for how the bandleader ostensibly received the title "the King of Jazz" is related in a Walter Lantz cartoon insert. Set in Africa, it comically shows Whiteman being chased by wild animals and ultimately being crowned as the "King of Jazz." In one very brief portion, Crosby, as part of the musical background provided by the Rhythm Boys, sings a brief sequence accompanying images of Paul Whiteman running away from lions. Although it is clearly Crosby who is singing the vocal on "My Lord Delivered Daniel," along the lines of a traditional spiritual, Crosby is totally anonymous. At this point in his career, of course, Crosby had not yet gone solo, and though his brief contribution is distinctive it is otherwise not identifiable.

Much different was the reference in the rather odd early 1932 Merrie Melodies cartoon, *Crosby, Columbo, and Vallee,* directed by Rudolf Ising. The humor of the short apparently was designed to show the influence of radio crooners, which was in this cartoon so pervasive that it penetrated even to the rather primitive life of Native Americans, who are depicted in a rather crude, stereotypical way. The song around which the cartoon is centered focuses on the way in which the triumvirate of radio crooners manages to steal the affections and interests of the Indian maidens to whom the braves are attached, and the Indians, of course, are bothered by this fact to the point that they are singing the song while doing a war dance. The cartoon then shifts to show how one young Indian brings his sweetie a big new radio, on which she listens to the crooners. At one point, a little brook makes sounds that resemble the voice of Crosby. In this cartoon, the theme of the irritation felt by the ordinary males toward crooners like Crosby is introduced, and this theme will reappear throughout the next few years in the early 1930s. In a sense, the theme parallels the plots in the Mack Sennett comedies Crosby was making at the time; in them, Crosby frequently would win the affections of females through his radio singing, much to the irritation of potential fathers-in-law and rivals for the affections of the girls. This theme shows up dramatically in two Warner Bros. cartoons released in the spring of 1936. The first of these cartoons is a Friz Freleng short called *Let It Be Me* that concerns itself with old-fashioned country values in contrast with the new-fashioned city values. The cartoon is really a morality tale that depicts adoring hens that listen on the radio to their favorite crooner, a rooster named Mr. Bingo, who turns out to be an undependable, self-centered, vain Lothario. Mr. Bingo cares little about the hens who adore him and even less about the rooster boyfriends who despise him. On a car trip through the countryside in his roadster, with a horn that gives off a characteristic Crosby-esque "bub-bub-boo," he picks up Emily, a chicken who is a big fan of his, sweeps her off her feet, and takes her to the city with him, much to the bewilderment of her boyfriend Lem, who wants to marry her. At a posh nightclub, Mr. Bingo offers her drinks, but upon seeing a Mae West-type entertainer, he rejects Emily and has her ejected from the establishment because he has found someone new. Impoverished in the city, Emily has to sell flowers to survive. Lem, still pining for Emily, loses his temper listening to Mr. Bingo on the radio. After destroying the offending radio receiver by smashing it on the floor, he leaves for the city. He shows up at the radio station, beats up Mr. Bingo, and rescues his love. In a happy epilogue, Lem and Emily are the picture of domesticity in their ideal country home; but when one of their little chicks offers the familiar Crosby "bub-bub-boo," the implication is anything but old-fashioned morality, and it oddly prefigures the hilarious ending when Crosby shows up as the son of Bob Hope and Dorothy Lamour at the end of the 1945 romp, *The Road to Utopia*. The fact that the parents throw an object at their bewildered chick suggests either their embarrassment about or their rejection of any part of Mr. Bingo and his value system. (This cartoon essentially was remade two years later as *A Star Is Hatched* with a hen who vocally resembles Katherine Hepburn; the concluding gag is almost identical.)

The theme in this offering thus depicts the Crosby rooster as a representation of slick, decadent urban life in contrast to the more dependable, if less flashy, values of the rural area in which Lem and Emily live. Mr. Bingo's image is that of someone who earns his fortune in an unworthy way and spends his money on ostentation and the empty pursuit of females and high times. Crosby, then, in this film, is shallow and superficial, someone for whom decent male roosters would have contempt. The beating that he receives at the radio station is well deserved for his mistreatment of Emily, and the audience is expected to cheer the punishment he receives. This image is clearly far from the usual impression audiences have of Bing Crosby. Visually, Mr. Bingo does not really resemble Crosby in any way; but the fact is, probably most Americans at this point knew Crosby primarily from the radio, even though his film career was beginning to thrive. Later, the visual caricature would accompany the vocal similarities, but at this point, at least in this film, it is the sound that mimics Crosby.

Later that spring, another Leon Schlesinger release, again directed by Freleng, painted a similar negative picture of Crosby. This cartoon, entitled *Bingo Crosbyana*, apparently went too far, at least from the perspective of Crosby, who did not appreciate the image it created of him. According to Jerry Beck and Will Friedwald, in their outstanding reference *Looney Tunes and Merrie Melodies: A Complete Illustrated Guide to the Warner Bros. Cartoons,* "Crosby's attorneys . . . [pursued possible] legal action" in reference to the cartoon; the authors quote the *Hollywood Reporter* in observing that the suit represented a "potential threat to cartoon producers who caricature stars" and they refer to the article's point that the "Crosby corporation has demanded that Warners cease distribution and exhibition of the reel . . . [because] the Crosby voice is imitated and the character of BINGO CROSBYANA is shown as a 'vainglorious coward.' "[1] What prompted this fuss was a silly little cartoon about insects: Bingo Crosbyana is a crooning fly who impresses all the female flies with his singing and guitar playing. Inexplicably, he is, pardon the expression, a "Spanish fly" with a sombrero, who also does some impressive flying, thereby irritating once again the boyfriends of the females who admire his daredevil antics. When a spider threatens the community of flies, Bingo is nowhere to be found, and the other flies have to attack the spider. Later, when the spider has been subdued, Bingo comes out again, but now he has lost his following.

Again, the visual depiction has nothing to do with Bing Crosby's appearance but the voice quite obviously matches that of the familiar radio crooner. The cowardly behavior and the showing off in the flying sequence in this cartoon again seem to bear little resemblance to the later image of Bing Crosby or, for that matter, to reality. The resentment of the other flies is obvious, and the fact that there are no likeable qualities to this Crosby character reveals a continuing depiction of crooners as objects of contempt.

An early 1937 Tex Avery cartoon, *I Only Have Eyes for You,* emphasizes the power that crooners have over females. Katie Canary rejects her poor speaking suitor, so he secures the services of a ventriloquist, Professor Mockingbird, who can imitate the popular crooning ability of a certain well-known contemporary singer. By mouthing the songs being sung by the hidden ventriloquist, the boyfriend attracts the affections of Katie Canary, who is quick to turn to the previously-spurned boyfriend, until she discovers that the voice is actually that of the mimic. As a result, she winds up caring for Professor Mockingbird. Again, the ability of the voice of the Crosby-esque crooner to attract female attention is seen as a quality that is problematic for a protagonist who does not measure up to the appeal of the singer. However, what is somewhat different in this cartoon is that the character attempts to use, mimic, and adopt the attractiveness that has affected his girlfriend.

This largely negative image changed in subsequent cartoons later in the decade. For instance, in late 1936, Warner Bros. released a cartoon called *Toytown Hall.* In it, a little boy who enjoys listening to the radio is told to go to bed by his mother, even though he wants to stay up to hear some of his favorite performers on the air. After his mother has tucked him in, all of his toys come to life, and, paralleling popular radio programs, they put on a program for him. The host of *Toytown Hall* is a caricature of Fred Allen, whose radio program at the time was known as Town Hall Tonight. One of his guests turns out to be the same Bing Crosby caricature as the rooster in *Let It Be Me,* but in this case it is clear that the child is delighted with the performance of the bird and the Crosby figure is seen as a positive one.

Crosby also shows up in another cartoon that celebrates contemporary radio performers, the 1937 release *The Woods Are Full of Cuckoos.* In this cartoon, overseen by future Jerry Lewis director Frank Tashlin, an assortment of radio and movie celebrities are transformed into animals putting on a radio revue. The writers had a field day coming up with animal names that provided puns on the names of the performers being spoofed: names like W. C. Fieldmouse, Sophie Turkey, Dick Fowl, Deanna Terrapin, Al Goatson, Jack Bunny, Fred McFurry, Louella Possums, and Fats Swallow must have had audience members groaning. Crosby is represented as a crow named Bing Crowsby and the depiction is certainly nothing like the earlier negative portrayals.

The Penguin Parade was another revue-type cartoon, this one released in the spring of 1938 and prepared by Tex Avery. In this cartoon centering on familiar celebrities as penguins and walruses in a nightclub near the South Pole, Crosby's appearance is that of a featured singer, Bon Crispy, who sings the tune "When My Dreamboat Comes Home" in a style that is indisputably Crosby. Again, the character now has neutral qualities and is introduced as "our popular crooner." Much of the humor involves sight gags and outrageous puns, such as the name of the pianist, Fats Walrus.

A pun also figured in a brief Crosby reference in the 1938 Tashlin cartoon *Wholly Smoke* with Porky Pig. To demonstrate his toughness, Porky attempts to show he can smoke, resulting in his becoming ill and hallucinating in a tobacco shop; this gives Tashlin the opportunity to bring smoking materials to life with predictable puns and sight gags. One of the gags, briefly, is a play on the name Corona, which becomes "Crooner" with pictures of Bing Crosby and Rudy Vallee. The reference now is to Crosby's visual image as opposed to his voice, which had dominated earlier cartoon representations.

As Crosby gradually became better known to the public, other characteristics referring to him began to show up in cartoons. For instance, in Tex Avery's clever 1941 cartoon *Porky's Preview,* animals go to a theater to watch a stick cartoon drawn by Porky Pig and see an episode of the film referring to the lack of success of Bing Crosby's horse at the Santa Anita racetrack. These continuing references to Crosby's supposed lack of success as a stable owner reappear in several other cartoons, such as Avery's late 1941 cartoon *The Bug Parade,* a collection of sight gags presented like blackouts referring to the insect world; in this short, one of the episodes shows a particularly slow horsefly who, it turns out, has been a little too close to Bing Crosby's horse. In Bob Clampett's 1944 cartoon *The Old Grey Hare,* Bugs Bunny and Elmer Fudd are projected into the future to the year 2000; Elmer reads a newspaper with several gag headlines, one of which refers to the fact that Crosby's horse has not reached the finish line yet. The gentle "ribbing" is similar to some of the jokes made on radio programs at the time, not just about Crosby, but about other public figures: comedy programs made fun of W. C. Fields's drinking, John Barrymore's "ham" acting, Jolson's egomania, Fred Allen's baggy eyes, and, of course, Jack Benny's stinginess. Such insider teasing made listeners feel as if they knew the celebrities more personally. With the radio bringing these personalities into the living rooms of the audience, such mocking, whether contrived or not, became a way for people to identify—and identify with—these performers.

The horse gag reappears in one of the most enjoyable of the Merrie Melodies celebrity cartoons, the wonderful 1941 Tex Avery short *Hollywood Steps Out.* The cartoon is filled with wonderful facial caricatures of dozens of Hollywood stars who ostensibly are having a night out at Ciro's nightclub. After the cartoon surveys some of the performers who are present, the stage show begins with Bing Crosby serving as master of ceremonies. By now, Crosby is recognizable with his bedroom eyes, his large ears, and his laid back persona. The easygoing style that characterized his film characters and his radio appearances on the Kraft Music Hall, is instantly recognizable. In the cartoon, each time he begins to introduce the next act, a race horse and jockey come out from the wings of the stage and the horse nuzzles Crosby, who keeps trying to push it away. The cartoon is very funny, and the representation of Crosby is remarkably realistic and familiar.

A Crosby caricature is also portrayed in another emcee role five years later in Robert McKimson's *Hollywood Canine Canteen,* a depiction of the famous Hollywood Stage Door Canteen, but with dogs instead of celebrities coming to dance with the enlisted dogs. Again, the film is a wonderful excuse to see caricatures of Hollywood performers and big band leaders, this time as canines, and again, the writers delighted in making puns with the names of well-known musical figures like Kaynine Kyser and Ishcapoodle, "Hairy" James, Tommy "Dorgy," Lionel "Hambone," Leopold "Bowwowski," "Boney" Goodman, and other performers such as "Schnauser" Durante. The Bing Crosby caricature again is the perfect, laid-back master of ceremonies; he is shown as friendly, cool, and unflappable, and audiences would have recognized the parallels instantly.

This image of Crosby, the easygoing, friendly celebrity is apparent, at least by implication, in another Bugs Bunny cartoon, the 1944 short *What's Cookin' Doc?,* which depends heavily on the audience's awareness of Hollywood. The cartoon depicts the Academy Awards ceremony and the wacky rabbit's expectations of receiving an Oscar. When the audience first sees Bugs after the introduction that sets the location, the rabbit is presiding over his table, waving at celebrities and then imitating them. The assumption is that Bugs knows them well enough that they will appreciate his mimicking them; after all, he is a celebrity too. Of course, one of the stars whom Bugs greets is Crosby, and after waving at him, Bugs launches into lower and lower "scat" singing, until he goes so low that he "burps." Though Bugs seems momentarily embarrassed, he quickly recovers and continues in his confident manner. The fact that his imitation may have insulted Crosby does not seem even relevant, since the expectation is that it was done all in fun and that surely Crosby would not have taken umbrage.

Bugs Bunny was not the only Looney Tunes star to imitate Bing Crosby. Daffy Duck took a crack at imitating Crosby in *Hollywood Daffy.* In this 1946 film, the movie-crazy duck is making his first tourist visit to Hollywood with the goal of seeing as many stars as he can. He decides to try to sneak by a studio guard at "Warmer" Bros. studios, and he tries to disguise himself as various performers and figures from Jimmy Durante and Charlie Chaplin to the Oscar statue itself, all to no avail. Obviously, his imitation of Crosby is no more successful than his other attempts.

But all of these cartoons only briefly make reference to Crosby's characteristics. Three other shorts from Warner Bros. go much further, and they really document thoroughly the changed image of Crosby in the 1940s. The first of these productions is the 1940 Bob Clampett short, *Slap-Happy Pappy,* with Porky Pig. The cartoon revolves around the well-publicized eagerness of Eddie Cantor, who had four daughters, to have a son, and around the fact that Bing Crosby and his wife Dixie were the proud parents of four sons. Playing off that well-known bit of celebrity information, the film begins with Porky learning that Eddie Cackler's wife Ida is due to have chicks; but when the chicks hatch, they are all females, to Eddie's disappointment. Just then, the Crosby rooster is taking a stroll with all his little roosters, and Eddie asks him how he manages to produce so many males. The reply, in that characteristic, amiable, laid-back voice, explains, "Well, Eddie old man, I'll tell you." He then shows how his singing inspires hens to give birth to rooster sons. Eddie races back to Ida to do his rendition of a song to motivate her, but the results do not match what the Crosby rooster is able to achieve.

This cartoon evokes the domestic image of Crosby, now settled into comfortable married life, but still a heart-throb. Although the primary focus of the cartoon is to contrast Crosby with an Eddie Cantor caricature, the relaxed, pipe-smoking, and casual Crosby is clearly in view. The transformation from the crooner Lothario of some of the earlier cartoons could not be more striking.

A remarkably similar theme can be found in one of the most memorable cartoon depictions of Crosby, the 1944 Frank Tashlin short, *Swooner Crooner.* This film, which was an Oscar nominee, depicts Porky Pig as manager of the Flockheed Eggcraft Factory, which is in full production to support the war effort. The presence of a new, very thin singing rooster named Frankie, clearly resembling the sensation Frank Sinatra, has created problems because when he sings, the hens stop laying in order to see him perform. So Porky advertises for a new singing rooster "to keep the hens producing." After hearing auditions from roosters who sing in the styles of Nelson Eddy, Al Jolson, Jimmy Durante, and Cab Calloway, and rejecting all of them, Porky finally finds the Crosby rooster singing "When My Dreamboat Comes Home." With his high forehead under a rumpled hat and with an open sports shirt, half-closed eyes, and a pipe, the Crosby rooster is the picture of the white, suburban, middle class family man. As he sings, the hens begin laying again and he is hired. The Frankie rooster challenges the Crosby rooster and as the two roosters sing, production of eggs goes beyond anything achieved before. Surrounded by piles and piles of eggs, Porky inquires of the two how they were able to inspire the production increase and they demonstrate by singing to him, whereupon the giggling Porky himself begins to lay a pile of eggs.

In his outstanding article on parody and caricature in Warner Bros. cartoons in *Film History,* Donald Crafton pays particular attention to this film. Crafton argues that in the cartoon the contrast between the Frankie rooster's effect of turning the hens into frenetic, unproductive bobby-soxers and, by comparison, the Crosby rooster's ability, with his gentle, crooning voice, to encourage extraordinary egg production, thereby re-establishing a renewed sense of stability and purpose, is significant. Aside from being a celebration of the entertainment industry's ability to help the war effort by providing a means of reducing anxiety and tension, Crafton maintains that the cartoon shows a distinction between the sexual appeal of Sinatra and that of Crosby. Where "Sinatra's voice urges the women toward unproductive release, evoked in masturbatory gratification," the Crosby rooster "on the other hand provides erotic distraction, but . . . [with] effects [that] are channeled into egg-making"; that is, "Crosby's fatherly, nonaggressive sexuality is preferable because it results in a socially tolerated sexual outlet for women: reproduction."[2] Certainly, the sexual attractiveness of the Crosby figure in *Swooner Crooner* is far different from the characterizations some years earlier, and it is clear that the Crosby figure is now viewed as reliable, non-threatening, domestic, and mainstream. Now he represents fully American values in the war effort and he is presented as reassuring and comforting.

However, a late 1947 release, the Arthur Davis cartoon *Catch as Cats Can,* is slightly darker in its portrayal of good, old dependable Bing Crosby. In this Sylvester the cat cartoon, Crosby is a parrot with all of the usual external trappings (pipe, sportshirt, etc.) who nonetheless is uncharacteristically concerned with his own position. Specifically, he is upset with the attention given to a Sinatra-like canary, and he helps the feline with various schemes to try to have his rival eliminated by the hungry cat. This plot provides excuses for various Roadrunner-like efforts to trap the canary, all of which backfire and lead to disaster for the cat. Finally, in frustration, in the last scene Sylvester has instead chosen to eat the Crosby parrot. In the process, he now has assumed some of Crosby's recognizable characteristics, as he wears a comfortable hat and smokes a pipe. In a sense, Crosby has been totally absorbed into American life.

In 1949, Crosby's involvement with cartoons became more direct with his narration of the memorable section of Disney Studios' *The Adventures of Ichabod and Mr. Toad* depicting Washington Irving's "Legend of Sleepy Hollow." In contrast to the narration of "The Wind in the Willows" section by familiar British voices like those of Basil Rathbone and Eric Blore, Crosby's easygoing telling of the tale was as American, as reassuring, and as comfortable as a father sitting around a campfire to tell a ghost story. Certainly it would be going too far to suggest in any way that Ichabod Crane was a caricature of Bing Crosby. However, some interesting parallels do exist. The Crosby-esque ears are rather pronounced on Ichabod and he does seem reminiscent of the comic Crosby in the "Road" pictures. He is fond of the ladies in the town. He is opportunistic. He enjoys eating and he is somewhat lazy and easygoing. He is willing to play tricks on Brom Bones, his rival for the hand of Katrina Van Tassel, and he basically has some cowardly qualities. All he needs is Bob Hope to serve as a foil. While this parallel may be difficult to accept, there is no doubt that at least in one scene, the connection is suggested. When Ichabod is entertaining the ladies of the town at the piano, he gives out with a characteristic "ba-ba-ba-boo!" Audiences in 1949 undoubtedly found this connection as funny then as it is today.

By the late 1940s and early 1950s, near the end of the so-called golden age of the Hollywood cartoon, caricatures of Bing Crosby revealed him to be a universally recognized show business icon. For instance, in a 1947 Little Lulu cartoon *A Bout with a Trout* made at Famous Studios for Paramount, Lulu ditches school to go fishing; her guilt causes her to dream, and the song "Swinging on a Star" serves as a background to the lesson she must learn. One of images depicted in the stars to which the song refers is a picture of Bing Crosby. Crosby is a figure of wisdom who is persuading Lulu to return to do what is right and proper. Several years later in a 1954 Paramount short entitled *Popeye's Twentieth Anniversary* celebrating the anniversary of the sailor man's first cartoon, Crosby is depicted as one of the Paramount contract players and celebrities who congratulate the spinach eater on his animated longevity. In such films, Crosby is not even a caricature; he is a show business institution.

Warner Bros. cartoons also acknowledged this fact, but as usual they did it in a typically Looney Tunes way. Playing against the notion of Crosby's status in the pantheon of American show business and culture, but referring to Crosby's earlier obscurity at the beginning of his career, is Robert McKimson's 1950 short *What's Up, Doc?* In this film, Bugs Bunny is seen as a wildly successful movie star, complete with Hollywood-style sunglasses, and as he chews on carrots from a fancy cigarette case he is asked by the "Disassociated Press" to tell his life story. Resembling the format of musical biopics like *Yankee Doodle Dandy,* the short takes Bugs's life from rags to riches and shows his early show business struggles to become noticed. In one hilarious and telling scene, he is down on his luck, sharing a park bench with other performers who are having an equally bad run of luck. They include legendary figures like Jolson, Benny, Cantor, and, of course, Bing Crosby. Jolson sees a very prosperous-looking Elmer Fudd, whom he identifies as the well-known vaudeville superstar who is in search of a partner. Each of the performers then tries to audition for him, but Fudd will have nothing to do with them until he sees Bugs, whereupon he enthusiastically greets him, telling him he needs him in his act. The joke in the scene is that Fudd asks Bugs, "Why are you hanging around with these guys? They'll never amount to anything." In this manner, Warner Bros. cartoons are confirming that Crosby now has moved from obscurity to legendary status, from crooner to American icon. The transformation has been completed in cartoons as well as in reality.

Crosby was known to Americans on the radio, in records, in film, and in stage appearances. He was a star not just to adults but also to the children who enjoyed the cartoons as well. Therefore, it is not surprising that we would see his image represented in so many cartoons during this period, and it is equally certain that his image changed over the years as the public got to know him. That change had to be shown if the caricature was to be in any way meaningful to audiences. And as Bing Crosby was transformed from crooner to icon in America, so he was transformed in cartoons.

Notes

1. Jerry Beck and Will Friedwald, *Looney Tunes and Merrie Melodies: A Complete Illustrated Guide to the Warner Bros. Cartoons* (New York: Henry Holt, 1989), 46.

2. Donald Crafton, "The View from Termite Terrace: Caricature and Parody in Warner Bros. Animation," *Film History* 5, no. 2 (June, 1953), 207.

Part 3

HISTORICAL PERSPECTIVES ON CROSBY

12

Not Just "The Crooner": Bing Crosby's Research and Business Endeavors in World War II

Deborah Dolan

Most Americans today have some awareness of Bing Crosby's fame as a musical and film entertainer during the World War II era, and perhaps even as a war bond promoter. Fewer are probably aware of the full extent of his involvement in promoting bonds, providing morale-boosting entertainment, and visiting military camps and hospitals. It is unlikely, however, that more than a very small number of Americans are aware of his other endeavors in the areas of invention, manufacturing, and equipment repair in support of America's WWII war effort, as these were overshadowed by his more public efforts in fundraising and entertainment at home and abroad. It is this aspect of his contributions, in the context of a nation preparing for and participating in full-scale war mobilization, that I will address here.

When one begins to explore the role of Bing Crosby in World War II, one finds numerous and repetitive mentions of his involvement, as well as that of other celebrities, in selling U.S. war bonds. It takes a bit of investigating to get beyond these brief references, and it was while doing this additional research that I serendipitously found reference to Crosby's war-related research and business efforts.

Even before war broke out, Bing Crosby had developed a reputation as an astute businessman. As early as 1940, he was awarded the U.S. Junior Chamber of Commerce Distinguished Service key as the man under thirty-five years old who had contributed the most to his community during the previous year.[1] How did Bing Crosby become involved in a business that would test over 15,000 inventions between 1941 and 1943? John B. Rathnell, a motion picture writer and friend, had been a machine-gun officer and ordnance expert in World War I. When the War

Department called him back to teach that subject to officers in the late 1930s, he advised Crosby that there would be an increasing need for entrepreneurs to develop new weapons, and suggested that Crosby go into the research and development of such weapons. Bing Crosby and his brother Bob, also involved in the entertainment business, were well aware that fame and popularity could be fleeting, and that it was a good idea to have something else to fall back on.[2] Thus Bing and his brothers Bob and Larry agreed to try the plan for a year and founded the Crosby Research Foundation in February of 1940 with the objective of testing, developing and marketing war and civilian use inventions. Rathnell later opened the office in Pasadena, California, in December 1940.[3]

During the first year, they looked only at ideas with military value and hired engineers to refine the items to the point of real potential value, with the idea that they would then bring those items to the attention of the government. This original plan, however, didn't succeed, as the government labs were too busy with their own existing projects to take over the final development of these potential products. When they attempted to bring the items directly to manufacturing outfits, they found that commercial ventures had put the bulk of their resources into the immediate production of war materials and were not interested in conducting further research and development. At this point, they changed their model and focused on finding inventions that could be made commercially viable for immediate production, items that were war goods but could be used in a postwar civilian economy.[4]

As mentioned earlier, the Crosby Research Foundation tested over 15,000 inventions between 1941 and 1943. Some of those inventions included a radio-controlled "iron pig" or "blind pig," which, loaded with TNT, could be forwarded to enemy emplacements; a lens that would enable pilots to see better in fog; and a stereoscopic fluoroscope that would enable military surgeons to better view bullets, shrapnel, or severed nerves embedded in soldiers' bodies, reducing the time in surgery. Some inventions, including a better tool for fastening plane cowlings to decrease vibration stress, and a device that would measure how much ice was on an aircraft's wings, would also have postwar civilian purposes. These items would then be farmed out to various manufacturers, who, again, had halted or reduced their own research and development programs. Some inventions originally thought to be of military value were picked up by the government, but not to be used as they were originally intended. One such example was a "Molotov Breadbasket," which was originally designed to scatter bomblets. While the military turned the idea down, the Department of Agriculture picked it up as a seed-scatterer to be used in humanitarian food efforts.[5]

Another venture in which Crosby's early business acumen would create a successful business enterprise was the Del Mar Turf Club, an exclusive California horse racing venue, which attracted people from afar to see and be seen with the Hollywood stars of the day. In 1935, through a series of political maneuverings, it was decided that the San Diego County Fair would be held on the old Del Mar Golf Course. The 241 acres were purchased for approximately $35,000 from South Coast Land Company, and a grant application was made to the federal Works Progress Administration (WPA) for approximately $500,000 for development of the property.[6] After the grant was awarded, William Quigley, a stockbroker and racing fan, acquired the franchise for a major thoroughbred racetrack and approached Bing Crosby, who was also known to be a horse breeder. Crosby not only supported the idea, but also acquired a ten-year lease on the property for use after the fair. Thus Crosby was the primary mover in making the eventual Del Mar Turf Club a reality in the life of southern Californians.[7] He would come to hold a major interest in and become president of the Turf Club, a franchise he owned with fellow actor Pat O'Brien, automobile distributor Charles Howard (best known for his ownership of the racehorse Seabiscuit), and Los Angeles attorney Kent Allen.[8]

Shortly after the attack on Pearl Harbor, the track, stables, grandstands, and clubhouse were requisitioned by the government for various military purposes in January 1942. First it was used to house soldiers who were sent to the West Coast to guard strategic areas of the southern California coast against potential attack by the Japanese in early 1942. In the latter part of 1942 it was used as a temporary staging for Marines who were on their way to the Pacific theatre. In 1943 the government relinquished its use of the property.[9] This created a new problem—what would become of the club?

An interesting point regarding the wartime use of the Del Mar Turf Club is that in addition to providing entertainment and exhorting the public to support the war effort by buying war bonds and contributing to various relief efforts, Crosby also utilized his celebrity status to explain government programs such as gas rationing, and the successful implementation of these programs was often attributed to his promotion of them.[10] Ironically, at the time, this very gas rationing program in California seemed to put the Del Mar Turf Club in danger of closing, at least for the duration of the war.[11] This was due to the Club's location, fifteen miles from San Diego and one hundred miles from Los Angeles at a time when the average San Diegan was issued a gas rationing sticker which allowed only four gallons per week.[12]

Until World War II, San Diego was a quiet, relaxed area without a strong industrial base. Naval expenditures, tourism, and real estate formed the bulk of the area's revenues. The attack on Pearl Harbor, however, led to an almost immediate transformation of the city into an industrious wartime center. The changes were so rapid, including an increase in San Diego's population from 200,000 in 1941 to 500,000 in 1944, that they were referred to as the Blitz-Boom.[13]

Fortunately for Crosby and his partners, California was so rapidly increasing aircraft production schedules at this time that manufacturers were seeking to subcontract work out. In May of 1943 it was announced that the Del Mar Turf Club would be converted to an aircraft parts manufacturing plant. Fred Poggi, a friend of Crosby, who was a retired mechanical engineer and had also served as a gunnery officer in World War I, brought this plan to fruition. The manufacturing plant set up at the track first received small contracts from a variety of manufacturers for projects such as cockpit floors of the Liberator, a Convair bomber used by the U.S. Navy, and exhaust manifold parts from Solar and Ryan. The large space available, however, later led to the acquisition of a contract to manufacture wing subassemblies for the Douglas plant in Long Beach, California, in 1943.[14] These wing assemblies, sometimes referred to as "Bing's Wings," went on the Flying Fortress bomber used by the U.S. Air Force, which flew in every war theater during World War II and is to this day one of the most famous aircraft in the world, particularly known for its bombing of industrial targets in Germany.[15] Thus the Del Mar plant contributed to the delivery of 28,000 completed aircraft and 5,000 plane equivalents (delivered for spare parts) by Convair, including B-24 Liberator Bombers as well as a variety of other training and transport planes between the end of 1941 and 1945.[16]

One of the common iconic images from the World War II era is that of Rosie the Riveter, the woman who stepped into traditionally male jobs in heavy manufacturing plants. And while this image is accurate, it was not as common as is sometimes thought. At the height of the war, only twenty-three percent of the entire workforce consisted of married women.[17] In San Diego, women aircraft workers never exceeded forty percent of the total number of aircraft workers.[18] At the Del Mar plant, however, ninety percent of the workers were women. Why? At first, the plant actually had difficulty getting large subcontracts because the major contractors were concerned that they would not be able to get enough labor in that distant area. But most of the women who were employed at Del Mar were local women, wives and daughters of nearby farmers who otherwise would not have worked outside of the home. Others moved to the area to be close to their husbands who were on nearby military bases; they were typically not able or willing to travel to San Diego for work and worked outside of the home because of the proximity of the Turf Club plant. Unlike some other plants, the Turf Club plant had a waiting list of women who wanted to work there.[19]

Bing Crosby and his partners clearly benefited from the fact that Del Mar was put to use in a million dollar operation and was thus maintained rather than lying unused and neglected. But personal gain was not a primary motivating factor. According to Marge Willett, secretary to plant manager Fred Poggi, "Until the war is won, Mr. Crosby thinks it is unpatriotic to consider use of the track for anything that will not help the war effort. He has repeatedly said that the plant has been dedicated to a war purpose and that it will be kept that way until victory." In addition, Poggi himself reported, "Bing told me he'd be satisfied if we could meet expenses of maintaining the track in condition good enough so it can quickly be restored to its original use after the war."[20]

It would be natural for one to question the lack of serious desire for personal or business gain that is attributed to Bing Crosby regarding these ventures by various people. And while it is clear that he did receive some personal satisfaction from these activities, he had other business interests that were making a profit for him. And his professional career certainly did not need any kind of a boost. By 1942, he had already completed thirty-four films and was already a top box-office draw throughout the United States.[21] In his own autobiography, James Cagney describes the rapturous applause for Crosby by the audience of 130,000 celebrating " 'I am an American' Day" at Soldier Field in Chicago because of the incredible impact it had on him—the response of the crowd to Bing was so overwhelming that it left Cagney with goosebumps.[22] He reportedly also received the largest round of applause ever at the Canteen, where he was entertaining troops.[23] It was also a time when he won the *Photoplay* magazine gold medal award for "Most Popular Actor" for the fifth year in a row.

These research and business endeavors at the Crosby Research Foundation and the Del Mar Turf Club had a significance beyond the development of war-related inventions and the production of aircraft subassemblies. They also provided a sense of community in working for the war effort. Much has been written about the role of Hollywood in producing war propaganda films dressed as entertainment. Because most of Crosby's films at the time were musical comedies, they did not as readily lend themselves to propaganda purposes as did dramatic films. An important role that activities such as those discussed here, as well as the selling of war bonds, played was that of maintaining morale and creating the sense of a unified society with a common goal—to support the troops and win the war.[24]

This presents only a very brief summary of some of Crosby's endeavors in support of his country during World War II. Bing Crosby was known to be an astute businessman, and so his business involvement in the war effort, as well as any resulting benefit to him, is not particularly surprising or unique. Although others were in charge of the day-to-day management, these enterprises required time and energy—time and energy spent in addition to the whirlwind of fundraising and entertainment events at which he performed, which speaks to his stamina as well as to the multifaceted nature of his talents and gifts. Did he receive personal and financial benefit from his business interests? Yes. But they also took their toll in time spent away from family, and general health and well-being.

Another thought that comes to mind is "Why Bing?" What was it about this individual that led him to be so deeply involved in such a variety of activities in support of the war effort? Was it his religious upbringing and adult involvement in his faith? Was it his religious high school education and attendance at Gonzaga College, which is known for its philosophy of promoting social action? Was it a basic philosophy of taking advantage of opportunities as they arose and putting forth one's best efforts in all areas? While in his private life he experienced many of the personal issues that the average person does, in his public and business life he was known always to be a professional. Because Crosby was known as a quiet and rather reserved person in his personal life and feelings, some of these questions are not directly answerable from information available to the public. Perhaps Crosby himself put it best as his character in *Road to Zanzibar*—"Some fellas got it, and some fellas aint got it. I got it."

Notes

1. Malcolm Macfarlane, *Bing Crosby: A Diary of a Lifetime* (Leeds, UK: International Crosby Circle, 1998); Malcolm Macfarlane, *Bing Crosby Day by Day* (Lanham, MD: Scarecrow Press, 2001); The Bing Crosby Internet Museum.

2. Andrew R. Boone, "Talent Scouts for War," *Nation's Business*, February 1943; *American Magazine*, "Bing's Secret Weapon," December 1943.

3. Boone, "Talent Scouts for War"; and Macfarlane, *Day by Day*.

4. Boone, "Talent Scouts for War."

5. Harold Keen, "Race Track Production Line," *Flying*, May 1944.

6. "A Brief History: 1900–1935—Horse Racing Provides a Steady Source of Funds," Del Mar Fairgrounds web site, http://www.sdfair.com/index.php?fuseaction=about.history_1900 (accessed 10 July 2007).

7. Del Mar Fairgrounds, A Brief History.

8. Keen, "Race Track Production Line."

9. Macfarlane, *Day by Day*; and Keen, "Race Track Production Line."

10. Scrimger, Liner Notes.

11. Keen, "Race Track Production Line."

12. Lucinda Eddy, "War Comes to San Diego," *Journal of San Diego History* 39, nos. 1–2 (1993).

13. Ibid.

14. Macfarlane, *Day by Day*.

15. United States Air Force Museum.

16. Richard F. Pourade, "Water—The Real Key to a City's Survival," in *The History of San Diego: City of the Dream* (La Jolla, CA: Copley Books, 1977).

17. Karen Anderson, *Wartime Women: Sex Roles, Family Relations, and the Status of Women During World War II* (Westport, CT: Greenwood Press, 1994), 4.

18. Maurice Albert Tomkins, "Military and Civilian Aspects of San Diego During the Second World War" (master's thesis, San Diego University, 1982), 99; Keen, "Race Track Production Line."

19. Keen, "Race Track Production Line."

20. Ibid.

21. Barbara Bauer, *Bing Crosby* (New York: Pyramid Books, 1977).

22. James Cagney, *Cagney by Cagney* (Garden City, NY: Doubleday, 1976).

23. Macfarlane, *Day by Day*.

24. Lawrence R. Samuel, *Pledging Allegiance: American Identity and the Bond Drive of World War II* (Washington, DC: Smithsonian Institution Press, 1997).

13

Bing's Entertainment and War Bond Sales Activities During World War II

Malcolm Macfarlane

"What did you do in the war, daddy?"

If Bing Crosby's children had asked him that, they would no doubt have a gotten a very modest and understated reply, because, as we know, that was his style. But what did he do? Did he enlist and fly bombing missions like Clark Gable? Did he fight on the front line like Audie Murphy? Was he classified as being medically unfit like Frank Sinatra? Did he register as a conscientious objector like Lew Ayres? Well, actually, he did none of those things.

After the attack on Pearl Harbor, the House and Senate required that all men aged twenty to forty-four years register for the draft, and Crosby, who was then aged thirty-eight, duly did so. From interviews he gave around that time he fully expected to be called up. However, as a married man with dependents, he was a long way down the priority list for being drafted.[1]

Crosby had been as shocked as anyone following that day of infamy in late 1941. His career was reaching its peak with his huge record sales and the popularity of his film, *Birth of the Blues,* which premiered two days after Pearl Harbor. He was the star of the prestigious radio program, *The Kraft Music Hall,* and in the show broadcast on Christmas Day 1941, he sang "White Christmas" for the first time on the air.

Crosby wanted to do as much as possible for the war effort, pending being drafted, but it soon became evident that he was unlikely to be conscripted because of his age, his family, and possibly because he was considered an "essential industry." It does seem that he was very embarrassed about not being called up and it was evidently decided that Crosby could do more to help the war effort by entertaining and boosting war bond sales than by donning a uniform.[2,3] Crosby's embarrassment about his absence from the armed forces ended on December 5, 1942, when the War Department suspended the induction of men thirty-eight years of age or older.

In the meantime, Crosby had been keeping his end of the bargain handsomely, and his workload was excessive for the rest of the war years. He was virtually the "Voice of America," as he articulated the feelings of Americans everywhere in his war time broadcasts. Crosby was contracted by Kraft to deliver his weekly radio show for thirty-nine weeks each year, and around this commitment he worked constantly on the war effort. As the decade progressed, it was said that his voice was being heard somewhere in the world every minute of every day.

Early in 1942, Crosby was honored by a request from General MacArthur, on behalf of his soldiers, to send the *Kraft Music Hall* radio show by shortwave to the American forces besieged in the Philippines at Corregidor. He also started to become involved in golf matches to raise funds for the American Red Cross and the Professional Golfers' Association (PGA) War Relief Fund. He took two weeks off from his Kraft show in February of that year to tour various locations in Arizona and Texas where he played in front of huge crowds. After the matches, he would auction off items in exchange for sales of war bonds. He also entertained at army camps in the evenings and thus developed an ideal pattern for his future wartime excursions. After the tour, he filmed *Road to Morocco* for two months, and during this time he and Dixie opened the family home in Hollywood to the public for a day to aid the American Women's Voluntary Services (AWVS). As soon as filming was over in May, Crosby went to Chicago to join the Hollywood Victory Caravan for the last seven shows of its tour. This was a traveling extravaganza of eighteen top Hollywood stars; Crosby worked alongside such stars as James Cagney, Cary Grant, Bob Hope, Laurel and Hardy, Charles Boyer, Groucho Marx, and others. Around the nightly shows, Crosby and Bob Hope had a daily challenge golf match at each location, which again raised funds for the Army and Navy Relief Funds. The Victory Caravan succeeded in generating war bond sales of over $1 billion, an incredible figure for those days.

On May 26, 1942, the War Department officially established the Armed Forces Radio Service (AFRS) to keep American forces informed and entertained, and Crosby was quick to become involved. Within days, he recorded his first guest shot in a *Command Performance* show. The Command Performance series was recorded weekly on transcription discs for shipment to overseas forces instead of being broadcast live, and Crosby's experience of recording for radio in this way was to have a major impact on his show-business activities after the war. Other major weekly AFRS shows were *Mail Call* and *GI Journal,* and Crosby was a regular participant in both.

In July and August 1942, during his break from the weekly Kraft show, Crosby went off on tour again as the star of a United Service Organization (USO) Camp Show with Phil Silvers.[4] They began their trip at Camp Lewis, Washington, and continued through Washington State into Wyoming and Colorado, with Crosby also fitting in fundraising golf matches, visits to hospitals, and personal appearances to sell war bonds. As soon as this junket ended, Crosby traveled to Washington, D.C. for a major war bond rally that inaugurated the "Salute to our Heroes" drive. He then departed on a three-week hectic excursion starting at Binghampton, New York, and finishing in Houston, Texas. Crosby kept to the same daily formula as before, which enabled a wide cross section of people to see him while at the same time raising vast amounts of money.

Crosby then returned to the weekly Kraft show and to the filming of *Dixie*. Weekends, however, were free, and again, golf matches proved an ideal method of entertaining and raising money. Bob Hope often joined Crosby for these weekend capers. On October 31, 1942, Crosby's recording of "White Christmas" reached number one on the charts for the first time and stayed there for eleven weeks. This song had a huge impact on servicemen, particularly those overseas.

1943

During the war, the Kraft radio shows had audiences of up to fifty million people and Crosby was able to deliver many inspiring messages in support of the war effort. When his Kraft commitments ended in April 1943, Crosby again went off on tour to locations as diverse as Chicago, New York, Memphis, Washington, D.C., Atlanta, Georgia, Birmingham, Alabama, and Nashville, Tennessee. His six-week trip brought him acclaim from the press wherever he went.[5]

On his return to Hollywood, Crosby also took part in other events to raise funds and one of these was a two-hour star-studded show from the Hollywood Bowl in front of 20,000 people. Crosby's contribution to the nation's morale at this time cannot be overstated—and then he was persuaded to take the part of a priest in a movie called *Going My Way*. Filming started in August 1943 and if Crosby thought his popularity had reached its peak, he was to be pleasantly surprised.

By this time, the government's need for funds was immense and there were regular launches of new War Loan offers. Crosby was invariably involved in the introduction of these offers and September 1943 saw him launch, with Dinah Shore, the Third War Loan in a nationwide broadcast. That month of September 1943 was when V-Discs were issued for the first time. These discs were prepared for the exclusive use by servicemen and featured airshots by famous artists, including Bing Crosby. Crosby also recorded special material for V-Disc use, some in a singalong format.

His recording activities continued rapidly and October 1943 saw him commit to wax another song that was to be a huge favorite of servicemen. "I'll Be Home for Christmas" was enough to bring a tear to the most hardened veteran's eye.[6] But this was just what the public and the servicemen wanted in those difficult days and it was a huge seller for Crosby. His next film was *Road to Utopia* with Bob Hope and Dorothy Lamour, and it was no surprise when Crosby's recording of "White Christmas" appeared in the pop charts again in December 1943.

1944

The Fourth War Loan drive commenced on January 17, 1944, and Crosby fronted a one-hour radio show on all four networks to launch it. At the end of January he and Bob Hope put on a two-day golf event at the Lakeside Club in front of large crowds. After the golf event, a war bond auction was held and Crosby took part as an auctioneer with Frank Sinatra, Bob Hope, and Kay Kyser. Kay Kyser paid $20,000 to hear Crosby and Sinatra sing together, and in response they duetted "People Will Say We're in Love." Within days, Crosby recorded another song, "I'll Be Seeing You," that was important to servicemen. This too became a number one hit, but not before his recording of "San Fernando Valley" reached the top of the charts and held the number one position for five weeks.

Crosby then filmed *Here Come the Waves*, and while this was before the cameras, his movie *Going My Way* had its world premiere at the Paramount in New York and went on to be the top box office attraction of 1944 in the United States. The critics were unanimous in their praise.[7]

Crosby had committed to go on an overseas tour but before he departed, he worked hard to get the Fifth War Loan off the ground. A war bond golf match against Bob Hope helped sell $700,000 worth of war bonds. That night Crosby served as master of ceremonies for a show at the Hollywood Bowl before a capacity crowd of 20,000.

Crosby was expecting to go to the Pacific and had all the necessary inoculations in readiness. But in mid-August he joined Overseas Unit 329 of the USO for a trip to Europe. The unit sailed on the converted liner "Ile De France" from New York to Greenock, Scotland, with Crosby giving four shows a day to the servicemen on board.[8] He toured the U.S. military bases in England, putting on show after show for a week before flying to France to get closer to the front line. The day before he went to France he obtained a new nickname after he broadcast to Germany speaking phonetic German. Reporter Bob Musel dubbed him "Der Bingle" in recognition of his apparent fluency.

Crosby flew into Cherbourg, France, with Fred Astaire and they entertained together at several locations before Crosby went off to follow the Third Army for three weeks, giving several shows a day with his troupe.[9] Many years later, Crosby was interviewed by noted Canadian broadcaster, Gord Atkinson, who subsequently wrote:

While on his lengthy overseas tour in 1944, Bing couldn't do a show without bringing a little bit of home to the front lines with "White Christmas." At the time of our last interview his thoughts went back to those bittersweet wartime days. "Well, it was always a kind of a wrench for me to sing the song," he confessed. "I loved it of course, but at the camps and in the field hospitals, places where spirits weren't too high anyway, they'd ask for the song—they'd demand it—and half the audience would be in tears. It was a rather lugubrious atmosphere that it created, which you can understand, because of its connotation of home and Christmas, and here we were thousands of miles from either one. It was a rather sorrowing experience to have to sing it for these men and women when it made them feel sad. But I guess in retrospect that it was a glad kind of sadness.[10]

After his French tour, Crosby returned to England for a few days to entertain at several camps and then he sailed back to New York on the Queen Mary, and again Fred Astaire was there.[11] Overall, it was quite a trip, during which Crosby lost ten pounds. Astaire later wrote in his autobiography:

Once in a while I've been asked what has been the most satisfying and rewarding experience in my career. The answer is readily available. Nothing I've ever done stands out like my trip overseas to entertain the troops in England and France during the last war. If I never do anything else, I'll always take satisfaction in knowing that I helped some of our soldiers relax for a few moments when they needed amusement and entertainment.[12]

1945

As the third year of the war got under way, Crosby began filming *The Bells Of St. Mary's* with Ingrid Bergman. During the making of this film, he went to the Academy Awards presentation and, much to his surprise, he received the Oscar for best actor for his performance in *Going My Way*. *Going My Way* received seven Oscars altogether, including best song for "Swinging on a Star."

On Monday, May 7, 1945, Germany surrendered to the Allies, and Sunday, May 8, was named as VE Day. By chance that was the day when Crosby appeared on *The Chapel of the Air* hour on the Mutual Network talking about finding time for prayer. This was the first of Father Peyton's Rosary broadcasts and it achieved nationwide coverage as it was a national day of thanksgiving.[13] That night, Crosby and Bob Hope starred in the Seventh War Loan program, which was broadcast on all networks.

When his radio and filming commitments were completed later that month, Crosby went on another tour from Chicago, through various locations including Montreal, Boston, and Washington, D.C., where, in front of a crowd of ten thousand, he received a "GI Oscar" in recognition of his wartime entertainment of allied troops.[14]

His next film was *Blue Skies* with Fred Astaire, and during the filming the Japanese surrendered.[15] Crosby's war was almost over. He recorded a *Command Performance Victory Extra* radio show for broadcast on August 15, VJ (Victory over Japan) Day, and fittingly he sang "White Christmas" at the end of it.

The details and statistics of Crosby's activities that follow are outstanding, but apart from these bald figures, many, many members of the armed forces had warm memories of him during wartime. Whether it was in the escapist "Road" films or movies such as *Holiday Inn, Going My Way,* or *The Bells of St. Mary's,* Crosby, with his portrayal of an apparently "regular" guy, helped everyone to forget the daily grind of the war. He won *Yank* magazine's GI poll as the person who had done most for the morale of overseas servicemen. His radio shows provided light relief, but he also usually ended them with a suitable patriotic rallying call. In addition, we must remember his recordings, which were certainly therapeutic at the time, and still remain so today. Also, we must not forget that through all of this he had the occasional personal problem; his house burnt down in 1943 and his wife took an overdose, which nearly killed her in January 1945.[16]

So back to that question, "What did you do in the war, Daddy?" Well, we know that Crosby took great satisfaction in having helped some of the soldiers to relax, but he could have legitimately replied, "I entertained the nation through all available media, helping to sustain morale." In fact, in the three years and eight months of the war, Crosby made eight full-length films,[17] twelve short films (including guest appearances), and more than seventy programs for the Armed Forces Radio Service,[18] appeared in at least 190 other radio programs,[19] recorded 160 songs for commercial release—and out of these, an incredible fifty-four were top-thirty hits, including nine number-one hits. In addition, his songs "White Christmas" and "Swinging on a Star" won Oscars for the best song in a film in their respective years. A total of seventy-one V-Discs were issued containing his material, some of which was specially recorded. In all, Crosby spent a total of twenty-five weeks touring to entertain servicemen, not including his numerous weekend trips.

He could have also mentioned his fund-raising activities, which resulted in the sales of millions of dollars of war bonds, and the many funds he raised for the USO, Red Cross, and other charities. So even he would have had to admit that he certainly played his part in helping the Allies win the war.

"Going My Way?" he had asked. We certainly were in those difficult days!

Notes

1. The Clarification Directive issued on July 27, 1942, stated that the order of priority for being drafted was: (a) Single men with no dependents—1A; (b) Single men with financial dependents and employed in non-essential industries—3A; (c) Single men with financial dependents and employed in essential industries—3B; (d) Married men, maintaining bona-fide family relationships, with no children and in non-essential industries—3A; (e) Married men, maintaining bona-fide family relationships, with no children and in essential industries—3B; (f) Married men, maintaining bona-fide family relationships, with children and in non-essential industries—3A; and (g) Married men, maintaining bona-fide family relationships, with children and in essential industries—3B.

2. During the Fall of 1942, when interviewed by Dick Mook for *Silver Screen* magazine (date unknown), the subject of Crosby not being conscripted came up and Mook wrote, "He paused a moment and a sombre note crept into his voice. 'You know, Dick, I feel pretty foolish not being in the service right now myself.' "

3. "When war came to the United States as 1941 was drawing to a close, Bing hastened to shape his schedule so that he could best contribute to winning it. At first he was for joining the Navy or Army, but official Washington pointed out that he could best help by contributing his time and talents in the entertainment of service personnel, and in boosting war bond sales rather than by enlisting. He was also assigned the task of helping select programs to be transcribed for the Armed Forces. From that time on, Bing's first reaction to any request made to him was 'What will it do to help win the war?'" Ted Crosby, *The Story of Bing Crosby* (Cleveland: World Publishing, 1946), 222.

4. United Service Organizations Web page at http://www.uso.org/. In 1940, America's military was rapidly growing in response to the increasing threat which preceded entry into World War II. President Franklin Delano Roosevelt challenged six private organizations—the YMCA, YWCA, National Catholic Community Service, the National Jewish Welfare Board, the Traveler's Aid Association, and the Salvation Army—to handle the on-leave recreation needs for the members of the Armed Forces. The six organizations pooled their resources and the United Service Organizations—which quickly became known as the USO—was incorporated in New York State on February 4, 1941. By 1944, USOs were found in over 3,000 locations throughout the United States primarily staffed by the USO's most precious resource, volunteers. President Roosevelt became the first USO Honorary Chairman, a position accepted by every President who followed.

5. For instance, Bob Rule of the *Nashville Tennessean* wrote on June 3, 1943: "He was marvelous at the bond auction. Immediately, when he walked out on the platform and took

over the microphone, he captivated the crowd. His easy manner endears him to you. Never have I seen a more receptive audience. . . . In twelve years of sports writing, this person has never met a man of Crosby's personality. He's the most sincere, easiest to talk with individual I've ever had the pleasure of contacting—absolutely tops."

6. *Look* magazine (date unknown) reviewed "I'll Be Home for Christmas" as follows: "The lyric and melody of this number by Kim Gannon and Walter Kent reach the ultimate in sentimentality."

7. Bosley Crowther of the *New York Times* (May 3, 1944) made the following comments about *Going My Way:* "Having hit about as high in his profession as any average man would hope to hit—and that is to say the top notes in the musical comedy league—Bing Crosby has switched his batting technique (or had it switched for him) in his latest film . . . old Bing is giving the best show of his career." *Going My Way* completed a record-breaking ten-week run at the New York Paramount where over a million people paid a total of $847,000 to watch it!

8. The trip across the Atlantic took five days: "Crosby worked harder than anybody; he endeared himself to everyone aboard the ship. He was miserably, agonizingly seasick through most of the crossing; nevertheless he insisted on putting on four one-hour shows a day so that all the troops could be entertained, 2,500 at a time—a gruelling schedule for any entertainer, even one who could keep his lunch down, which Crosby could not, as a rule. He could have made it easier on himself; the ship's officers who got three meals a day and had a very pleasant private wardroom to eat them in, sympathetically invited Crosby to join them, but he declined. If two meals a day in the mess hall were all the fighting men got, he said mildly, then that would be good enough for him, and he took his green-faced place in the shuffling queue with the troops. He did not spurn the officers' hospitality entirely; the ship's officers had liquor, which the troops did not, and Crosby could occasionally be prevailed upon to join the officers for a single highball in the evening. But then he invariably made it a point to leave shortly before eleven o'clock in order to spend an informal hour with Captain Lauder's Coast Guard gunners as they changed the watch, amiably chatting and joking, and agreeably singing any nostalgic old song that anyone asked for." Don Stanford, *The Ile De France* (New York: Appleton-Century Crofts, 1960), page numbers unavailable.

9. "One afternoon, Bing was entertaining troops in an abandoned factory somewhere in Alsace-Lorraine just two miles from German positions, but after one song his audience was called away to deal with a German attack. There was a nice story about another one of his adventures. After mass one Sunday morning, Bing, with a lieutenant at the wheel of their jeep, started off for their destination. After they had traveled ten or fifteen minutes, Bing Crosby became worried because the telephone lines strung up in the battle zone by the Army had run out. Bing later said: 'When that happens you know you've gone too far. It was raining and most of the road markers had been washed away. Then we got to a town and I asked the lieutenant if he knew where we were. I remembered seeing this town on a map earlier. Do something for me,' Bing told the officer. 'Turn this thing around and get us out of here.' The lieutenant turned around. That night Bing mentioned to the commanding officer where he'd been during the day. 'But you couldn't have been in that town,' the commander protested. 'I sure as hell was,' Bing told him. 'That town's in German hands,' the officer insisted. 'Well,' Bing shot back, 'we had it for two minutes today.' " Bing Crosby, *Call Me Lucky: Bing Crosby's Own Story,* as told to Pete Martin (New York: DaCapo Press, 1993; reprint of original 1953 printing), 294–95.

10. Gord Atkinson, *Gord Atkinson's Showbill* (Carp, Ont.: Creative Bound, 1996), 201.

11. Astaire added, "I ran into Crosby again and we had some laughs relating our experiences. Arriving in London, we were loose for a day or so awaiting the alert to embark for home. I had chosen the boat trip and so did Cros. We were shipped on the Queen Mary and it was loaded, but loaded. The boys were sleeping in the halls, on the stairs, and every place. It was a good trip, with several deviations to avoid submarines.

"There were a great many bomber boys on this trip. They were being transferred from the European to the Pacific area mostly, as they told me. Some were just going on long leave. They were dead tired. Cros and his group and I entertained on the boat a number of times in a special setup in the main dining hall, also in the hospital sections for the many returning wounded." Fred Astaire, *Steps in Time* (London: William Heinemann, 1960), 278.

12. Crosby, *Call Me Lucky,* 203–4.

13. *Variety's* review of *The Chapel of the Air* program: "Crosby said that the Family Rosary was recited at his home every day, that he wanted his four boys to love their country, God and their home, that he wanted to believe in the efficacy and practice of prayer both at home and in church. Through daily family prayer, continued Crosby, all children and all adults will come closer to God. Crosby had a simple but perfectly phrased script which he read superbly." *Variety* (May 16, 1945).

14. When the news came through of Japan's surrender, Gord Atkinson wrote: "It seemed that everyone at Paramount headed for the studio square, site of a war bond billboard with large images of Hitler, Mussolini and Tojo. A big letter 'X' had been painted over the first two caricatures. Suddenly voices began calling for Bing, which eventually broke into a chorus of 'Crosby, Crosby, Crosby.' A few moments later Bing appeared carrying a bucket of black paint and a brush. A ladder was put in place and Bing began climbing towards the billboard. . . . With two sweeps of his brush, Bing placed an 'X' over the image of Tojo, and the crowd let out with a loud cheer—and took off in every direction to celebrate." Atkinson, *Showbill,* 20–21.

15. His day at Boston on June 9, 1945, was typical as reported the next day: "Mobbed by bobbysoxers wherever he went, Bing Crosby went through a grueling twelve hour schedule in greater Boston, yesterday, to wind up as airy as ever at the bedsides of paralyzed war-wounded, at 8 o'clock last night, ready with a song and a gag, despite the fact that he had attended a ship launching, played a stiff exhibition golf match, starred at a Bond Rally, signed (by actual count) 1754 autographs and gone without supper so that he could sing for the wounded. A less durable personality would have wound up halfway through the schedule with his nerves dragging on the floor but Bing had to be told it was the patients' bedtime at Cushing General Hospital in Framingham to stop him and he went to take a train to Washington where, today, he will be presented the GI Oscar award, at Walter Reed Hospital, for his USO entertaining tours in Europe." *Boston Sunday Post,* June 10, 1945.

16. Macfarlane, *Bing Crosby Day by Day,* 248, 291.

17. Crosby made the following films during the war: full-length (eight): *Holiday Inn, Road to Morocco, Dixie, Going My Way, Road to Utopia, Here Come the Waves, The Bells of St. Mary's, Blue Skies*; shorts and guest appearances (twelve): *Don't Hook Now, Now About Christmas, Swingtime with the Stars, My Favorite Blonde, Star-Spangled Rhythm, The Princess and the Pirate, The Shining Future, Hollywood Victory Caravan, Duffy's Tavern, Meet the Crosbys, All-Star Bond Rally,* plus a special Paramount newsreel appealing to the youth of the nation to return to school. In addition, he sang the songs for the soundtrack mimed so successfully by Eddie Bracken in the film *Out of This World.*

18. Armed Forces Radio Service shows in which we know Crosby participated during wartime (December 7, 1941–August 15, 1945) total more than seventy and include *Command Performance* (thirty appearances), *Mail Call* (thirteen appearances), *GI Journal* (nineteen appearances), *Song Sheet* (at least five appearances), *Personal Album* (many appearances), *Front Line Theater,* and *Jubilee* (at least twice). In addition, his regular *Kraft* show was transcribed for the Armed Forces.

19. Crosby's other major radio appearances added up to at least 190 and included the *Kraft Music Hall* (135 appearances), *Lux Radio Theatre* (*Road to Morocco, Sing You Sinners, Dixie*), *Screen Guild Players* (*Too Many Husbands, Going My Way, Holiday Inn, Birth of the Blues*), *Silver Theater* (two appearances), *The Telephone Hour, Walgreen Birthday Party, The Ray Bolger Show, The Frank Sinatra Show* (twice), *The Bob Hope Show* (twice), *Your Hit Parade* (twice), *The March of Dimes Show* (three times), *Philco Ra-*

dio Hall of Fame, The Andrews Sisters Show, Quiz Kids, Paul Whiteman Presents, Johnny Mercer's Music Box (twice), *Duffy's Tavern, Soldiers with Wings* (twice), *Between the Lines, The Elgin Watch Christmas Special* (twice), *Pan-American Day program,* War Loan launch broadcasts (four times), *Treasury Star Parade* (three times), special programs regarding the war effort (*Christmas Eve at the Fronts, Salute to Our Armed Forces,* USO show), Religious programs (*Five Will Get You Ten, Chapel of the Air*), a special Spanish program, a tribute to FDR after his death, *Redbook* radio show, *Cavalcade of America, On the Scouting Trail, Report to the Nation,* plus seven programs during his European tour and numerous local radio spots.

14

Bing Crosby's Magnetic
Tape Revolution

Martin McQuade and Pete Hammar

Bing Crosby played a vital role in the development of entertainment technology. His financial backing of Ampex Corporation in the late 1940s led to that company's successful introduction in America of the German invention of professional magnetic tape recording, a fundamental technology that even today remains the basis for all broadcasting, audio and video production, and computer science. By helping launch an electronics revolution in communications, Crosby vastly transformed the world of show business, which he had dominated for so long, and in the process hastened the growth of American broadcasting.

A set of serendipitous events set this technological revolution in motion. The trigger was Crosby's increasing dissatisfaction with the demands of live radio. Starting in 1935, Crosby was the host of *The Kraft Music Hall* on the NBC radio network and transformed that weekly program into the premier musical variety show of the time. The demands of live broadcasting were many, including the need to perform each weekly program twice, once for East Coast and Midwest audiences, and again later for the live West Coast feed. "Live" meant no chance to correct mistakes; embarrassing and even career-damaging bloopers went right out to millions of listeners. Production values were limited by what the cast and crew could do in one live take.

By 1945 Crosby desperately wanted a change from the rigors of live radio. Rumor had it that if he was forced to continue doing live broadcasts on NBC or on any other network, Crosby would quit radio altogether and concentrate on films and records, two media at the time, both of which allowed for retakes and editing. The two major radio networks, NBC and CBS, insisted on producing live broadcasts. Since the networks' inception, they had banned the playing of recordings on the air because the audio quality couldn't match live sound. Crosby had reached an impasse and seemed to have no choice but to go live on the air if he wanted to remain on network radio. NBC, CBS, and the other radio networks had the last word, or so it seemed.

At that time American radio technicians had only electrical transcription (ET) discs with which to record sound. An ET was a large, sixteen-inch-diameter acetate or lacquer disc cut on the spot in the studio with a running time of just a few minutes. Recording a thirty-minute show required several ETs. A carefully mastered, first-generation ET sounded acceptable to most radio listeners, but a show that had been edited on multiple ETs sounded badly distorted. Editing a show to reduce its running time or to remove bloopers was a clumsy process requiring the operator to make copies of copies until he completed the final edited disc or discs. As the technician recorded multiple generations of edited sound, the ET's distortion, noise from needle scratch, and the inevitable "pops" and "ticks" built up as well. It was no wonder that NBC and CBS had prohibited ETs on their networks.

In 1941 the U.S. Department of Justice broke up the NBC radio network into its two component parts, "Red" and "Blue," claiming that the company had grown too large and was engaging in monopolistic trade practices. The Blue network subsequently became the American Broadcasting Company, while the Red network remained the National Broadcasting Company. At first very few "name" performers wanted to be associated with the fledgling ABC, although the new network eagerly courted talent. Hearing about Crosby's unhappiness with live shows, ABC executives made the key deal that gave their new network the necessary boost: once his contract with *Kraft* on NBC expired in May of 1946, ABC said it would allow Crosby to produce and broadcast a new show using the sixteen-inch electrical transcription discs, an unheard of decision in American network radio at the time.

With this concession to America's biggest star, ABC hedged its bets by making only one requirement: the program's Hooper rating, the predecessor to today's Arbitron and Nielsen ratings, could not drop below sixty from a theoretical high of a hundred. If Crosby's rating went below sixty, he would be contractually required to go back to doing live broadcasts. In reply, Crosby and his manager-brother Everett Crosby made a contractual stipulation that would change history: ABC had to provide Crosby's producers with state-of-the-art recording devices—whatever those were. The kind of recording technology didn't matter as long as it was the latest and the best.

On September 18, 1946, *Philco Radio Time Starring Bing Crosby* was recorded on multiple discs using state-of-the-art Scully ET disc lathes rented from NBC and edited disc to disc for the first broadcast on October 16. For the remainder of the 1946–47 season, that pattern was repeated: the show was recorded once, so-called "live to disc," which allowed Crosby to leave for the week to pursue his other career interests and to relax and play golf while the technicians edited the discs and then played them on the air twice, once for each half of the country.

Once Crosby tasted the freedom of edited radio broadcasting, he never wanted to go back to the constraints of his "live" past. Without sacrificing his trademark spontaneity, Crosby could eliminate material that wasn't to his liking, tighten dialogue and comedy routines, tell off-color jokes that he knew would not be heard on the air in or-der to warm up the studio audience, perform different takes of songs, and even aug-ment laughter and applause, an early use of the laugh track. The Crosby shows began to sound tighter and more coherent than anything else on radio, while still giving au-diences that relaxed and casual mood that only Crosby could create. However, be-cause of the awkward disc editing techniques and the lingering problem of multigenerational disc distortion ruining the show's sound quality, Crosby still feared that he would be compelled to revert to live broadcasts, the thing he hated most. One man, John T. Mullin, possibly saved Crosby's radio career.

Jack Mullin, an officer in the U.S. Army Signal Corps during World War II, had been assigned to travel throughout postwar Germany to research the advanced technology that the Germans had used during the war. Mullin knew that the Ger-mans had been using some kind of high fidelity means of recording for time-de-layed radio broadcasts, the reason he had heard live-sounding symphony concerts at three o'clock in the morning on German radio all throughout the war. Mullin had seen low fidelity magnetic tape field recorders used by the German military, and knowing the machines' sonic limitations, assumed tape wasn't good enough for ra-dio use. He was thrilled when a British officer directed him to the high fidelity AEG Magnetophon studio tape recorders and their BASF and Agfa tape, which was still in postwar use at a radio station near Frankfurt.

Mullin returned to his Signal Corps laboratory in Paris, retrofitted several of the low fidelity German military field Magnetophons [sic] with American electronics to record hi-fi sound, and filed his reports to his headquarters in the United States. In addition, carefully following GI regulations using standard mail sacks, Mullin shipped home to San Francisco two surplus AEG machines, spare parts, and fifty reels of BASF/Agfa tapes, all of which the U.S. Army would have otherwise thrown away. When he arrived home shortly after Thanksgiving, 1945, he and a colleague, Bill Palmer of WA Palmer Films in San Francisco, created a partnership that led to the creation of the first high fidelity tape recorders in America. Com-bining the German magnetic head assemblies and mechanical tape transports that Jack had brought from Europe with American electronics of their own design, the two men built two working tape machines which together could record over a half hour of very high fidelity audio. Mullin and Palmer named their modified Magnetophons the "Magnetrack" system.

Equipped with the two recorders and their stash of only fifty reels of German ac-etate and plastic magnetic tape, Mullin and Palmer set out to generate interest in this novel method of recording sound. Tape's high audio quality, with its ex-tremely low distortion and wide frequency range, was complemented by its long playing time of over fifteen minutes, far longer than was practical with an ET disc. Tape's ease of editing created another sensation. Never before had anyone in America been able to edit an original recording and play it back without loss of quality. A pair of scissors, some sticky tape, and dexterous fingers were all the tape operator needed to create editing miracles that were simply impossible with disc recording. Even trained audio professionals couldn't tell where most edits had been made. The new recording technology stunned and thrilled American radio and recording technicians, producers, and performers.

On May 16, 1946, Mullin and Palmer demonstrated the Magnetrack system in San Francisco to a large group of Bay Area electronics and radio professionals. In the audience were engineers from Ampex Corporation based in nearby San Carlos, California, a small company founded by Russian expatriate Alexander M. Poniatoff. With half a dozen employees, Ampex had been making small radar motors and generators for wartime Allied military use. Once the war ended and the commissions dried up, Ampex had to find a postwar product in order to stay in business. The WA Palmer Magnetrack prototypes gave Ampex the answer. With Mullin's and Palmer's guidance Ampex began, in the fall of 1946, to build the prototype of their Model 200A, which became the first commercially produced, professional, high fidelity tape recorder in the United States. The company had little working capital, but incorrectly assumed that a successful prototype and the resulting orders would open financing floodgates. Only later did they realize that without Bing Crosby they would have failed; even after the initial successful demonstration of their product and an enthusiastic reception by Hollywood producers and talent, no California bank would loan them a nickel. Venture capital was largely unknown in those days.

Mullin and Palmer followed their May 1946 demonstration with other public and private demos in the Bay Area and in Hollywood. Two of Bing Crosby's agents, Hugh King and Basil Grillo, heard about the exciting new recording technology and visited Palmer's San Francisco studio. They were astonished when they realized that the music they thought they were hearing from a live orchestra somehow shoehorned up into the loft was really coming from a Magnetrack tape recorder and a good-quality loudspeaker! They reported this miracle to Bing and Everett Crosby, as well as to Bing's technical producer, Murdo MacKenzie. Everyone in the Crosby organization immediately recognized the huge implications of this technical marvel.

As the second season of *Philco Radio Time* was about to begin, the Crosby brothers invited Mullin and Palmer to tape record the first show on August 10, 1947, using the two Magnetracks and several of Jack's precious reels of German tape. The program would also be recorded, as always, on the Scully ET disc lathes that ABC shared with NBC in the recording department of the NBC West Coast studios on Sunset and Vine in Hollywood. After the recording session, armed with only a pair of scissors and Scotch tape, Mullin edited the show with a precision that astounded both technicians and talent. The quality of the final edit was so good that almost no one could tell what was live and what had been taped. One radio executive even insisted that taped sounded better than live! At that moment Crosby made the decision to use the new technology to produce all of his shows and asked Mullin to be his chief recordist under a contract with WA Palmer Films of San Francisco.

With only two operational high fidelity tape recorders in the entire country, Mullin needed to limit the use of his Magnetracks so that they didn't wear out prematurely before the American made replacement machines arrived. His small supply of blank German tape was also dwindling. When the Crosbys asked him which

American company would provide U.S. built machines, Mullin answered that Ampex would be ready soon. The Crosbys invited Ampex to demonstrate their prototype Model 200A on October 1, 1947, the day of that first-ever, tape-produced radio show broadcast. Ampex held the demo in Crosby's listening room in the NBC studios in Hollywood. Playing tapes that Mullin had already recorded, the Ampex machine ran continuously all day and worked perfectly, reassuring the Crosbys and others that this exciting new technology had truly arrived in America.

ABC didn't trust Mullin's edited tapes or the Magnetracks themselves well enough to use them directly on the air during the 1947–48 season. Instead, network technicians dubbed Mullin's finished, edited tapes to several first-generation, sixteen-inch ET discs for airing, a procedure repeated for most of that season until the first Ampex machines arrived and tape was considered reliable enough for direct on-air use.

In the fall of 1947, although the news from Ampex in San Carlos was good—their new prototype worked perfectly and reliably and they were ready to go into mass production—the little company was in dire need of cash. Meanwhile, ABC executives were getting nervous about trusting their network to a few young California inventors and tried to get out of the tape deal, but the Hollywood entertainer reminded the New York executives of their 1946 contract with him: ABC was required to buy the best and latest recording technology to produce and broadcast Crosby's show, and tape recording was clearly superior to ET disc recording. ABC still balked, insisting the Scully ET recording lathes they were renting from NBC counted as the "latest recording technology." Bing and Everett Crosby strongly disagreed and pushed ABC to adopt tape as the network's new recording method.

Realizing the enormous potential of the new technology for both Crosby's radio and recording career, and as a business opportunity, the Crosbys helped convince ABC to accept tape and thus help launch it in the United States. Under the umbrella of Bing Crosby Enterprises (BCE), the show business entrepreneurs promised ABC that they would financially support Ampex and also become Ampex's main distributor, thus guaranteeing a successful outcome. Tiny WA Palmer Films was left out of the deal.

ABC agreed, and Crosby immediately sent Ampex a check by regular U.S. Mail—without so much as a cover letter—for $50,000. To Alex Poniatoff and his Ampex engineers, the unexpected money seemed to fall from heaven in their moment of financial desperation. The huge unsecured loan, which was equal to about $1 million today (an average technical job in California in 1947 paid around $2,500 a year, while today similar work nets about $50,000), enabled Ampex to buy the materials and hire the workers needed to build the production version of the Model 200A. In April 1948 the first two machines from the Ampex assembly line went to Mullin in Hollywood to record the *Philco* show. More recorders went to ABC's WLS Chicago affiliate to time-shift the program for the Eastern and Central time zones, while yet more Ampex machines went to New York and Hollywood to fill an instant demand for the incredible new recording technology. By April 1948, when Crosby and the networks took delivery of the first Ampex machines, Minnesota Mining and Manufacturing Company (3M) had introduced a line of perfected recording tapes, "Scotch No. 111" and "Scotch No. 112." Everyone—Mullin, Palmer, the Crosby organization, and ABC executives—breathed a sigh of relief when American made tape recorders and tape began to be delivered in volume.

The difference in quality between Crosby's disc based broadcasts of 1946–47 and the tape broadcasts of 1947–48 was startling. Crosby's Hooper ratings shot back up to where they had been when the show started on ABC in 1946, before the distorted ET sound quality had driven away listeners. As soon as the taped shows aired, the network was inundated by approving phone calls and letters from listeners around the country, demonstrating that the public did in fact notice technical quality. A new age dawned as producers and artists, including Burl Ives, Eddie Cantor, Bob Hope, and Jack Benny, realized the advantages of tape-edited and tape-delayed performances and joined the runaway technology bandwagon that Mullin, Palmer, Ampex, and Crosby had created. Crosby continued to broadcast regular weekly radio shows produced on tape until 1963, establishing an unparalleled radio career.

One immediate beneficiary of magnetic recording was Crosby's guitarist, Les Paul, who figured out how to use tape to improve his unique method of "sound-on-sound" that resulted in a kind of multilayered sonic effect and helped make stars of Les and his wife, Mary Ford, in the 1950s. Another beneficiary was Crosby himself, who was now liberated to take his radio show on the road, with forays to San Francisco, Spokane, Chicago, New York, and even Vancouver. Crosby told his recordist, Jack Mullin, that he liked San Francisco and Washington State audiences best.

As the Ampex distributor for all sales west of the Rocky Mountains—by 1949 the contract with Ampex had been amended so that East Coast sales were handled by a New York company—Bing Crosby Enterprises and its people became crusaders for the new tape technology in all aspects of life. Besides acting as Crosby's chief recordist and engineer, Mullin was his leading salesman. In 1949, along with a young tape enthusiast named Tommy Davis, who would later become an Ampex vice president, Mullin made historic sales trips to Point Mugu Naval Air Station and to Edwards Air Force Base, both in southern California, where he showed military personnel how to use tape to record radio telemetry and other flight data. In this way, Crosby Enterprises pioneered the instrumentation tape recording field that would become an indispensable part of America's aeronautical and space development programs. Airplanes, rockets, and spacecraft all transmitted telemetry—real-time data about a craft's technical performance and other flight information. Recording and replaying this data in non-real-time allowed engineers to re-fly missions over and over to analyze aircraft performance. Out of this technology pioneered by Mullin at Crosby Enterprises came the famous black box, used in most commercial aircraft to assess performance and determine the cause of crashes.

Instrumentation tape formed the basis of later forms of magnetic recording used in computers. From mainframes to today's PC and computer-based servers used in radio and TV broadcasting, most computers need magnetic tape and magnetic disc drives to function. Most of that technology was derived from, or at least inspired by, the early research that began with those first Crosby Enterprises instrumentation demonstrations using Ampex recorders.

In 1950 Mullin figured out how he could record video on magnetic tape, something that had been theorized but never seriously tried, and suggested that he could do for Crosby's budding TV career what he had done for the singer's radio career—put Crosby on tape. Mullin's video recorder used fixed, audio-type heads with tape moving at a high rate of speed to record the large bandwidth necessary for the television signal. Up to then, the only way to record the TV image was with film using the kinescope—or "kinney"—process, which produced pictures of poor quality. A videotape recorder (VTR) with quality as good as live, using editable and reusable tape had been the Holy Grail of the television industry since TV's introduction in America in 1946. Aided by a $100,000 investment from Crosby, Mullin set up the Electronics Division of Bing Crosby Enterprises to develop America's first videotape recorder.

With his assistant, Wayne Johnson, and a small team of engineers, Mullin quickly developed what became known as "Crosby Video," the world's first prototype of a working VTR and the precursor of today's videocassette recorder. Over the next six years the Crosby Video project overcame a number of difficult technical problems. All the while, Crosby continued to funnel money into his engineers' video experiments.

Mullin worked independently of his sales client, Ampex Corporation, though he made no secret of his video work. When Ampex managers heard about Crosby Video, they started their own VTR research and development department headed by Charles P. Ginsburg and a staff of one, a young engineer named Ray Dolby, later of Noise Reduction fame. Without the stimulus of Crosby Video, Ampex might not have begun its own successful video project, and Dolby Noise Reduction might never have happened.

Crosby and his technical team were disappointed when Ampex won the race and introduced the first practical, commercial VTR, the Ampex VR-1000, in April 1956. Rather than using the fixed video heads found on Crosby Video, which limited the machine's performance, the Ampex engineers employed spinning video heads that Crosby, RCA, and BBC engineers had rejected as impractical for a VTR. When Mullin informed Crosby that Ampex had beaten them, he was far from being crestfallen. The ever-optimistic Crosby asked his chief engineer what else the machine could be used for besides video. Jack told Crosby that the Crosby VTR would make an excellent data recorder. Crosby recouped some of his R&D money on the sale of several Crosby Video machines custom-built as instrumentation recorders. In the same year, 1956, Crosby sold his Electronics Division to 3M, which renamed the operation the Mincom Division of 3M. Mullin went to work for Mincom, where he continued his pioneering work in professional audio and data recording. Crosby's sale of his Electronics Division signaled the end of Crosby Enterprises' involvement in electronics research and development.

For the next two decades, right up to his death in 1977, Crosby appeared on television in a huge array of his own programs and specials as well as numerous guest spots—some recorded on magnetic tape, mostly using Ampex audio and video recorders! He also formed Bing Crosby Productions, which boasted popular TV hits such as *Ben Casey* and *Hogan's Heroes*, and a sitcom called *The Bing Crosby Show*. In 1981, he received a posthumous accolade from the Video Hall of Fame for being "an innovator in videotaping TV programs."

Bing Crosby Enterprises provided the basis for the rapid development in America of magnetic tape recording for audio, data, and video. Crosby's fantastic vision and progressive management style led to a sea change in world communications, just one facet of his amazing legacy. Crosby's other entrepreneurial pursuits, along with his contributions to the live performance arts and to the world of sports, revealed a man of extraordinary versatility, intellect, generosity, and talent, who magnificently enhanced life in the twentieth century.

15

The Bing Crosby Fan Clubs

F. B. (Wig) Wiggins

Bing Crosby was born in Tacoma, Washington, on May 3, 1903, and died in Madrid, Spain, on October 14, 1977. During the three decades since his death, fan clubs have played an indispensable role in working to preserve Crosby's incomparable musical legacy for the continued enjoyment of the general public around the world. Without their efforts, it is unlikely that his once widely popular recordings and films would have remained as well known as they are today.

Various Bing Crosby fan clubs have come and gone over the years, but two major organizations—one in the United States and one in Great Britain—have been at the forefront of endeavors to keep Crosby's memory alive during a period of dramatic change in popular music tastes and a sharp decline in the attention paid by the media to vocalists of the first half of the twentieth century, Bing Crosby included.

Even though Bing Crosby's once dominant position as a leading star on radio, in films, and on records has faded considerably since his death (except, of course, for the annual rediscovery of his talents during the Christmas holiday season), the activities and membership roles of his two leading fan clubs have continued to expand to the point that they are now even more influential than they were during Crosby's lifetime.

The original, officially approved Bing Crosby fan club was organized in the United States in 1936, some five years after he leapt to nationwide stardom via his radio programs on the Columbia Broadcasting System (CBS), his early series of musical films for Paramount Pictures, and his best-selling recordings for the Brunswick, and later Decca, record labels.

Named "Club Crosby," for sixty-seven years this American organization published a regular newsletter (later a semi-annual magazine) called *Bingang,* and attracted members from many different countries around the globe. Club Crosby has been recognized by Guinness World Records as the oldest continuously-active fan club in the world.

His foremost overseas fan club began in Great Britain in 1950 as the "British Bing Club," later renamed the "International Crosby Circle." This club also acquired members from many other countries, including the United States. It has long-issued a quarterly publication called *Bing* and has sponsored books on related subjects.

Both Club Crosby and the International Crosby Circle have attracted a growing membership in recent years, and significant numbers of these have been younger enthusiasts in their twenties, thirties, and forties—even a few teenagers—thus disproving the belief that remaining Crosby fans are only oldsters who still remember Bing from more than a half century ago.

As an active member of both the American and British clubs for more than thirty years myself, I was extremely pleased when I learned that Hofstra University was organizing an unprecedented academic conference about Bing Crosby's major influence on American (and international) popular culture that would take place in November 2002, just after the twenty-fifth anniversary of his death, and six months prior to celebrations of the centennial of his birth in May 2003.

I was even more pleased to be asked to become a member of the planning committee for the conference, and to advise Hofstra on themes and participants for the various events it would encompass. It was an honor to represent the Bing Crosby clubs in this manner.

Many fan club members came from all over the world to attend the highly successful Hofstra conference, and they enthusiastically concluded that it had provided an outstanding opportunity to spark greater general awareness of Bing Crosby's leading role in defining American entertainment throughout his remarkable fifty-year career.

After the conference, the American and British fan clubs merged under the combined name of the "International Club Crosby" in order to strengthen their ongoing efforts to further honor Bing Crosby as the preeminent popular entertainer of the twentieth century.

Our new joint magazine, also called *Bing,* is professionally printed and illustrated, with full-color covers, and it contains some sixty pages per issue. It is distributed quarterly (in April, August, and December) to more than a thousand worldwide members of the combined club. Articles include news of current and forthcoming activities involving Crosby, in-depth interviews with his fellow artists and other contemporaries, plus reviews of new books, CDs, videos, and DVDs featuring him.

The International Club Crosby also publishes and distributes books and other publications about major aspects of Crosby's career. Recent volumes have included comprehensive histories of his radio programs and television appearances, as well as several new biographical studies.

Individual club members also are active in promoting Bing Crosby in other ways, such as working with major entertainment companies in various countries to encourage the commercial release of his recordings and films, arranging and participating in public tributes and retrospective film showings across this country and abroad, as well as appearing on radio and television programs.

The International Club Crosby always welcomes new members. For further information, please contact me:

F. B. (Wig) Wiggins
American/Canadian Representative
International Club Crosby
5608 North 34th Street
Arlington, Virginia 22207

Conclusion: Bring Crosby—Architect of Twentieth-Century Style

Will Friedwald

Whenevcr the late Nat King Cole announced that he was going to sing his hit "Nature Boy," he had a standard introduction that he used at most every concert. He described it as a song that asked the big questions about life, such as "Why am I here? Where I am going? Where am I going to park?"

The future is a snap—it's the past that's impossible to explain. The crucial question that we're all asking in the new millennium is not necessarily "where are we going?" but rather, "how did we get here?" So many notions on so many subjects were completely altered during the last century on every topic from transportation to the role of government to Civil Rights, so the question of how we made the transition from there to here is not an easy one.

In the more than one hundred years since the birth of Bing Crosby in 1903, it seems that the sphere of human activity that has changed the most is communication. It might have been possible, a hundred years ago, to foresee that the thingamabobs that were then regarded as inventor's toys and occasional follies—the telegraph, the telephone, the phonograph, and the kinetoscope (movie camera to you and me)—could affect the way information was disseminated.

Jules Verne, H. G. Wells, or some other nineteenth-century science fiction writer might have been able to predict that there would be such a thing as mass communication—one person speaking out to many—the same way that one might have predicted that by 1975 everyone would have one's own private autogyro. What no one could have anticipated was how the new technology would have such a profound effect on the content of the messages it was more than merely transmitting.

Everything from how we communicate with those we love to how we do business and how we elect a president has been affected by the media. For instance, the cinema popularized the concept of young and beautiful faces. One hundred fifty years ago, an aging star like Sarah Bernhardt could play Juliet long into her sixties because few folks in the audience sat close enough to count the wrinkles beneath the greasepaint. (In ancient Greece, the actors wore masks, and as late as the nineteenth century the casting of roles didn't even have to be gender- or race-specific.) The modern newspaper made whole new kinds of writing possible—not just the telegraphic journalism of Walter Winchell and his assorted ghosts, but such great prose stylists as Ring Lardner and Damon Runyon. An immediate, stylistic approach to communication grew out of the tabloids and led to the dramatic works of Ben Hecht and Charles MacArthur, among many others. New wrinkles in the development of building materials made the innovations of Frank Lloyd Wright possible.

No less an architect than Wright, Bing Crosby is one of the great innovators of twentieth-century style. Crosby forever changed the way we hear the human voice, and he was the first great musician to develop a performance style largely in response to technology—specifically the advent of electrical recording in the 1920s. It was the microphone that made modern mass media possible—recordings, talking pictures, and broadcasting—and Crosby was the first to fully fathom its implications. The larger-than-life personalities that dominated Broadway theater and the vaudeville stage clearly had no place in this new, intimate art form, and neither did the high shrill voices heard on cylinders and early disc records in the teens. Bing popularized the deep, rich tones that people came to love so much.

And, like Wright, Runyan, and the others, while there might have been a technological imperative at the root of Crosby's innovations, his artistry and the impact he had on world culture was ultimately more driven by emotion than electronics. It wasn't just the sound of his voice and the way it was transmitted through the vacuum tube that made Crosby a twentieth-century legend, it was the heart behind the voice. More than being able to convey a beautifully dark, romantic baritone, Crosby was among the earliest to realize that the microphone made it possible to achieve a much more profound connection with his audience.

Along with the deep voice came a casualness, a relaxed approach that was part cultivated, part natural, and all Crosby, which may have been the biggest factor in how Crosby achieved credibility with his listeners. This was reflected in, among other things, a heightened sensitivity towards the lyrics of a song. Crosby was the first to take the "mass" out of mass media and bring a sense of intimacy to coast-to-coast communication. That is, he had the ability to make his singing personal to a mass audience—to make listeners at home forget that they were part of an advertiser's demographic so they could concentrate on the most direct contact imaginable between singer and listener. Crosby re-transformed the audience from a collective, a mob, back into individuals.

Crosby was greatly aided in his achievements by two genres that were developing, independent of each other, at least a decade before the microphone came into use in the music industry—modern popular song and jazz. Jerome Kern's 1912 song "She Didn't Believe Me" is often described as the first modern pop song; for whatever reason, the music industry would not produce the first modern popular singer until Crosby's first flowering nearly twenty years after that. Jazz first became a national craze a few years later during World War I, thanks to its initial exposure on recordings. Tin Pan Alley gave Crosby the raw material and Dixieland provided him with the raw inspiration. In putting the two together, Crosby invented the art form retrospectively referred to as American popular singing.

Crosby was the first to work out the entire equation, to see how all these elements could be brought together. Professor Lewis Porter of Rutgers may be the first scholar to actually divine the meaning of the word "jazz."[1] Although it later became associated with sex and music, it's been documented that as early as 1912, Americans were using the term "jazz" as a slang word for "energy." At that time, it was common to say that when you intended to make something more interesting, more exciting, you were going to "jazz it up." That was a well-known colloquialism long before jazz as a musical form was born in New Orleans. When the teenaged Bing Crosby described his first experience watching the great Al Jolson, he was very specific: he didn't use the term emotion, he didn't use the term excitement, the word he used was "electricity." As Crosby put it, "no man in my memory could generate such electricity in the theatre." By Crosby's maturity, the word jazz was used to describe a kind of music, but in the art of Bing Crosby it still meant energy and electricity.

Crosby completed the equation by bringing the twin-headed hydra of jazz and electricity to American popular music. We often talk about the dehumanizing effect of technology, as in some kind of Alvin Toffler book, but the truth is, electrical sound transmission has served to bring people together, to make communication (be it musical or otherwise) more intimate, more up close and personal, and the architect of all that was the man whom we honor, Bing Crosby.

Note

1. Lewis Porter, *Jazz: A Century of Change* (Belmont, CA: Wadsworth Press, 1997).

PERSONAL COMMENTS

Sing, Bing, Sing

Kathryn Crosby

Dr. M. W. Sullivan, my Trustee, wrote *Sing, Bing, Sing* in a reading text in the 1960s. That was the first phrase in easy reading. Bing is the first name in easy singing.

He has left a legacy of joyous music. The poets of song, Burke, Mercer, Robin, Porter, Cahn, Hart, Hammerstein, Berlin, wove their magic with his tones, his inflections.

Like the troubadours of old, he shared our sorrows, comforted us in our losses. He stirred us to patriotic action in times of national crisis. He reflected our dreams—and he made us laugh.

Perhaps he put it best when he sang:

> It's been a joy, I can't deny, though some may think
> I took things lightly.
> But man and boy, I looked on high
> And never failed to thank Him nightly.
> When I look back, I can't forget
> The friends I've met
> And the things they've done.
> I thank them all;
> It's been great fun.
> As for me, I have no doubt:
> That's what life is all about.

SING, BING, SING.

Thoughts on Relationships:
Father, Son, Grandson

Steven Crosby

Having a grandfather by the name of Bing Crosby was, to say the least, very interesting. Everyone hears of stories of individuals who have a famous father or mother or some distant relative, and of the benefits and some burdens that accompany fame. In my situation, being somewhat removed as a grandson, the relationship was far simpler and more straightforward. In other words, it was the fairly typical grandfatherly relationship, the normal give and take that anyone might expect.

On the other hand, my father, Gary Crosby—an actor, singer, entertainer—had a very different relationship with this father, Bing Crosby, one that spanned the many emotions, from love to anger. In some ways, it might be said to be typical of a strong father and a strong-willed son. A closer look may provide some insight into the question that has always been raised when speaking about Bing Crosby: "Was he a mean father?"

As we all know, my dad wrote a book, *Going My Own Way*, about himself and *his* father. If we read the book without thinking about typical parental relationships—especially those involving fathers and sons, and particularly the oldest male child—we might conclude that father and son disliked one another intensely. But the truth is that there was a mutual respect between the two men, although their interactions were often difficult and trying.

My dad grew up at a time—the 1930s, 1940s, and early 1950s—when men's emotions were not expressed, but rather were expected to be buried. A man showed emotion by fighting, not by talking; it was a world far different from ours today. At the same time, my dad, like most of us, had his own personal demons; his were manifested in the form of alcoholism. And while he stopped drinking in the early 1960s, it took him many years to comprehend and to acknowledge all of the "stuff" he had inside him. Some of that was parent-related. Remember, Bing's first wife, Dixie, died when my dad was just eighteen years old. The pain of watching a parent die must affect the feelings of the child. Further, the enormity of the name "Bing Crosby" played a part in my father's trying to find his own place in society, and the entertainment industry played another role, creating pressures that were not expressed openly and leading to many unresolved issues between father and son.

The book my dad wrote was cathartic for him in many ways, but it should be remembered that it was written from the point of view of one man, from his perspective, experience, and a particular moment in his history. We cannot forget that as we look at the reasons for his writing the book—here was a genuine opportunity for him to articulate feelings, better understand himself, and think about the consequences of his actions. I do know that many people questioned the intent of the book, but there is always some truth in one's writings. It again comes down to the personal perception and experience of those involved with one another. In cases of family memories, why does each person in a family remember an event differently from the other family members? The answer probably lies in the perspective from where one views or experiences the events described.

From my perspective, my grandfather treated me with respect, encouragement, and love. A good example of his affection for me occurred during my senior year at the University of Santa Clara. I was approached by the university to find out if my grandfather would perform at a fundraiser for the university as part of an annual show—the "Golden Circle" dinner party. Performers in previous years included Frank Sinatra, Bob Hope, and Andy Williams. I was a bit nervous about asking my granddad—and it was at that moment that I truly realized the enormity and importance of this man—because with one positive response, he could raise $250,000 for my school. I called him on the telephone and asked if I could drive up to his home in Hillsborough, just south of San Francisco, and speak with him. He said, "Sure."

When I arrived, his ever-present and quite entertaining butler, Alan Fisher, answered the door and brought me to the study where my grandfather was seated. He said, "What can I do for you?" I took a deep breath and asked the question: "Would you do me a favor and perform for a large fundraising event for my university?" He looked at me and smiled ever so slightly and said, "Sure—when is it?" With that statement, I felt a cool breeze come across my body and the uneasiness left. I later found out that he was happy to do it, was proud of me for going to college, and further pleased that I was on my way to law school the following year.

As anyone might guess, the performance at the university was superb. The entire family was present on stage, along with Rosemary Clooney singing and Joey Bushkin playing the piano. The audience loved it, the university was very grateful, and there was one extremely happy college senior sitting in the audience beaming brightly.

It is clear that the relationships I've described, both my father's and grandfather's with me, and mine with each of them, were separate and distinct. I learned a great deal from them about the importance of listening and of understanding and of valuing humility; they both taught me many lessons, each in his own style and manner. I have much to be thankful for from both of these very important men—both with public personas—but one clearly cast a long shadow over all others. In other words, I am a very lucky man.

The Real Bing Crosby

Ken Barnes

If one were to examine the various books and articles that have been written about Bing Crosby since his death in 1977, most of them—with just two or three notable exceptions—have failed to completely reflect the real man and the true nature of his talent and accomplishments.

In his heyday of the 1930s, 1940s, and 1950s (and even well into the 1960s), he was easily the best-loved and most respected entertainer in the world. So great were his fame and success that even today no artist can begin to rival his accomplishments.

In a radio career spanning more than twenty-five years, he was number one for eighteen of those years.

As a screen actor, he was the world's number one box office star for five straight years (1944 to 1949) and, as a recording artist, notched up a staggering total of 368 chart entries including thirty-eight number one hits. There's little point in comparing him with Elvis Presley, The Beatles, Michael Jackson, or even Frank Sinatra because none of them even comes close to Crosby.

These are the facts and, without even mentioning his twenty-nine-year career as a TV performer, Bing's place in entertainment history is secure and unassailable. Why, then, is he regarded by the media as something of a forgotten man? I think the answer lies in the man he was. Behind his unparalleled success, Bing Crosby was a genuinely modest man and was anything but a self-promoter. As he approached maturity, he did nothing to hide the fact that he was no longer playing romantic leads. He was content to let the public think of him as an easy-going avuncular pipe-and-slippers suburbanite. He was, in fact, happy that he no longer needed to compete with his contemporaries or with "newer fellas" like Sinatra.

The media, and especially the pop world, have short memories. Today's artists play by a whole new book of rules ("You're only as good as your last hit") and to the new show-biz commentators, nostalgia is last Tuesday. How could a great artist who died thirty years ago possibly have any meaning for them? But even this isn't the whole case. Elvis Presley died thirty years ago—yet he is still talked about as though his talent and achievements were greater than Crosby's, which is not true. Let us suppose that Elvis—who died a bloated, burned-out wreck at just forty-two—had somehow managed to linger on until he was sixty or sixty-five, and not getting any prettier in the process. Would he still be idolized today? The answer is no. Well, at least, not to the same extent. Today's Presley is the result of a carefully maintained and diligently executed commercial exercise. As a personality, Presley was a grandstander in every sense of the word. With his outlandish attire and vocal eccentricities, he craved attention with his every move.

Bing was never like that. Consequently he is not regarded as particularly important. But as a singer and as a person he had taste, he had class, and he had the kind of intelligence that is not common among pop singers. How do I know this? I had the great privilege of working with him for three years on records, TV, and radio. When the opportunity arose in the summer of 1974 to produce an album with him, I grabbed it with both hands. For an English-born producer—who had grown up with Crosby's films and records—it was a chance not to be missed. As I flew up to San Francisco for my first meeting with him at his home, I was thinking of certain people—mainly journalists—who told me I would be disappointed when I met him. "He's not as nice as his image suggests," said one person who, I later discovered, had never met him.

Naturally, I paid no attention because my curiosity to find out for myself was greater than my interest in half-baked, second-hand opinions. Still, I couldn't help wondering. Would he be the casual blue-eyed charmer who had made over fifty films? Or would he be—as another person described him—"a cold and cantankerous curmudgeon?"

Well, in all honesty, I have to tell you that he was very much the Bing Crosby I had hoped to find—friendly, easygoing, and cooperative. At that first meeting—September 9, 1974—he impressed me as being a normal and communicative person and not at all star-like in his demeanor. The fact that he was not wearing his familiar hairpiece only added to this impression. While he made me feel welcome, I should add that he was a little more subdued than his generally outgoing screen persona. But this was understandable. After all, I was talking to the *real* Bing Crosby, not a scriptwriter's concoction and certainly not a journalist's manipulative creation.

His height was pretty much what I expected—about five feet eight (although it had been publicized as five feet ten or even five-eleven). I was surprised to see how much weight he had lost since his recent operation in which he'd had part of a lung removed. Yet in spite of this there was something decidedly robust about him that came mainly from his voice—rich, round, and strong, belying the effects of that operation. In fact, the voice was the most reassuring thing about him. Even in speech it always seemed to be lingering on the edge of melody. There was something eloquent in his choice of words and phrases, something rhythmic about his conversational delivery, as he seemed to blow out certain words like unburst bubbles in that endearing manner that belonged to him alone.

I spent about an hour with him at that first meeting. During that time he would occasionally look me up and down as though saying to himself, "Do I really want to work with this limey?" But this was only momentary and may have been just my imagination because the more we talked about music and songs the more genial he became.

We undertook to make one initial album for United Artists to be recorded partly in Los Angeles and partly in London. The first session took place in Hollywood in October of that year—two duets with his old friend, Johnny Mercer. It was a happy session and Bing—who was clearly delighted with Pete Moore as musical director—asked me if would care to extend the deal to two albums. Would I? The record company swiftly agreed and plans were made to choose and "routine" a further twelve songs for Bing to record in London the following February. The first time out we scored a hit single and a hit album "That's What Life Is All About."

As it turned out we eventually made a total of six albums—including his 50th Anniversary Concert at the London Palladium and a splendid duet album with the equally legendary Fred Astaire.

All of the recordings enjoyed international success, and the three years I spent in association with Bing were among the happiest of my career. Then in March 1977, he suffered a serious accident. While playing a concert in Pasadena, he was taking bows into a bright spotlight that obscured his view of the floor around him. He stepped backwards and fell some twenty-five feet, crushing a disc in his back.

His plans to play the London Palladium again later that year seemed dashed. He had also planned to make another album in London. That too seemed unlikely. But somehow in the ensuing months, he forced himself onto the road to recovery. As soon as he was able to stand, he took long walks each day and eventually resumed playing golf. The doctors, however, warned him not to play more than nine holes. Soon it became apparent that he would be coming to London. Apart from discussing the album and the Palladium, he made plans to shoot his Christmas show in London as well as record a duet album with Bob Hope. In the summer of 1977, all of these things he achieved—except one, the album with Hope.

He recorded his last commercial sessions in London on the mornings of September 12, 13, and 14. And while he looked frail—and was clearly in pain with his back still bothering him—he sang superbly. If anything, the voice was richer and stronger than on his previous albums. We talked about songs and routines regarding the duet album. He said Bob Hope was looking forward to it quite eagerly. "There's a lot of ham in that boy," he added. "But he's got a very good ear. So we should have some fun."

We also discussed two other future albums—one a project that would reunite him with jazz violin virtuoso, Joe Venuti. "We'll need a good guitar player on that one," said Bing, obviously harking back to the early days of Venuti and Eddie Lang. "How about Les Paul?" I asked. "Now you're talking," he smiled. There was also a proposed collection called "The Sporting Life," which would reflect Bing's love of golf ("Straight Down the Middle"), fishing ("Gone Fishin'"), and the race-track. For the latter, he mentioned doing a new version of Frank Loesser's "Fugue For Tinhorns," which he previously made with Sinatra and Dean Martin. "This time," he told me, "I'd like to take a whack at singing all three parts."

In the last month of his life, I met with him several times and I never saw an artist work harder: the TV special, the album, ten days at the Palladium, a final concert in Brighton on October 10th, and a final radio recording for the BBC on the morning of October 11th and a final photo session for the album cover in the afternoon. I had spent most of that day with him and dropped him off at the Dorchester, where he had a 3:00 pm business meeting. As we parted, he said "I'm going to Spain for a few days to play a little golf. I'll see you guys in California in about ten days, I guess, or two weeks."

He shook my hand warmly and we said goodbye. That was the last time I saw him.

Three days later, his sudden death on a Spanish golf course was headline news around the world. He was seventy-four. His death received greater coverage than that of Elvis Presley, who had passed away two months earlier. He was the only American entertainer to receive a memorial service in London's Westminster Cathedral—attended by two thousand people.

In the years since his death, a number of books and articles have sought to destroy the character of the real man. The most damaging was the one allegedly written by his eldest son, Gary Crosby—depicting him as a cold disciplinarian and child-beater. Much of this has since been factually refuted. But the damage that this book did is probably irreparable. People always like to believe the worst of a person—especially someone as famous as Bing Crosby.

I count myself fortunate to have known and worked with the real Bing Crosby and I can only report that, in my experience, he was as fine a man as anyone could wish to meet. Oh sure, he probably had some dark corners in his life and there must have been times when he made wrong decisions. But that's true of everybody. The point is that he carried his fame with dignity and class. And, oh, yes, he was a damn good singer to boot.

Selected Bibliography

Books

Adamson, Joe. *Bugs Bunny: Fifty Years and Only One Grey Hare*. New York: Henry Holt, 1991.
———. *Tex Avery: the King of the Cartoons*. New York: Popular Library, 1975.
———. *The Walter Lantz Story*. New York: St. Martin's Press, 1989.
Adler, Bill. *Fred Astaire: A Wonderful Life*. New York: Carroll & Graf Publishers, Inc., 1987.
Agee, James. *Agee on Film: Criticism & Comment on the Movies*. New York: Modern Library, 2000.
Ahlstrom, Sydney E. *A Religious History of the American People*. New Haven, CT: Yale University Press, 1972.
Albanese, Catherine L. *America: Religions and Religion*. 3rd ed. Belmont, CA: Wadsworth Publishing Company, 1999.
Amburn, Ellis. *Dark Star: The Roy Orbison Story*. New York: Carol Publishing Group, 1990.
Anderson, Karen. *Wartime Women: Sex Roles, Family Relations, and the Status of Women During World War II*. Westport, CT: Greenwood Press, 1994.
Aristotle, *The Nicomachean Ethics*. Translated by W. D. Ross. Oxford: Oxford University Press, 1984.
Astaire, Fred. *Steps in Time*. London: William Heinemann, 1960.
Atkinson, Gord. *Gord Atkinson's Showbill*. Ontario, Canada: Creative Bound, 1996.
Bach, Bob, and Ginger Mercer. *Our Huckleberry Friend: The Life, Times & Lyrics of Johnny Mercer*. Secaucus, NJ: Lyle Stuart, 1982.
Baker, Russell. *There's a Country in My Cellar*. New York: Morrow, 1990.
Balio, Tino. *Hollywood as a Modern Business Enterprise (1930–1939)*. Berkeley, CA: University of California Press, 1995.
Barnes, Ken. *The Crosby Years*. New York: St. Martin's Press, 1980.

Barrier, Mike. *Hollywood Cartoons*. London: Oxford University Press, 1999.

Barrios, Richard. *A Song in the Dark: The Birth of Musical Film*. New York: Oxford University Press, 1995.

Bauer, Barbara. *Bing Crosby*. New York: Pyramid Books, 1977.

Beatles Anthology, The. San Francisco: Chronicle Books, 2000.

Beck, Jerry, and Will Friedwald. *Looney Tunes and Merrie Melodies: A Complete Illustrated Guide to the Warner Bros. Cartoons*. New York: Henry Holt, 1989.

Bendazzi, Giannalberto. *Cartoons: One Hundred Years of Cinema Animation*. Bloomington, IN: Indiana University Press, 1994.

Bergreen, Laurence. *As Thousands Cheer: The Life of Irving Berlin*. New York: Viking, 1990.

Black, Gregory D. *Hollywood Censored: Morality Codes, Catholics, and the Movies*. New York: Cambridge University Press, 1994.

————. *The Catholic Crusade Against the Movies, 1940–1975*. New York: Cambridge University Press, 1997.

Blanc, Mel. *That's Not All Folks!* New York: Warner Books, 1989.

Bloom, Harold. *The Anxiety of Influence*. New York: Oxford University Press, 1973.

Bookbinder, Robert. *The Films of Bing Crosby*. Secaucus, NJ: Citadel Press, 1977.

Boskin, Joseph. *Sambo: the Rise and Demise of an American Jester*. New York: Oxford University Press, 1986.

Brasch, Walter. *Cartoon Monickers*. Bowling Green: Bowling Green University Popular Press, 1983.

Brodkin, Karen. *How Jews Became White Folks, and What That Says about Race in America*. New Brunswick, NJ: Rutgers University Press, 1999.

Brooks, Peter. *The Melodramatic Imagination*. New Haven, CT: Yale University Press, 1976.

Burch, Noel. *Life to Those Shadows*. Translated and edited by Ben Brewster. Berkeley, CA: University of California Press, 1990.

Burke, Johnny, and Jimmy Van Heusen. *Going My Way*. 1944. Copyright Bourne Music, New York, all rights reserved.

Butler, Frank, Frank Cavett and Leo McCarey, screenwriters. *Going My Way*. 1944.

Butler, Joseph. *Fifteen Sermons Preached at the Rolls Chapel*. London: Knapton, 1726.

————. *The Analogy of Religion, Natural and Revealed, to the Constitution and Course of Nature*. London: Knapton, 1736.

Cabarga, Leslie. *The Fleischer Story*. New York: Nostalgia Press, 1977.

Cagney, James. *Cagney by Cagney*. Garden City, NY: Doubleday, 1976.

Canemaker, John. *Felix: The Twisted Tale of the World's Most Famous Cat*. New York: Pantheon Books, 1991.

Catherine of Siena. *Catherine of Siena: The Dialogue*. Translated by Suzanne Noffke. Mahwah, NJ: Paulist Press, 1980.

Cawley, John, and Jim Korkis. *The Encyclopedia of Cartoon Superstars*. Las Vegas: Pioneer Books, 1990.

Climacus, John. *The Ladder of Divine Ascent*. Translated by Colm Luibheid and Norman Russell. Mahwah, NJ: Paulist Press, 1982.

Cohan, Steve. "'Feminizing' the Song-and-Dance Man: Fred Astaire and the Spectacle of Masculinity in the Hollywood Musical." In *Screening the Male: Exploring Masculinities in Hollywood Cinema*, edited by Steve Cohan and Ina Rae Hark. London: Routledge, 1993.

Coleman, Ray. *Lennon*. New York: McGraw-Hill Company, 1984.

————. *McCartney: Yesterday . . . and Today*. Los Angeles: Dove Books, 1997.

Couffer, Jack. *Bat Bomb: World War II's Other Secret Weapon*. Austin, TX: University of Texas Press, 1992.

Crafton, Donald. *Before Mickey*. Cambridge, MA: MIT Press, 1982.

————— . "The View from Termite Terrace: Caricature and Parody in Warner Bros. Animation." In *Reading the Rabbit: Explorations in Warner Bros. Animation*, edited by Kevin S. Sandler. New Brunswick, NJ: Rutgers University Press, 1998.

Crosby, Bing, and Pete Martin. *Call Me Lucky*. New York: Simon & Schuster, 1953.

Crosby, Gary, and Ross Firestone. *Going My Own Way*. Garden City, NJ: Doubleday, 1983.

Crosby, Ted. *The Story of Bing Crosby*. Cleveland, OH: World Publishing, 1946.

Culhane, Shamus. *Talking Animals and Other People*. New York: St. Martin's Press, 1986.

Davis, Kenneth C. *Don't Know Much About History*. New York: Perennial, 2001.

De Cordova, Richard. *Picture Personalities: The Emergence of the Star System in America*. Urbana, IL: University of Illinois Press, 1990.

Delamater, Jerome. *Dance in the Hollywood Musical*. Ann Arbor, MI: UMI Research Press, 1981.

DeLong, Thomas A. *The Mighty Music Box*. Los Angeles: Amber Crest Books, Inc., 1980.

Dick, Bernard F. *Engulfed: The Death of Paramount Pictures and the Birth of Corporate Hollywood*. Lexington: University Press of Kentucky, 2002.

Dodge, Consuelo. *The Everly Brothers: Ladies Love Outlaws*. Starke, FL: CIN-DAV, Inc., 1991.

Dolan, Jay. *The Immigrant Church: New York's Irish and German Catholics, 1815–1865*. Notre Dame, IN: University of Notre Dame Press, 1983.

Dostoevsky, Fyodor. *The Eternal Husband and Other Stories*. New York: Bantam Books, 1997.

Dyer, Richard. "A Star is Born and the Construction of Authenticity." In *Stardom: Industry of Desire*, edited by Christine Gledhill. London: Routlege, 1990.

Eberly, Philip K. *Music in the Air: America's Changing Tastes in Popular Music, 1920–1980*. New York: Hastings House Publishers, 1982.

Eliot, T. S. "Tradition and the Individual Talent." In *Selected Essays, 1917–1932*. New York: Harcourt, 1950.

Ellis, John Tracy. *American Catholicism*. 2nd ed. Chicago: University of Chicago Press, 1969.

Everett, Walter. *The Beatles as Musicians: Revolver Through Anthology*. New York: Oxford University Press, 1999.

Ewen, David. *American Songwriters*. New York: The H. H. Wilson Company, 1987.

Finch, Christopher. *The Art of Walt Disney*. New York: Harry Abrams, 1973.

Finke, Roger, and Rodney Stark. *The Churching of America, 1776–1990: Winners and Losers in Our Religious Economy*. New Brunswick, NJ: Rutgers University Press, 1992.

Friedwald, Will. *Jazz Singing: America's Great Voices from Bessie Smith to Bebop and Beyond*. New York: Da Capo, 1996.

Froehle, Bryan T., and Mary L. Gautier. *Catholicism 2000: A Portrait of the Catholic Church in the United States*. Maryknoll, NY: Orbis Books, 2000.

Furia, Philip. *Irving Berlin: A Life in Song*. New York: Schirmer Books, 1998.

Gabler, Neal. *An Empire of Their Own: How the Jews Invented Hollywood*. New York: Doubleday, 1988.

Giddins, Gary. *Bing Crosby: A Pocketful of Dreams, The Early Years, 1903–1940*. Boston: Little, Brown and Company, 2001.

Giles, Sara. *Fred Astaire. His Friends Talk*. New York: Doubleday, 1988.

Gillman, Peter, and Leni Gillman. *Alias David Bowie: A Biography*. New York: Henry Holt, 1986.

Gilmore, Mikal. "Dylan at a Crossroads Once Again." In *The Bob Dylan Companion: Four Decades of Commentary*, edited by Carl Benson. New York: Schirmer Books, 1998.

Glancy, H. Mark. "Dreaming of Christmas: Hollywood and the Second World War." In *Christmas at the Movies: Images of Christmas in American, British and European Cinema*, edited by Mark Connelly. New York: I. B. Tauris, 2000.

Gluck, Shema Berger. *Rosie the Riveter Revisited: Women, the War, and Social Change*. Boston: Twayne Publishers, 1987.

Goldman, Herbert G. *Jolson: The Legend Comes to Life*. New York: Oxford University Press, 1988.

———. *Banjo Eyes: Eddie Cantor and the Birth of Modern Stardom*. New York: Oxford University Press, 1997.

Grant, John. *Encyclopedia of Walt Disney's Animated Characters*. New York: Disney Press, 1993.

Guralnick, Peter. *Last Train to Memphis*. Boston: Little, Brown and Company, 1994.

Hammond, Phillip E. *Religion and Personal Autonomy: The Third Disestablishment in America*. Columbia, SC: University of South Carolina Press, 1992.

Handy, Robert T. *A Christian America: Protestant Hopes and Historical Realities*. 2nd ed. New York: Oxford University Press, 1984.

———. *Undermined Establishment: Church-State Relations in America, 1880–1920*. Princeton, NJ: Princeton University Press, 1991.

Head, Sydney W., and Christopher H. Sterling. *Broadcasting in America*. Boston: Houghton Mifflin Co., 1991.

Herberg, Will. *Protestant—Catholic—Jew: An Essay in American Religious Sociology*, Garden City, NY: Anchor Books, 1960.

Holliss, Richard, and Brian Sibley. *Walt Disney's Snow White and the Seven Dwarfs & the Making of the Classic Film*. New York: Simon & Schuster, 1987.

Inge, M. Thomas. "Washington Irving's Agrarian Fable." In *Perspectives on American Culture*. West Cornwall, CT: Locust Hill Press, 1994.

Irving, Washington. "The Legend of Sleepy Hollow." In *History, Tales and Sketches*. New York: Library of America, 1983.

Izod, John. *Hollywood and the Box Office, 1895–1986*. New York: Columbia University Press, 1988.

Jablonski, Edward. *Harold Arlen: Rhythm, Rainbow and Blues*. Boston: Northeastern University Press, 1996.

———. *Irving Berlin: American Troubadour*. New York: Henry Holt and Company, 1999.

James, William. *The Varieties of Religious Experience*. London: Longmans, 1902.

John of the Cross. *The Complete Works of Saint John of the Cross*. Translated by E. Allison Peers. 3 vols. Wheathampstead: Anthony Clarke, 1974.

Jones, Chuck. *Chuck Amuck*. New York: Farrar, Strauss, and Giroux, 1989.

Karlin, Fred. *Listening to the Movies: The Film Lover's Guide to Film Music*. New York: Schirmer Books, 1994.

Karpp, Phyllis. *Ike's Boys: The Story of the Everly Brothers*. Ann Arbor, MI: Popular Culture, 1988.

Kempis, Thomas A. *Imitation of Christ*. Translated by Richard Whitford and Harold C. Gardiner. New York: Doubleday, 1955.

Keyser, Les, and Barbara Keyser. *Hollywood and the Catholic Church: The Image of Roman Catholicism in American Movies*. Chicago: Loyola University Press, 1984.

King, Barry. "Articulating Stardom." In *Star Texts: Image and Performance*, edited by Jeremy G. Butler. Detroit: Wayne State University Press, 1991.

Klein, Norman. *Seven Minutes: The Life and Death of the American Animated Cartoon*. New York: Verso, 1993.

Lawrence, John Shelton, and Robert Jewett. *The Myth of the American Superhero*. Grand Rapids, MI: William B. Eerdmans, 2002.

Lenburg, Jeff. *The Encyclopedia of Animated Cartoons*. New York: Facts on File, 1999.

Lott, Eric. *Love and Theft: Blackface Minstrelsy and the American Working Class*. New York: Oxford University Press, 1993.

Macfarlane, Malcolm. *Bing Crosby: A Diary of a Lifetime*. Leeds, UK: International Crosby Circle, 1998.

————. *Bing Crosby Day by Day*. Lanham, MD: Scarecrow Press, 2001.

Mahar, William J. *Behind the Burnt Cork Mask: Early Blackface Minstrelsy & Antebellum American Popular Culture*. Urbana, IL: University of Illinois Press, 1999.

Maltin, Leonard. *The Disney Films*. New York: Crown Books, 1973.

————. *Of Mice and Magic*. New York: New American Library, 1980.

Marshall, J. D. *Blueprint on Babylon*. Phoenix, AZ: Phoenix House 1978.

Marty, Martin E. *Modern American Religion, v. ii: The Noise of Conflict, 1919–1941*. Chicago: The University of Chicago Press, 1991.

————. *A Short History of American Catholicism*. Allen, TX: Thomas More, 1995.

Mazur, Eric Michael. *The Americanization of Religious Minorities: Confronting the Constitutional Order*. Baltimore: Johns Hopkins University Press, 1999.

McDonald, Paul. *The Star System: Hollywood's Production of Popular Identities*. London: Wallflower, 2000.

Merritt, Russell and J. B. Kaufmann. *Walt in Wonderland*. Baltimore: Johns Hopkins University Press, 1994.

Miles, Margaret R. *Seeing and Believing: Religion and Values in the Movies*. Boston: Beacon Press, 1996.

Miller, James. *Flowers in the Dustbin: The Rise of Rock and Roll, 1947–1977*. New York: Simon and Schuster, 1999.

Moore, R. Laurence. *Religious Outsiders and the Making of Americans*. New York: Oxford University Press, 1986.

Morella, Joseph, and Edward J. Epstein, and Eleanor Clark. The *Amazing Career of Bob Hope*. Carlstadt, NJ: Rainbow Books, 1973.

Mueller, John. *Astaire Dancing: The Musical Films*. New York: Alfred A. Knopf, 1985.

Murray, William. *Del Mar: Its Life and Good Times*. Del Mar, CA: Del Mar Thoroughbred Club, 1988.

Nathan, Hans. *Behind the Burnt Cork Mask: Early Blackface Minstrelsy & Antebellum American Popular Culture*. Norman, OK: University of Oklahoma Press, 1962.

Neale, Steve. "Masculinity as Spectacle: Reflections on Men and Mainstream Cinema." In *Screening the Male: Exploring Masculinities in Hollywood Cinema*, edited by Steve Cohan and Ina Rae Hark. London: Routledge, 1993. Originally published in *Screen*, 24, 6, 1983.

New Grove Dictionary of American Music, The. London: MacMillan Press, 1980.

Osterholm, J. Roger. *Bing Crosby: A Bio-Bibliography*. Westport, CT: Greenwood Press, 1994.

Paramount Press Books. 1933–34; 1943–44. Special Collections, Fairbanks Center for Motion Picture Study. Los Angeles.

Paskman, Dailey and Sigmund Spaeth. *Gentlemen Be Seated: A Parade of Old-Time Minstrels*. New York: New American Library, 1977.

Peary, Gerald and Danny Peary. The *American Animated Cartoon*. New York: E. P. Dutton, 1980.

Porter, Cole. "I Love You Samantha." Copyright 1956 Cole Porter. Copyright renewed, assigned to Robert H. Montgomery, Jr. Trustee of the Cole Porter Musical & Literary Property Trusts. Chappell & Co. owner of publication and allied rights throughout the world. All rights reserved. Warner Bros. Publication U.S. Inc., Miami, FL 33014.

————. "True Love." Copyright 1956 Cole Porter. Copyright renewed, assigned to Robert H. Montgomery, Jr. Trustee of the Cole Porter Musical & LiteraryProperty Trusts. Chappell & Co. owner of publication and allied rights throughout the world. All rights reserved. Warner Bros. Publication U.S. Inc., Miami, FL 33014.

Porter, Lewis. *Jazz: A Century of Change*. Belmont, CA: Wadsworth Press, 1997.

Pourade, Richard F. "Water—The Real Key to a City's Survival." In *The History of San Diego: City of the Dream*. La Jolla, CA: Copley Books, 1977.

Ray, Robert B. "Tracking." In *Present Tense: Rock and Roll and Culture*, edited by Anthony DeCurtis. Durham, NC: Duke University Press, 1992.

Riley, Tim. *Hard Rain: A Dylan Commentary*. New York: DaCapo Press, 1999.

Rogin, Michael. *Blackface, White Noise*. Berkeley, CA: University of California Press, 1996.

Roof, Wade Clark. *A Generation of Seekers: The Spiritual Journeys of the Baby Boom Generation*. San Francisco: Harper San Francisco, 1993.

Rosen, Jody. *White Christmas: The Story of an American Song*. New York: Scribner, 2002.

Sampson, Henry T. *That's Enough Folks!: Black Images in Animated Cartoons 1900–1960*. Latham, MD: Scarecrow Press, 1998.

Samuel, Lawrence R. *Pledging Allegiance: American Identity and the Bond Drive of World War II*. Washington, DC: Smithsonian Institution Press, 1997.

Schickel, Richard. *The Disney Version*. New York: Simon and Schuster, 1968.

Schneider, Steve. *That's All Folks: The Art of Warner Bros. Animation*. New York: Henry Holt, 1988.

Schofield, Mary Anne. *The Bashful Quixote: Bing Crosby as Reluctant War Hero*. Villanova University, 2002. Unpublished manuscript.

Sennett, Mack, and Cameron Shipp. *King of Comedy*. Garden City, NY: Doubleday, 1954.

Shepherd, Donald, and Robert F. Slatzer. *Bing Crosby: The Hollow Man*. New York: St. Martin's Press, 1981.

Shull, Michael, and David E. Wilt. *Doing Their Bit: Wartime American Animated Short Films*. Jefferson, NC: McFarland, 1987.

Singer, Ben. *Melodrama and Modernity*. New York: Columbia University Press, 2001.

Smith, Eric Liddle. *Bert Williams: A Biography of the Pioneer Black Comedian*. Jefferson, NC: McFarland & Co., Inc., 1992.

Southern, Eileen. *Music of Black Americans: A History*. 2nd ed. New York: W. W. Norton & Co., 1983.

Spada, James. *Grace: The Secret Life of a Princess*. Garden City, NJ: Doubleday 1987.

Stanford, Don. *The Ile De France*. New York: Appleton-Century Crofts, 1960.

Staveacre, Tony. *Slapstick! The Illustrated History*. London: Argus & Robertson Publishers, 1987.

Stephenson, Ralph. *Animation in the Cinema*. London: Tantivy Press, 1973.

Swanson, Kenneth. *Uncommon Prayer*. Columbus, MS: Genesis Press, 1987.

Théberge, Paul. "'Plugged in': Technology and Popular Music." In *The Cambridge Companion to Pop and Rock*, edited by Simon Frith, Will Straw, and John Street. Cambridge, UK: Cambridge University Press, 2001.

Thomas, Bob. *The One and Only Bing*. New York: Grosset and Dunlap, 1977.

———. *Astaire: The Man, The Dancer*. New York: St. Martin's Press, 1984.

Thomas, Frank, and Ollie Johnston. *Disney Animation: The Illusion of Life*. New York: Abbeville Press, 1981.

Thompson, Charles. *Bing: The Authorized Biography*. London: Allen 1975.

Thompson, J. *Bob Hope: Portrait of a Superstar*. New York: St. Martin's Press, 1981.

Toll, Robert C. *Blacking Up: The Minstrel Show in Nineteenth-Century America*. New York: Oxford University Press, 1986.

Wenner, Jann, ed., *Twenty Years of Rolling Stone: What a Long, Strange Trip It's Been*. New York: Friendly Press, Inc., 1987.

Wilder, Alec. *American Popular Song: The Great Innovators 1900–1950*. New York: Oxford University Press, 1972.

Wilder, Laura Ingalls. *Little Town on the Prairie*. New York: Harper & Row, 1941.

Williams, Paul. *Bob Dylan: Performing Artist, The Middle Years, 1974–1986*. Novato, CA: Underwood-Miller, 1992.

Wills, Garry. *Bare Ruined Choirs: Doubt, Prophecy, and Radical Religion*. Garden City, NY: Doubleday and Company, Inc, 1972.

Woll, Allen L. *The Hollywood Musical Goes to War*. Chicago: Nelson Hall, 1983.

Wakeman, John, ed. *World Film Directors*. Vol. 1 *(1890–1945)*. New York: The H. H. Wilson Company, 1987.

Wuthnow, Robert. *The Restructuring of American Religion: Society and Faith Since World War II*. Princeton, NJ: Princeton University Press, 1988.

———. *After Heaven: Spirituality in American Since the 1950s*. Berkeley, CA: University of California Press, 1998.

Zochert, Donald. *Laura: The Life of Laura Ingalls Wilder*. Chicago: Henry Regnery Co., 1978.

Zukor, Adolph. The *Public Is Never Wrong: My Fifty Years in Motion Pictures*. New York: Putnam's, 1953.

Articles

American Magazine. "Bing's Secret Weapon." December 1943.

Bacon, James. "Bing May Sing Good-bye to Song and Start as an Actor at Age 50." *Los Angeles Times*, 2 May 1954.

Barnett, Lincoln. "Bing, Inc." *Life*, 18 June 1945.

Baskette, Kirtley. "Pennies from Heaven." *Modern Screen*, July 1945.

Boone, Andrew R. "Talent Scouts for War Ideas." *Nation's Business*, February 1943.

Boston Sunday Post, 10 June 1945.

Business Week. "Guiding Inventors," 8 August 1948.

Crafton, Donald. "The View from Termite Terrace: Caricature and Parody in Warner Bros. Animation." *Film History* 5, no. 2 (June 1953).

Crosby, Bing. "Bing Scans His Elgin." *New York Times*, 12 December 1954.

Crowdus, Gary and Dan Georgakas. "Thinking About the Power of Images: An Interview with Spike Lee." *Cineaste* 26, no. 2 (2001).

Crowther, Bosley. "'Going My Way,' Comedy-Drama with Bing Crosby and Barry Fitzgerald, at Paramount—New Film Palace." *New York Times*, 3 May 1944.

———. "Clerical Callers: 'Going My Way' Gives a Human Picture Of Men of God for a Change." *New York Times*, 7 May 1944.

———. "Crosby Acts in 'Country Girl.'" *New York Times*, 16 December 1954.

———. "Screen: 'Say One for Me,'" *New York Times*, 20 January 1959.

Cue. "Bing Goes Dramatic." 27 November 1954.

Curry, Andrew. "Men in Blackface." *U.S. News and World Report*, 8–15 July 2002.

Davies, Jim. "Let's Duet Together." *The Guardian*, 19 August 1994.

Eddy, Lucinda. "War Comes to San Diego." *Journal of San Diego History* 39, nos. 1–2 (1993).

Fortnight. "Crosby Turns Actor." 19 January 1955.

Fricke, David. *Simon and Garfunkel, Old Friends*. CD liner notes. Columbia Records, 1997.

Friedwald, Will. "Bing: His Legendary Years—An Appreciation." Booklet with 4-CD Set. MCAD4/C4-10886, 1993.

Gehring, Wes. "On the 'Road' with Hope and Crosby." *USA Today Magazine*, November 2000.

Gusfield, Joseph R. "Moral Passage: The Symbolic Process in Public Designations of Deviance." *Social Problems* 15, no. 2 (Fall 1967).

Harford, Margaret. "'The Country Girl' Wins Praise." *Hollywood Citizen News*, 22 December 1954.

Hilburn, Robert. "Record Rack: This Year's Dylan is a Sonic Dynamo." *Los Angeles Times*, 9 September 2001, calendar section.
Hollywood Reporter. "Paramount Buys Odets B'way Play." 2 March 1951.
———. *Little Boy Lost.* 8 July 1953.
———. "'Country Girl' is Powerful Drama with Superb Acting." 29 November 1954.
Hopper, Hedda. "What Is Today's Bing Like?" *Los Angeles Times*, 13 June 1954.
———. "Bing's First Half Century." *Chicago Tribune*, 13 June 1954.
Keen, Harold. "Race Track Production Line." *Flying*, May 1944.
Lemore, Henry M. "The Lighter Side." *Los Angeles Times*, 10 November 1955.
Life. "Bing on Binge." 6 December 1954.
Look. Review of "I'll Be Home for Christmas" performed by Bing Crosby. Date unknown.
———. "Bing Crosby and Grace Kelly Try for Academy Awards." 14 December 1954.
Los Angeles Times. "Bing Crosby, Judy Garland Win Awards." 2 March 1955.
McBride, Carrol "Mac." E-mail correspondence. "Bing Crosby and Del Mar Turf Club." 7 January 2003.
Mook, Dick. *Silver Screen.* Fall 1942.
Mooring, William H. "Hollywood in Focus: What Happened to the Anti-Red Pledge?" *The Tidings*, 5 February 1954.
Mosby, Aline. "Alcoholic Role Had 'Groaner' Worried." *Beverly Hills Newslife*, 13 December 1954.
Newsweek. "The Country Girl." 6 December 1954.
New Yorker, 25 December 1954.
New York Times. "'Going My Way' Gets Film Critics' Honor." 28 December 1944.
———. "Crosby 'Best of 1944' in Trade Paper Poll." 8 January 1945.
———. "Crosby, Bergman Win Film Awards." 16 March 1945.
———. "'St. Mary's' Lists 4 on 'Oscar' Ballots." 28 January 1946.
———. "Bing's Country." 21 June 1953.
New York Times Magazine. "The Country Girl." 14 November 1954.
O'Connor, Dick. "Bing Crosby Views 30 Years of Success." *Herald Express*, 21 February 1955.
Pacific Stars and Stripes. "House Says 'Keep Secret.'" 3 October 1945.
Pam, Jerry. "'Country Girl' Hit—Crosby Excellent." *Newslife*, 23 December 1954.
Pix. "Movie: Crosby Plays a Drunk." 15 January 1955.
Popular Mechanics. "Hunting New Weapons of War." November 1941.
———. "Proving Ground for Inventions." December 1945.
Pryor, Thomas M. "Hollywood Scene: Perlberg-Seaton Portrait." *New York Times*, 19 August 1956.
Rochlen, Kendis. "Candid Kendis: Bing Eyes Work with Combo." *Los Angeles Mirror-News*, 21 February 1955.
Rule, Bob. *Nashville Tennessean,* 3 June 1943.
Santoro, Gene. "Lilt: Seductive Hawaiian musical forms have regularly swept the mainland and changed its music." *Atlantic Monthly*, November 1994.
Saturday Review, 18 December 1954.
Scheur, Philip K. "Producer-Director Stick But Not Stuck." *Los Angeles Times*, 4 April 1954.
———. "Bing Crosby's Acting Comes of Age with Alcoholic Role in 'The Country Girl.'" *Los Angeles Times*, 12 December 1954.
Scrimger, Mark. *Bing Crosby: The War Years.* CD Liner Notes. Cleopatra, 2000.
Smith, Wendy. "Gary Giddins: The True Life of a Crooner." *Publishers Weekly.* 11 December 2000.
Teachout, Terry. "Bing Crosby" (book review). *Commentary* 111, 4 April 2000.
Thomas, Bob. "Bing Crosby, Nearing 50, Considers Retirement." *Citizen News*, 8 March 1954.

Titcomb, Caldwell. Letter to the Editor. *The Chronicle of Higher Education*, November 1998.

Tomkins, Maurice Albert. "Military and Civilian Aspects of San Diego during the Second World War." Master's thesis, San Diego State University, 1982.

Variety. "The Chapel of the Air." 16 May 1945.

——— . "Bing Crosby Seen Exiting Radio, Too." 3 March 1954.

——— . "Squelching Campaign Against 'Country Girl.'" 13 April 1954.

——— . "Strange Sensitivity About Crosby—Although Unreleased and Unseen, Paramount Gets Protests on Bing's Drunk Role." 14 April 1954.

——— . "The Country Girl." 29 November 1954.

Way, Frank H. "Death of the Christian Nation: The Judiciary and Church-State Relations." *Journal of Church and State* 29, no. 3 (Autumn 1987).

Webb, Robert. "Pop: It's In the Mix: The Independent's Guide to Pop's Unlikeliest Collaborators." *The Independent* (London), 22 September 2000.

Weiler, A. H. "Happenings Hereabout: 'Going My Way' Set Record—Giant Mural for the Roxy." *New York Times*,. 16 July 1944.

Westbury, Ruth. "'Country Girl' Adult Picture." *Los Angeles Examiner*, 12 December 1954.

Wilson, John K. "Religion Under the State Constitutions, 1776–1800." *Journal of Church and State* 32, no. 4 (Autumn 1990).

Wood, Thomas. "Bing Crosby, Mousetrap Builder." *New York Times Magazine*, 6 June 1948.

Films

Adventures of Ichabod and Mr. Toad, The. Walt Disney, 1949.

Bells of St. Mary's, The. RKO, 1946.

Big Broadcast, The. Paramount, 1932.

Bingo Crosbyana. Warner Bros., 1936.

Blue Skies. Paramount, 1946.

Bug Parade, The. Warner Bros., 1941.

Country Girl, The. Paramount, 1954.

Country Girl, The. Undated press release, Paramount Studio.

Country Girl, The. File. Margaret Herrick Library at the Center for Motion Picture Study.

Crosby, Columbo, and Vallee. Warner Bros., 1932.

Dixie. Paramount, 1943.

Going My Way. Paramount, 1944.

Happy Holidays with Bing and Frank. Hart Sharp, 2003.

Here Is My Heart. Paramount, 1934.

High Society. Metro-Goldwyn-Mayer, 1956.

Patrick, John, screenwriter. *High Society*. MGM, 1956.

Holiday Inn. Paramount, 1942.

Binyon, Claude, and Elmer Rice, screenwriters. *Holiday Inn*. Paramount, 1942.

Hollywood Daffy. Warner Bros., 1946.

Hollywood Steps Out. Warner Bros., 1941.

It's a Wonderful Life. Liberty Pictures, 1946.

King of Jazz. Animated by Walter Lantz. Universal, 1930.

Let It Be Me. Warner Bros., 1936.

Little Boy Lost. Paramount, 1953.

Old Grey Hare, The. Warner Bros., 1944.

Riding High. Paramount, 1950.

Road to Zanzibar. Paramount, 1941.

Say One for Me. Twentieth Century-Fox, 1959.
Simpsons, The. "Marge Be Not Proud." December, 17 1995.
Sinatra: The Classic Duets. Hart Sharp, 2003.
Swooner Crooner, The. Warner Bros., 1944.
Too Much Harmony. Paramount, 1933.
Waikiki Wedding. Paramount, 1937.
Welcome Stranger. Paramount, 1947.
What's Cookin' Doc? Warner Bros., 1944.
White Christmas. Paramount, 1954.
Woods Are Full of Cuckoos, The. Warner Bros., 1937.

Web Sites

Big Cartoon Database. http://www.bcdb.com/
Bing Crosby Internet Museum.
Chambers, Kevin. Peace on Earth. http://www.chapel42.com/peace_on_earth/index.htm.
Christgau, Robert. http://www.robertchristgau.com.
Del Mar Fairgrounds. http://www.delmarfair.com/history.asp.
Dwight's Journal of Music. http://www.iath.virginia.edu/utc/minstrel/miar46et.html.
Everly Brothers, The. http://www.bellenet.com/everly.html.
Koenig, Peter R. "The Laughing Gnostic: David Bowie and the Occult." http://www.cyberlink.ch/~koenig/bowie.htm.
Life Overseas. http://www.kcmetro.cc.mo.us/pennvalley/Biology/lewis/crosby/life%20overseas6-18-45.htm.
Lyrics Café. "Nat King Cole Lyrics: 'Red Sails in the Sunset.'" http://www.lyricsafe.com.
National Public Radio. Harriet Baskas (interview). "Bing Crosby remembered a quarter century after his death." 14 October 2002 http://www.npr.org/templates/story/story.php?storyId=1151660
Pacific Stars and Stripes. http://www.interviewresearch.com/1945_pacific_stars_and_stripes.htm.
Twin Music Lyrics. "Peace on Earth/Little Drummer Boy." http://www.twin-music.com/lyrics_file/bowie/extra/peace.html.
United States Air Force Museum. "Boeing B-17G 'Flying Fortress.'" http://www.wpafb.af.mil/museum/air_power/ap16.htm.
USO Web page. http://www.uso.org/.

Recordings

Beatles First Live Recordings, The. Hamburg, Germany, 1962. Pickwick Records, 1979.
Bing!: His Legendary Years, 1931–1957. MCA, 1993.
Harrison, George. *George Harrison*. Dark Horse Records, 1976.
Sinatra, Frank. *Frank Sinatra and Friends: 60 Greatest Old-Time Radio Shows*. 15-CD Set. Schiller Park, IL: Radio Spirits, 2000.

List of Contributors

KEN BARNES is the author of several books, including *Sinatra and the Great Song Stylists* (Allen) and *The Crosby Years* (St. Martin's Press). Ken is a man of many parts: broadcaster, songwriter, music publisher, record producer, and filmmaker. One of Britain's busiest record producers of the 1970s and eighties, he worked internationally producing albums with such legendary artists as Bing Crosby, Fred Astaire, Peggy Lee, Rosemary Clooney, Frankie Laine, and Jack Jones. Today he runs a thriving film documentary company producing commercials and special edition DVDs for such clients as Universal Pictures and Fox Home Entertainment. In addition to his reputation as a musicologist, he is also a respected film historian. He lives in Benfleet, Essex, UK, with his wife Anne.

SAMUEL L. CHELL teaches and publishes in the areas of English literature and composition, film studies, and music. His book on the poetry of Robert Browning, *The Dynamic Self: Browning's Poetry of Duration*, was published in 1984. He continues to publish articles and reviews on Victorian literature in various journals, ranging from *CLIO* to *Christianity and Literature*. His articles on film and jazz have appeared in journals such as *Film Criticism* and *Journal of Popular Music and Society*, as well as in several book-length anthologies. For fifteen years Chell served as a regular reviewer of musical and dramatic performances for the *Kenosha News* and currently hosts a weekly jazz show on public radio.

KATHRYN CROSBY was married to Bing Crosby from 1957 until his death in 1977. A graduate of the University of Texas, with an R.N. degree, she has had a long career in entertainment. On stage, she appeared in more than thirty productions, including *The Lion in Winter* and *Hello Dolly* in Russia. Some of her films include *Forever Female, Rear Window, Arrowhead, Living It Up, Mister Cory, Operation Mad Ball,* and *Anatomy of a Murder.* She starred in the epic fantasy, *The Seventh Voyage of Sinbad.* With Bing Crosby, she appeared in many television specials and continues to perform on stage in productions based on her two books, *My Life with Bing* and *My Last Years with Bing.*

STEVEN CROSBY manages Vulcan Inc.'s Corporate Communications, which encompasses public, media, community, and government relations on a local and national level. His additional duties include marketing, advertising, graphic design, and internal communications. Vulcan, Inc. is the umbrella company for investor and philanthropist Paul G. Allen, co-founder of Microsoft.

JOHN MARK DEMPSEY is an associate professor of radio-television at Texas A&M University–Commerce. He has published four books: *The Jack Ruby Trial Revisited: The Diary of Jury Foreman Max Causey*; *The Light Crust Doughboys Are on the Air!*; *Eddie Barker's Notebook: Stories That Made the News (and Some Better Ones That Didn't!)*; and *Sports-Talk Radio in America: Its Context and Culture.*

BERNARD F. DICK is professor of Communication and English at Fairleigh Dickinson University (Metropolitan Campus, Teaneck, New Jersey). He is the author of *The Anatomy of Film,* now in its eighth edition. His most recent books are *Engulfed: The Death of Paramount Pictures and the Birth of Corporate Hollywood* (2001), *Hal Wallis, Producer to the Stars* (2004), and *Forever Mame: The Life of Rosalind Russell* (2006).

DEBORAH DOLAN is an assistant professor and serves as Social Sciences Librarian at Hofstra University. She is the subject specialist for undergraduate and graduate programs in psychology and related fields. Currently she is teaching in the Library Research and Information Literacy Instruction program at Hofstra; she has previously taught in several psychology departments in the United States.

MICHAEL FEINSTEIN is arguably the single most knowledgeable and dedicated musical anthropologist and archivist the Great American Songbook has ever known (a fact not lost on the Library of Congress, which recently elected Feinstein to the National Sound Recording Advisory Board, an organization dedicated to safeguarding America's musical heritage). Feinstein himself performs regularly at concert halls and at the nightclub that bears his name in the Regency Hotel in New York City. His repertoire as a singer/pianist includes songs by many great American songwriters, such as George Gershwin, Irving Berlin, Jerome Kern, Johnny Mercer, Duke Ellington, and Harry Warren. He has made more than two dozen CD recordings.

WILL FRIEDWALD is a leading authority on jazz singing and adult popular music. He is the author of several books on the subject, including Tony Bennett's autobiography, *The Good Life*, *Jazz Singing*, and *Sinatra! The Song is You*. The latter is the first full-length musical biography of Frank Sinatra. In 1996, *Sinatra!* received the ASCAP Deems Taylor Award for Excellence in Music Criticism. In 2002 he published *Stardust Melodies*, a biography of twelve of America's most popular songs. Since 1984, Friedwald has written regularly about music for the *Village Voice* and also appears frequently in the *New York Times* and other major publications. He currently writes a column on jazz and popular music for the *New York Sun*.

JEANNE FUCHS is professor emerita in the Department of Comparative Literature and Languages at Hofstra University. She has an essay "George Sand: Notorious Woman, Celebrated Writer" in the *Lincoln Center Theater Review* (Fall/Winter 2006) devoted to Tom Stoppard's *The Coast of Utopia*. She is co-editor with Ruth Prigozy of *Frank Sinatra: The Man, the Music, the Legend* (University of Rochester Press, 2007) and has a monograph on Jean-Jacques Rousseau, *The Pursuit of Virtue: A Study of Order in La Nouvelle Héloïse* (Peter Lang 1993). She has also written on Molière, Marivaux, and Alfred de Musset.

GARY GIDDINS won a National Book Critics Circle Award for *Visions of Jazz* and a Ralph J. Gleason Award for *Bing Crosby: A Pocketful of Dreams, The Early Years, 1903–1940*. He has written biographies of Louis Armstrong and Charlie Parker, which were the basis of documentaries he directed for PBS. His essays on movies, music, and books were recently collected in *Natural Selection*. Giddins was jazz critic for the *Village Voice* for thirty years, 1973–2003, during which time he won a record six Deems Taylor Awards for Music Criticism.

PETE HAMMAR is an entertainment technology historian who has worked in broadcasting and in the entertainment technology field for forty years. He has authored and edited numerous feature articles for the professional electronics trade press and has appeared on radio and television programs featuring the history of entertainment technology, including The History Channel, The Learning Channel, National Public Radio, The Voice of America, CBS, NBC, and ABC. Hammar created the Ampex Museum of Magnetic Recording, documenting the history of the medium and its importance in the development of radio and television. The Ampex collection is now a part of the Silicon Valley Archives at Stanford University. He is a fellow of the Society of Motion Picture and Television Engineers (SMPTE).

M. THOMAS INGE is the Robert Emory Blackwell Professor of Humanities at Randolph-Macon College in Ashland, Virginia, where he teaches American studies, interdisciplinary humanities, and Asian literature. He lectures on and writes about American humor and comic art, film and animation, Southern literature and culture, and William Faulkner. Recent publications include *Conversations with William Faulkner* and *Charles M. Schulz: Conversations*, both from the University Press of Mississippi; *Greenwood Guide to American Popular Culture*, a four-volume reference work from Greenwood Press; and new editions of Mark

Twain's *A Connecticut Yankee in King Arthur's Court* for Oxford University Press, and Sam Watkins' memoir of the Civil War, *Company Aytch*, for Penguin Books. His illustrated biography of William Faulkner has been published by the Overlook Press.

MALCOLM MACFARLANE is the author of *Bing Crosby: Day by Day*, which was published by Scarecrow Press in Maryland in 2001. He has edited *BING* magazine, published by the International Club Crosby, since 1993. A fellow of the Chartered Institute of Bankers and a former Rotarian, he retired from a senior banking position in the United Kingdom in 1999. Macfarlane has been involved in many radio and TV productions about Bing Crosby and has also written a number of liner notes for Crosby CDs.

ERIC MICHAEL MAZUR is associate professor and chair, Department of Religion at Bucknell University. His publications include *The Americanization of Religious Minorities: Confronting the Constitutional Order,* The Johns Hopkins University Press, 1999, and he has edited *Art and the Religious Impulse*, Associated University Presses, 2002; he has co-edited *God in the Details: American Religion in Popular Culture,* Routledge, 2001, and *Religion on Trial: How Supreme Court Trends Threaten the Freedom of Conscience in America*, AltaMira Press, 2004. He has also published many articles in scholarly journals.

MARTIN MCQUADE has dedicated much of his life to the study—and singing—of American popular music. Mr. McQuade graduated from New York University with a degree in Cinema Studies. His radio series, *Going Hollywood*, aired on WNYE-FM in New York for many years. In 2002 Mr. McQuade served as guest curator for Hofstra University's conference *Bing! And American Culture*. Since then, he has been Kathryn Crosby's special events coordinator, assisting her with the organization of several tributes and retrospectives honoring her husband, most significantly the 2004 New York Public Library series *Celebrating the Crosbys* and the 2005 Film Society of Lincoln Center 14-film review, *What a Swell Party*. McQuade is currently an American correspondent for the International Club Crosby.

ELAINE ANDERSON PHILLIPS is an associate professor of English at Tennessee State University in Nashville, Tennessee. She received her MFA in creative writing from Arizona State University and her PhD in English from Vanderbilt University. She specializes primarily in eighteenth-century British literature and has published articles on Samuel Richardson and Daniel Defoe.

RUTH PRIGOZY is professor of English and Film Studies at Hofstra University. She has published widely on F. Scott Fitzgerald as well as on Ernest Hemingway, J. D. Salinger, the Hollywood Ten, and film directors Billy Wilder, D. W. Griffith, and Vittorio de Sica. She has edited Fitzgerald's *This Side of Paradise*, *The Great Gatsby*, and *The Cambridge Companion to F. Scott Fitzgerald*. She is the author of

F. Scott Fitzgerald: An Illustrated Life. She has co-edited two volumes on detective fiction and film, one on the short story, one on Frank Sinatra, and two collections of essays on Fitzgerald. Her biography, *The Life of Dick Haymes: No More Little White Lies*, was published by the University Press of Mississippi in 2006.

WALTER RAUBICHECK is professor of English and chair of the department at Pace University. He has co-edited a book on the films of Alfred Hitchcock and published a number of articles on music, poetry, and American literature. One of his articles is included in *Frank Sinatra: The Man, the Music, the Legend* (University of Rochester Press, 2007).

LINDA A. ROBINSON is a PhD candidate in Radio-TV-Film at Northwestern University, and is currently teaching in the Radio-TV-Film Department at the University of Wisconsin–Oshkosh. In March 2006, she was an invited lecturer in the 2005–6 Chicago Film Seminar lecture series, one of only two students so invited. Since beginning her doctoral work in 2002, she has presented papers at numerous conferences, including the Society for Cinema and Media Studies and the Popular Culture Association/American Culture Association annual conferences. Her dissertation is entitled "Representation of Small-Town, Turn-of-the-Century America in Hollywood Cinema and Television, 1940–1965."

STEPHEN C. SHAFER has originated and taught courses on film and history at the University of Illinois at Urbana Champaign since 1974. The author of the 1997 book *British Popular Films, 1929–1939: The Cinema of Reassurance*, his articles have appeared in several other published collections and such journals as *International Labor and Working Class History.* His other publications have centered on British and American popular culture, literature, and history. In addition to his position as assistant professor of Cinema Studies at Illinois, he also serves as Assistant Dean in the College of Liberal Arts and Sciences.

DAVID E. WHITE is an associate professor of philosophy at St. John Fisher College, Rochester, NY. He has published in the area of philosophy of religion, most recently a new edition of the *Works of Bishop Butler* for the University of Rochester Press. Active in many professional associations, he is a vice-president of the International Institute for Field-Being, former Chairman of the Board of the Bertrand Russell Society, and vice-president of the New York State Philosophical Association. He is the founder of the Bishop Butler Historical Society and is a frequent speaker at professional conferences.

F. B. (WIG) WIGGINS has been a Bing Crosby collector since he bought his first 78 rpm record in 1944 (Crosby's "Don't Fence Me In") and has been a member of various American and International Bing Crosby clubs for the past thirty-five years. He is a retired Foreign Service Officer with the U.S. Diplomatic Service who served in Kenya, Guatemala, Indonesia, Italy, Malta, and Australia during his forty-year career with the government. He has represented the International Club

Crosby in the United States and Canada since 1991 and was a consultant with the planning committee for the Hofstra University conference on "Bing! Crosby and American Culture."

Index